Yale Studies in English, 186

D0913928

MALORY

Style and Vision in *Le Morte Darthur*

Mark Lambert

New Haven and London   Yale University Press

1975

Published with assistance from the
Kingsley Trust Association Publication Fund
established by the Scroll and Key Society of Yale College.

Library of Congress catalog card number: 74–29727
International standard book number: 0–300–01835–5

Designed by John O. C. McCrillis
and set in Baskerville type.
Printed in the United States of America by
The Murray Printing Co., Forge Village, Massachusetts.

Published in Great Britain, Europe, and Africa by
Yale University Press, Ltd., London.
Distributed in Latin America by Kaiman & Polon,
Inc., New York City;
in India by UBS Publishers' Distributors Pvt.,
Ltd., Delhi; in Japan by John Weatherhill, Inc., Tokyo.

I am grateful to the following for permission to reprint
passages from works protected by copyright:

Bantam Books, Inc., for a passage from *The Aeneid of
Virgil: A Verse Translation,* by Allen Mandelbaum, copyright © 1971 by Allen Mandelbaum.

Faber and Faber, Ltd., and Random House, Inc., for
"Musée des Beaux Arts," by W. H. Auden, copyright
1940 and renewed 1968 by W. H. Auden. Reprinted from
Collected Shorter Poems, 1927–1957, by W. H. Auden.

In memory of my father,

Joseph Lambert

Contents

Preface

The literature of medieval England offers many pleasures and several kinds of greatness. Yet there are, I think, only two books in this literature that one could say are now widely loved: Chaucer's *Canterbury Tales* and Malory's *Le Morte Darthur*. These are fondly remembered, and on occasion reopened, by many readers who otherwise let olde thynges pace; they are probably also the two medieval English works which have appealed most to the imaginations of later English writers.

These two books have certain things in common—above all, a strong sense of fellowship. But what seems to me most interesting about the prominence of the *Canterbury Tales* and *Le Morte Darthur* in our imaginations is not their similarities but their differences. Excellent as they both are, medieval as they both are, the artistic sensibility of the one writer is fundamentally unlike the artistic sensibility of the other. Chaucer characteristically broadens and enriches; Malory narrows, concentrates, intensifies. For us as for Dryden, the *Canterbury Tales* present God's plenty, and we love Chaucer's celebration of the sometimes bewildering variousness of that plenty. Malory we love for the earnestness with which he speaks of a world where there is one thing that matters.

That one thing that matters for Malory is nobility, knightliness. Yet no one would say *Le Morte Darthur* lives because of its political or ethical ideas. Malory is not important as a thinker. The central turth he offers us is an emotional one; we recognize in *Le Morte Darthur*, and thereafter recognize more clearly in ourselves, not what true nobility is, but what it is like to view some kind of nobility as the center and gauge of experience. More particularly, it is Malory's two last tales, telling of the ruin of Arthur's civilization, which are at once Malory's unique gift to us and (in the Johnsonian phrase) something "to which every bosom returns an echo."

I come to what is vital in Malory through an examination of his prose style. It is above all the texture of this narration which brings us two things basic to the experience of *Le Morte Darthur*: first, the sense of a world in which values are as palpable as material objects—the world of a believer, where emotions, landscapes and time itself exist in relation to knightliness rather than simultaneously with it; second, the tone of Malory's voice, his painstaking gravity, and the way that tone forms our attitudes toward the stories he tells.

There are a few things I should say before beginning. There is the question of unity in Malory's tales: in this tourney I do not ride. The unity controversy has been useful in that the scholars involved have looked carefully for links and inconsistencies in Malory, but it does seem to me that this minute attention to links has produced a certain critical myopia. Too often the question of unity or nonunity has been presented as an absolute choice, which it is not; there are many degrees and kinds of unification. (I should say here that I think D. S. Brewer essentially right in suggesting that in Malory we find connectedness, but not the kind of unity we expect in a novel. The important point is that "the tales are meant to be read in their present order.")[1] But it is not only the formulation of the question which is a problem. Of course we want to know whether Malory thought he was writing one work or eight—but is this really the most important and most interesting question we have to discuss? Finally we expect Malorian criticism (as we expect any criticism) to show us what this author has to give us, why he matters; and it seems to me that further investigations of Malorian unity along established lines will not tell us much more about why Malory matters. After twenty years of investigating unity it is time for us to take the fruit, leave the chaff, and rotate our crops.

The scope of my work, I should point out, is somewhat more modest than my title suggests. I believe what I have to say in this book is true, *mutatis mutandis*, of the style of Malory's *Works* as a whole, but I have not attempted a full study of all eight tales. There is little discussion here of "The Noble Tale of King Arthur and the Emperor Lucius," which is something of a special case both because it is based on an alliterative English poem and because it appears to be apprentice work. In my second chapter, where I compare Malory with his sources, I have concentrated on the "Tale of King

1. Review article, *Medium Aevum* 25 (1956): 22.

Arthur," the "Noble Tale of Sir Lancelot du Lake," and the "Tale of the Sankgreal." My third chapter focuses on the "Lancelot and Guinevere" and the "Morte Arthur."

Though the present work probably contains the usual number of "but surely . . ." footnotes, I am very conscious of what I owe to earlier writers on Malory, both those with whom I disagree and those with whom I agree. Two of these writers I should like to mention here.

As readers familiar with Malorian criticism will see, what I have to say about the characteristics of Malory's style is far closer to the ideas of P. J. C. Field than to those of any other critic.[2] Because Field seems to me more nearly right about Malory's prose than anyone else has been, and because he points to important things which had not been shown before, it has sometimes been convenient for me to take issue with Field's ideas on a particular subject rather than simply present my own. But I hope it is clear that it is the excellence and originality of Field's work which make his book such a useful reference point: *Romance and Chronicle* is certainly one of the very best studies of *Le Morte Darthur* we have had.

That I owe a great deal to Eugène Vinaver's scholarship and critical insight might go without saying—except that in the United States the debt of Malorians to Vinaver has too often gone without saying, or gone with too little saying. The Oxford edition of Malory is magnificent scholarship; I knew this when I began studying Malory as a graduate student, but one only comes to understand *how* splendid this work is after using it for hundreds of hours. Vinaver's ideas about structure have been the most discussed parts of his interpretation of Malory. Having to make an either/or choice, I suppose I would say Malory wrote one work rather than eight, as Vinaver maintains: but Vinaver has what seems to me a truer sense of who Malory was, how his imagination worked, and what he cared about than do the critics who have argued for unity. And these are the things which matter more.

Except for very short passages I quote Old French works both in

2. See his "Description and Narration in Malory," *Speculum* 43 (1968): 476–86, and *Romance and Chronicle: A Study of Malory's Prose Style* (Bloomington, Indiana, 1971).

the original and in English. My goal in preparing the translations was to represent as nearly as I could what it was Malory saw as he read the French. In most cases I have stayed as close as possible to the syntax of the original and have tried not to use a less general or more varied vocabulary than the romancers themselves employed. Here and there I archaize. Where my use of a modern English word in an archaic sense might cause confusion I have marked the word with an archaic spelling. The recent and very readable translations of *La Queste del Saint Graal* and *La Mort le Roi Artu* published in the Penguin Classics series[3] are not quite literal enough to be quoted in this study, but I am glad they were there for me to consult.

ACKNOWLEDGMENTS

This book began a number of years ago as a paper in E. Talbot Donaldson's graduate course in Middle English Literature, and grew into a 1971 dissertation directed by Marie Borroff. As dissertation or revision-of-dissertation it has been read by Dewey Faulkner, Dorothée Finkelstein, Alice Miskimin, and Richard Sylvester of Yale, and by Irma Brandeis and Andrews Wanning, once officially and still de facto my teachers at Bard College. Each of these eight readers has made this a better book.

My great debts in preparing the translations from Old French are to Marie Borroff and Irma Brandeis, who saved me from a number of inaccuracies and infelicities. Those errors which remain in the translations are of course entirely my own responsibility.

Most of all, this book exists because of the counsel, taste, tact, and patience of my wife.

M.L.

3. *The Quest of the Holy Grail*, translated and with an introduction by P. M. Matarasso (Baltimore, 1969), and *The Death of King Arthur*, translated and with an introduction by James Cable (Baltimore, 1971).

Short Titles and Abbreviations

In addition to the standard abbreviations of periodical and series titles, I use the following:

Alliterative Morte *Morte Arthure or the Death of Arthur*, ed. Edmund Brock. *EETS-OS* 8. London, 1871; reprinted 1961.

ALMA *Arthurian Literature in the Middle Ages: A Collaborative History*, ed. Roger Sherman Loomis. Oxford, 1959.

Alphabet *An Alphabet of Tales: An English Fifteenth Century Translation of the Alphabetum Narrationum of Etienne de Basançon*, ed. Mary Macleod Banks. *EETS-OS* 126–127. London, 1904–1905.

Brut *The Brut, or the Chronicles of England*, ed. F. W. D. Brie. *EETS-OS* 131, 136. London, 1906–1908.

Charles the Grete *Charles the Grete*, trans. William Caxton, ed. S. J. H. Herrtage. *EETS-OS* 36–37 (in one volume). London, 1881.

Chaucer *The Works of Geoffrey Chaucer*, ed. F. N. Robinson. 2d edition. Boston, 1957.

Sir Degrevant *Sir Degrevant*, ed. L. F. Casson. *EETS-OS* 221. London, 1944.

Didot Perceval *The Didot Perceval, according to the Manuscripts of Modena and Paris*, ed. William Roach. Philadelphia, 1941.

English Merlin *Merlin, or the Early History of King Arthur*, ed. Henry B. Wheatley. *EETS-OS* 10, 21, 36, 112. London, 1865–1899.

Essays on Malory *Essays on Malory*, ed. J. A. W. Bennett. Oxford, 1963.

Golden Legend	*The Golden Legend,* trans. William Caxton. 7 vols. London, 1900.
Huth Merlin	*Merlin: Roman en prose du XIIIᵉ siècle,* ed. Gaston Paris and Jacob Ulrich. Société des Anciens Textes Français. 2 vols. Paris, 1886.
La Mort	*La Mort le Roi Artu: Roman du XIIIᵉ siècle,* ed. Jean Frappier. 3d edition. Les Classiques Français du Moyen Age. Geneva and Paris, 1964.
Malory's Originality	*Malory's Originality: A Critical Study of Le Morte Darthur,* ed. R. M. Lumiansky. Baltimore, 1964.
Paris and Vienne	*Paris and Vienne,* trans. William Caxton, ed. MacEdward Leach. *EETS-OS* 234. London, 1964.
Ponthus	*King Ponthus and the Fair Sidone,* ed. Frank Jewett Mather. *PMLA* 12 (1897): 1–150.
Prose Legends	"Prosalegenden—die Legenden des MS Douce 114," ed. C. Horstmann. *Anglia* 8 (1885): 102–196.
La Queste	*La Queste del Saint Graal: Roman du XIIIᵉ siècle,* ed. Albert Pauphilet. Les Classiques Français du Moyen Age. Paris, 1923; reprinted 1967.
Reynard the Fox	*The History of Reynard the Fox,* trans. William Caxton, ed. Edward Arber. Westminster, 1895.
Stanzaic Morte	*Le Morte Arthur: A Romance in Stanzas of Eight Lines,* ed. J. Douglas Bruce. *EETS-ES* 88. London, 1903; reprinted 1959.
Vulgate	*The Vulgate Version of the Arthurian Romances,* ed. H. O. Sommer. 8 vols. Washington, 1909–1916.
Works	*The Works of Sir Thomas Malory,* ed. Eugène Vinaver. 2d edition. 3 vols. Oxford, 1967.

In quoting medieval texts I generally follow the spelling and punctuation of the editions cited. I occasionally depart from the paragraphing of those editions, however, and never mark expansions of manuscript abbreviations. Italics in quotations from medieval texts are added by me for emphasis of one kind or another.

Arabic numbers in citations of prose texts indicate page and (where marked by the editor) line number, except in the case of *La Mort* where my references are to paragraph and line. Poems are cited by line numbers.

When I mention Professor Vinaver without giving a page citation, the reference is to his note in *Works* on the passage being discussed.

1

Aspects of Period Style

Dialogue

In the following pages I am going to discuss a number of characteristics of prose style common to Malory and to his sources and his
contemporaries but rare in nineteenth- or twentieth-century narrative. Some of these characteristics are so alien to us that we tend
to think of them (if we think of them at all) not as devices but as
mistakes. But here I will assume these characteristics to be intrinsically as respectable and functional as any other rhetorical or
stylistic devices, and will try to find in them what Leo Spitzer calls
"a common spiritual etymon."[1]

We are interested in these devices because we are interested in
Malory and because his vision of the world is conveyed to us through
such features of style, not in spite of them. And Malory does indeed
have a vision of the world; he is a profoundly original writer. But
just as Malory did not invent most of his stories, neither did he invent a new way of constructing prose. He is important as a stylist
not because he does things other writers do not do, but because he
works certain parts of the common inheritance more fully than do
his predecessors and contemporaries. The experience of reading
Le Morte Darthur is unlike the experience of reading any other later
medieval work; but to a great extent this is because Malory's
prose seems more medieval than any other medieval prose.

This first chapter is about that common inheritance: a number of
stylistic features common to Malory, his sources, and his contemporaries. The second is about Malory's refinement of that stylistic
inheritance. A new image will illustrate my purposes. I might say

1. "Linguistics and Literary History," *Linguistics and Literary History: Essays in
Stylistics* (New York, 1962), p. 1. Spitzer is, however, speaking of a common root
for a number of deviations from normal period usage in one writer's work, not of
period usage itself.

that in this chapter I am looking for a common root-system: both in *Le Morte Darthur* and in each of the other medieval prose works cited below, a common root-system is indeed there, underlying the various stylistic features I will be discussing. But in many of the non-Malorian works there are additional root-systems: the image is not of a single tree but of a thicket, containing perhaps an old maple, a young pine, and various vines and brambles. Malory's genius is for discovering the single tree he wants in such a thicket and cutting away all the competing vegetation. In this first chapter I am going to be looking at the root-system and tree Malory keeps; in the second, at Malory as he does his work, clearing the ground, removing things foreign to his imagination.

Mixed Forms of Discourse

One of the minor characters in *Dombey and Son* is a boxer called the Game Chicken. His career is not made of easy wins, and in chapter 44 of the novel we find him explaining why his face is badly cut up. Though one doubts the Game Chicken would care to know this, his explanation, as Dickens presents it, is an excellent illustration of *le style indirect libre:*

> The Chicken himself attributed the punishment to his having had the misfortune to get into Chancery early in the proceedings, when he was severely fibbed by the Larkey one, and heavily grassed. But it appeared from the published records of that great contest that the Larkey Boy had had it all his own way from the beginning, and that the Chicken had been tapped, and bunged, and had received pepper, and had been made groggy, and had come up piping, and had endured a complication of similar strange inconveniences, until he had been gone into and finished.[2]

Syntactically, all of this is indirect discourse; it is the narrator who speaks. But the diction mixes the slang of the Chicken's vocation with the narrator's mock-formality ("had endured a complication of similar strange inconveniences"). Novelists delight in this in-

2. Quoted as an example of the indirect free style in G. L. Brooks, *The Language of Dickens* (London, 1970), p. 46.

direct free style, and quite properly so. The device's popularity depends upon one of the realistic novel's principal assumptions—that the individuality of each character's voice is important—and on one of the novelist's great skills—his ability to make us hear that individuality of speech. More often than not the indirect free style has a satiric function, but there is also a brio to it, an exuberance in craft. Syntax need not make everything explicit; with diction alone the novelist tells us which phrases come from which speaker. The hands may be the hands of Esau, but we know Jacob's voice.

Now in Malorian narrative there are mixtures of discourse which at first appear to be somewhat like the novelistic indirect free style; but as we study them more closely, we come to recognize that these romance mixtures are usually different in form and opposite in function: they do not play with the distinctiveness of the character's voice, but enhance its normativeness. For example:

> Than sir Bors lenyd uppon hys beddys syde and tolde sir Laun-celot how the quene was passynge wrothe with hym, "because ye ware the rede slyve at the grete justes." And there sir Bors tolde hym all how sir Gawayne discoverde hit "by youre shylde" that he leffte with the Fayre Madyn of Astolat. [*Works*, 1084]

Here we do not have an admixture of individualizing mannerisms contained within the structure of indirect discourse; rather, the structure itself is broken. The novelist plays with the individuating features of different voices while sustaining the structural identity of just one of those voices; Malory (in his use of "ye" and "youre" rather than "he" and "his") violates the structural unity of discourse, but does not individualize the voices of narrator and character. Essentially, we might say, the novelist makes us aware of a mixed content within a unified form; Malory, a mixture of forms with a uniform content. The modern reader, used to the modulations of the indirect free style, experiences Malory's mixture of forms as a bumpy shuttling back and forth.

These abrupt transitions in the form of discourse are not characteristic of Malory alone; we encounter them frequently in Middle High German, in Old French, and in Middle and Early Modern

English.[3] For instance, in Caxton's version of *Paris and Vienne* (1485) we come upon:

> . . . & whan parys sawe that/ he sayd to the freres/ that they shold vnfeter the doulphyn/ & that they shold opene the yates of the pryson/ & yf ony of the kepars awake I shal slee hym/ [69][4]

The medieval writer freely moves from "he" to "I" and back again in a manner we find quite disconcerting. If these transitions from third-person forms to first-person forms seem odd to us, another medieval device, closely related to these transitions, seems odder still: the "such a" summary. There is a good example in a life of Catherine of Siena translated into English in the fifteenth century. A man has promised Catherine that he will go to confession if she can say why he is reluctant to do so. Catherine is, of course, able to tell him:

> "ful dere broþer, we maye oþer-while bi hidde fro mennes yen, but neuere fro þe sighte of god. Þerfore *siche a* synne þat þou didist *in siche* tyme and *siche* place, is þat wherþurgh þe fende so confoundys þy þoghte siche a manere þat hee latis þe not be confessyd." [*Prose Legends,* 190][5]

In the *Book of the Duchess*, to take an example from Chaucer, Morpheus enters Seys's body and says to Alcione:

3. See Dr. Leon Kellner's edition of the Caxton *Blanchardyn and Eglantine, EETS-ES* 58 (London, 1890), "Introduction," pp. xcviii–c. Mixed forms are not altogether unknown in Victorian fiction, for example, but they are fairly rare. Here is an example from Thackeray's *Pendennis:* "Pen, with a laugh, said 'that at one time he [Pen himself] did think he was pretty well in Miss Amory's good graces. But my mother did not like her, and the affair went off' " (II.2).

4. For other examples of mixed forms, see *Didot Perceval,* 146. 1–3; *Huth Merlin,* I.121 ("Et elle li conte comment . . . que mes sires mieus amoit . . . "); *Reynard,* p. 51 (" . . . and chargyd hym not for to loke in the male . . . made the lettre and endited it . . ."); *Alphabet,* I.43 ("We rede how þe fadir . . . And so þou may safe my life"); *Ponthus,* 22 ("Aftir this itt is no question . . . to save hym from all evyll").

5. See also *Paris and Vienne,* 28 ("I wyl fyrst that ye say . . . that in suche a yere cam euery nyght syngyng . . .") and *Prose Legends,* 69 ("And his frendes leued so . . . and as she sayde, so þe ende proued").

> "My swete wyf,
> Awake! let be your sorwful lyf!
> For in your sorwe there lyth no red.
> For, certes, swete, I nam but ded;
> Ye shul me never on lyve yse.
> But, goode swete herte, that ye
> Bury my body, for *such a* tyde
> Ye mowe hyt fynde the see besyde. . . ." [201 ff.]

There are two things to notice about this device. One is that it is a great convenience for a writer, since it allows him to deal with a situation likely to come up fairly often in narrative: that is, an occasion when it is important for a character to present very specific information but when what matters for the author and his audience is the fact of specificity rather than the specific data themselves. There is no miracle unless Catherine knows exactly what day, what sin, what time, and what place were involved; but none of these data is itself of interest to the reader. If Alcione is to find the body she must know the right "tyde"; but for the narrative it matters only that she receive the information, not what the information is. "Such a sin that thou didst in such time": a crisp, very efficient way to do things. Yet for all its utility, this device simply could not be employed by a novelist; it is too great a deviation from the proprieties of realistic dialogue.

And this leads me to my second point: the "such a" device is in a significant way just the opposite of the indirect free style. Indirect free style is essentially an outcropping of the character's voice in the narrator's speech; the "such a" summary is an outcropping of the narrator's voice in the character's. More than a norm, it is almost a generic law: in a realistic novel the character's voice is inviolable; its marked characteristics may appear in the narrator's speech, but the opposite is impermissible. In medieval prose narrative, however, either kind of discourse may be "contaminated" by the other.

A further example: this time the most unnovelistic bit of dialogue I know. In the *Alphabet of Tales* there is a story about a woman who wishes to become a monk. She disguises herself as a man, and is accepted into a monastic community. Eventually, however, she is

accused of getting a girl pregnant. Still the woman will not reveal
her sex, and so she is punished. Then we are told, just *before* her
secret is finally discovered:

> So with-in a while sho dyed; and when þis abbott saw at sho
> was deade, he said vnto hys brethir "Loo! now may ye se what-
> kyn a syn sho did, & yitt sho shrafe hur neuer þerof, nor askid
> forgifnes." [I.23]

Here of course the narrator has attributed his own point of view and
knowledge to the abbot at the very moment when what the abbot
is saying shows that he cannot possibly have that knowledge; for
him "she" must be "he." There is a joke about an amateur play-
wright's drama in which a doctor returns from delivering a baby and
exuberantly announces to his wife: "Do you know who was born
tonight? Victor Hugo!" But this *is* a joke; and if the Victor Hugo
anecdote seems improbable, it is much more difficult to imagine
even the most inept of modern writers producing the transposition
of pronouns in the *Alphabet* story. Perhaps this story seemed odd even
to a fifteenth-century audience;[6] it would, I think, simply be impossible in the nineteenth or twentieth centuries.

In the indirect free style the reader cannot be left in doubt as to
the source of a particular expression; medieval mixed forms of discourse blur the distinctions between voices. Since the last example
discussed was the most striking mixture of forms I know, let me now

6. Though it is difficult to say exactly how odd. This transference of the narrator's knowledge to the ignorant character in the *Alphabet* passage recalls another
common device in late medieval fiction by which the ignorance of the character is
transferred to the informed narrator. The most familiar example here is in Malory's
"Tristram." The author refers to his character as "Trystramys" until Tristram
first calls himself "Tramtryste" (*Works*, 384.27). He is now called "Tramtryste" by
Malory also until a character appears (386.29ff.) who knows, but does not betray,
Tristram's true identity. The author now refers to his hero sometimes by one name,
sometimes by the other. Tristram identifies himself to Isolde at 392.2 and is thereafter consistently called "Trystramys" by Malory. Much the same situation is
found in *Ponthus* when the hero assumes the name "Surdyte." Obviously the
Alphabet kind of transference and the *Ponthus*-Malorian kind go in opposite directions. But the important thing is that both blur the awareness of character and of
narrator in ways we should now find bizarre.

turn to two which represent a minimal interweaving. In the first,
Reynard the fox is narrating one of his own adventures:

> . . . I was aferd/ And wold wel I had been thens/ but I
> thoughte I am therin/ I muste ther thrugh and come out as
> wel as I may/ . . . [*Reynard*, 98]

Everything from "I am therin" to the end seems to be direct discourse; but in direct discourse the forms should be "herein" and
"here through,"not"therin"and"ther thrugh,"which are narrator's,
not the character's words.

The second passage comes from *Paris and Vienne*:

> And thenne Parys maad hys ansuer sayeng that the beaulte of
> my lady vyenne was so grete that in al the world was none to
> hyr lyke/ that yf it pleased the Kyng I am redy for to furnysshe
> the Ioustes for hys loue ayenst the knyght yet another tyme/
> and to Iuste tyl that geffroy shold be vaynquysshed. . . . [16]

"My lady" and "I am" indicate the passage is direct discourse; yet
in direct discourse we should expect "is so grete," "is none to hyr
lyke," "yf it please the Kyng," and "shall be vaynquysshed" rather
than the verbal forms actually used. If one attempted to modernize
the punctuation here, and add quotation marks logically, the effect
would be uncomfortably choppy. Read in the original punctuation
the passage moves quite easily. What we have in such passages as
this and the one from *Reynard the Fox* are mixtures of forms so unobtrusive, transitions so fluid, that even the modern reader experiences the whole as a merger, almost a *tertium quid*, rather than one
form of discourse interrupting another. I suspect that by reading
over many passages like these two the modern reader might develop
a feeling for the fifteenth-century attitude toward the individual
voice: an attitude that manifests itself more startlingly in the other
mixed forms I have been discussing.

It would probably be useful to have a full study of these medieval mixed forms of discourse: a catalogue of types, a consideration of linguistic and chronological distribution, and a discussion
of related devices. At the moment, however, we want not so much to

know more about mixed forms themselves as to know about the meanings and implications of this device in Malory and his contemporaries. What vision of reality allows one voice to replace another so quickly? If the individuality of the speaking voice is unimportant, what is important? To find answers to these questions we must look at the broader stylistic context of these mixed forms.

Confirmation

"Confirmation" may be defined as a marked similarity between the vocabularies of narrator and character or of different characters in a relatively short passage. By calling such a similarity "confirmation" I am of course suggesting one function for it: this likeness makes us feel that the word or words being "confirmed" are the correct ones, the inevitable ones, to use for a particular referent. In a work with frequent "confirmation" (and hereafter I shall omit the quotation marks) the audience is encouraged to regard the vocabulary of a given speech as either correct or incorrect, accurate or inaccurate, rather than as expressive of personality, of a unique, individual point of view.

There is an obvious parallel between the effects of confirmation and of mixed forms of discourse. I said before that rapid movement from forms and word choices appropriate (that is, appropriate from a modern point of view) to the narrator's voice to forms and word choices appropriate to the character's voice or vice versa suggests a great closeness, at times almost a merging of the two voices. Narrator-character confirmation, in that it is an additional kind of likeness between the two voices, strengthens the impression of closeness or merger.

One wonders about the origin of this device: it might be viewed as arising from either the rhetorical fashions or the limited vocabulary of Old French. Confirmation is perhaps related to the popular and elegant figure *annominatio* for instance; on the other hand, there is much repetition of terms in the romances which is plainly traceable to negligence rather than design. Discussing the general style of the Vulgate *Suite du Merlin*, Alexandre Micha speaks of "la pauvreté du vocabulaire, aggravée par le laisser-aller de l'expression . . . passages où les mots sont repris à satiété, sans souci

d'alléger la phrase, de souligner la pensée par un terme plus précis.
. . ."[7] He suggests that the *Merlin* is poorer than other parts of the
cycle in vocabulary and variety of expression, but from a twentieth-
century point of view all the prose works I am discussing are notably
poor in variation, and Professor Micha's sentences could describe
long stretches of any one of them. Such passages as this one, quoted
by Micha from the *Merlin*, are typical of much late medieval narrative prose:

> Et li rois Bohort *feri* si Marganant parmi le hialme qu'il le fent
> tout jusques as dens; et li rois Artus *feri* si Sinelant qu'il abat un
> quartier de son hiaume . . . Et Ulfins *feri* si Balant qu'il l'abati
> mort sanglant. Et Bretel *feri* Cordant, et Keu Candenart, et
> Lucans *feri* Molec. . . .[8]

7. *"La Suite Vulgate du Merlin:* Etude littéraire," *ZRP* 71 (1951): 50. See also
Albert Pauphilet's *Etudes sur la Queste del Saint Graal* (Paris, 1921), p. 187, on
vocabulary and repetition in the *Queste* and other prose romances. On the other
hand, Margaret Schlauch suggests that in his prose Chaucer quite deliberately
exploits "repetition and the echo of cognate forms," sometimes for the sake of
clarity, and sometimes as a stylistic flourish. See Schlauch's "The Art of Chaucer's
Prose," in *Chaucer and Chaucerians: Critical Studies in Middle English Literature*, ed. D.
S. Brewer (University, Alabama, 1966), pp. 140–63.

On Malorian repetition, see Field's *Romance and Chronicle*, pp. 78–81.

8. Micha, p. 51. Italics and abridgement are Micha's. In the twentieth century
we find Gertrude Stein doing deliberately what according to Micha the author of
the *Vulgate Merlin* did because of the limitations of his talent: "Her sister having
left for America she lived alone on the top floor of a building on the corner of the
boulevard Raspail and the half street, rue Boissonade. There she had at the window
an enormous *cage* filled with *canaries*. We always thought it was because she loved
canaries. Not at all. A friend had once left her a *canary in a cage to take care of* during
her absence. Mildred as she did everything else, *took excellent care* of the *canary in the
cage*. Some friend seeing this and naturally concluding that Mildred was fond of
canaries gave her another *canary*. Mildred of course *took excellent care* of both *canaries*
and so the *canaries* increased and the size of the *cage* grew until in 1914 she moved to
Huiry to the Hilltop on the Marne and gave her *canaries* away. Her excuse was that
in the country cats would eat the *canaries*. But her real reason she once told me was
that she really could not bear *canaries*" (*The Autobiography of Alice B. Toklas*, 1933.
Vintage edition, New York, 1960, p. 120, italics mine).

Part of the rationale for the lack of variation here is fairly close to the effect of
correctness, accuracy and objectivity created by lack of variation in medieval prose.
The Stein repetition wonderfully mirrors the sense of being oversupplied with

[And King Bohort so *smote* Marganant through the helm that
he splits him to the very teeth; and King Arthur so *smote*
Sinelant that he cuts off a cantle of his helm . . . And Ulfins
so *smote* Balant that he cut him down dead and bleeding. And
Bretel *smote* Cordant, and Keu Candenart, and Lucan *smote*
Molec. . . .]

Formally considered, confirmation is repetition of this kind in a
passage containing more than one voice; that is, either dialogue
involving more than one character or a combination of narrative
and dialogue:

And thus as they hoved stylle they saw a *knyght com rydynge*
agaynste them. "Lo," seyde sir Trystram, "se where *commyth
a knyght rydynge* whyche woll juste wyth you." [*Works*, 689].

Whatever its origins, how does such confirmation work? We might
say that in the preceding passage, Tristram and the narrator are
two witnesses and we the audience are the jury. Each witness cor-
roborates the other's use of "knight-come-riding." Certainly there
is nothing inherently suspect in these words; we would accept them
as an accurate description of reality even if they came from only
one voice. But, having them from two, we are particularly sure of
their accuracy; more important, the corroboration makes us believe
in the accuracy of both witnesses: by the time we have had fifty
or one hundred such confirmations, we are trained to accept the
words of the Malorian narrator and the Malorian knights not as
statements made from particular points of view but as Truth.

It is the cumulative effect of confirmation, then, which is im-

---

canaries, but it also reflects a broader aesthetic program: "Gertrude Stein, in her
work, has always been possessed by the intellectual passion for exactitude in the
description of inner and outer reality. She has produced a simplification by this
concentration, and as a result the destruction of associational emotion in poetry and
prose. She knows that beauty, music, decoration, the result of emotion should never
be the cause, even events should not be the cause of emotion nor should they be the
material of poetry and prose. Nor should emotion itself be the cause of poetry
or prose. They should consist of an exact reproduction of either an outer or an
inner reality" (Ibid., p. 211). While one can discuss the effects of a style without
considering the author's intention, it is pleasant to know that the effects produced
by one style are related to the intentions of an author choosing a like style.

portant. Typically the device is found in clusters; it becomes part of the normal pattern of reality in the narrative rather than a way to underline crucial assertions.

These groupings are sometimes in a fairly rigid *a a b b c c* form, as in this Malorian conversation:

> So rode sir Trystram unto Joyus Garde, and there he harde in that towne grete *noyse* and cry.
>
> "What is this *noyse*?" seyde sir Trystram.
>
> "Sir," seyde they, "here is a knyght of this castell that hath be longe amonge us, and ryght now he is slayne with two knyghtes, and for none other *cause* but that oure knyght seyde that sir Launcelot was better knyght than sir Gawayne."
>
> "That was a symple *cause*," seyde sir Trystram, "for to sle a good knyght for seyynge well by his maystir."
>
> "That is lytyll remedy to us," seyde the men of the towne. "For and sir Launcelot had been hyre, sone we sholde have bene revenged uppon tho false knyghtes."
>
> Whan sir Trystram harde them sey so, he sente for his shylde and his speare. And lyghtly so wythin a whyle he had overtake them and made them turne and *amende* that they had mysse-done.
>
> "What *amendis* woldiste thou have?" seyde the one knyght. [690–91]

Elsewhere the romancer varies and muffles confirmation by making a confirmed word part of a doublet on one of its appearances, interlacing two or more confirmations, adding or deleting modifiers before confirmed words, having some confirmed words appear more than twice, etc. We see a number of the possibilities in this passage from the *English Merlin*:

> And Madalen rode with grete plente of peple, and were vj^{ml} and it ne myght not longe endure but that Gawein sholde haue ben loste, where-of it hadde ben grete damage and harme to all the *londe of logres*, but as the *socoure com oute of the Citee*, and were v^{ml} men of armes. When the childeren saugh the *socour that com oute of logres*, and the baner that doo of Cardoell brought, The

men of countrey that were with the childeren badde hem be
of gode counforte, for "loo! heere *cometh the Citee of logres yow
for to helpe and to sucoure.*" Whan the childeren vndirstode that
thei *of logres* were *come hem for to helpe* thei were gladde and
ioyfull. [II.200]

Here no single word stands out; we simply have a blurred impression of uniform, and therefore correct, diction. The sequence of
terms is "londe of logres . . . socoure com oute of the Citee . . .
socour that com oute of logres . . . cometh the Citee of logres . . .
for to helpe and to succoure . . . thei of logres were come hem for
to helpe." One should notice especially the variation by means of a
doublet in "soccoure" → "helpe and soccoure" → "helpe" and the
varied first elements in the "——— of logres" formulas.

In the novelistic indirect free style the reader should sense the
origin of each expression;[9] with romance confirmation we are sometimes unable to sort out the different voices. Here, in somewhat
abridged form is a passage from Malory's first tale:

So after the feste and journeye kynge Arthur drewe hym unto
London. And soo by the *counceil* of Merlyn the kyng lete calle
his barons to *counceil*, for Merlyn had told the kynge that the
sixe kynges that made warre upon hym wold in all haste be
awroke on hym and on his landys; wherfor the kyng asked
counceil at hem al. They coude no *counceil* gyve, but said they
were bygge ynough. "Ye saye well," said Arthur, "I thank
you for your good courage; but wil ye al that loveth me speke
with Merlyn? Ye knowe wel that he hath done moche for me,
and he knoweth many thynges. And whan he is afore you I
wold that ye *prayd* hym hertely of his *best avyse.*" Alle the barons
sayd they wold *pray* hym and *desyre* hym. Soo Merlyn was sente
for and fair *desyred* of al the barons to gyve them *best counceil.*
"I shall say you," said Merlyn. . . . "What were best to do in
this cause?" said al the barons. "I shal telle you," said Merlyn,
"myne *advys.* There ar two bretheren beyond the see. . . .
Wherfor this is my *counceil*: that our kyng and soverayne lord

9. See the remarks on Margaret Lips's *Le style indirect libre* (Paris, 1926) in
Jeanette M. A. Beer, *Villehardouin: Epic Historian* (Geneva, 1968), p. 97.

sende unto the kynges Ban and Bors by two trusty knyghtes
with letters wel devysed, that and they wil come and see kynge
Arthur and his courte to helpe hym in hys warrys, that he wolde
be sworne unto them to helpe hem in theire warrys agaynst
kynge Caludas. Now what sey ye unto thys *counceyle?*" "Thys
ys well *councelde*," seyde the kynge. [19–20; the ellipses represent
omissions of 72 and 92 words.]

Consider the term "counceil." The first time we come upon the
word it is clearly the narrator who chooses it. The same is true of the
second occurrence: although here it is being used in a somewhat
more technical sense. But what of its third appearance? Is this indirect discourse in which it is understood that what the king actually
said was "I ask counceil at you all?" or is it a freer kind of summary?
What of the next occurrence? Did the barons actually say "we can
no counceil gyve" or is this the narrator's expression? Such questions are unanswerable and seem virtually meaningless: repetition
of terms, both in true confirmation and by the narrator himself,
so lulls us into unawareness of differences in points of view and of
differences between various voices that we are not moved to sort
them out more exactly than the syntax of the narrative does.

Confirmation works together with mixed forms of discourse to
turn our attention away from the individuality of the speaking
voice. But the correctness of terminology suggested by confirmation
does more than this. It points, as do a number of the devices I will
consider later in this chapter, to the objective existence of moral
qualities and values. Confirmation in the following passage encourages us to believe not only that Ponthus and the narrator judge
correctly, but that "grete trouthe" and "stedfastnes" reside in and
are of the essence of what Sidone has done—they are not merely
expressions of an individual, personal reaction to her deeds:

When Ponthus hard the *grete trouthe* and *stedfastnes* of hir, the
teres fell doune from his eeyn, and aftre he smyled a litle, and
said, "Madame, by my trouthe ther was neuer fonde a bettre,
a fairer, ne a more *stedfaste* lady then ye be; and sith I see your
grete trauthe, I wolle hyde no thing frome you no lenger. . . ."
[*Ponthus,* 100]

At a number of points in this study we will find that the saint's life, particularly in its earnest, least "romantic" aspects, stimulates our understanding of romance. Consider a brief but very interesting confirmation in Caxton's version of the *Golden Legend* (1483). In the life of Saint Ambrose, Ambrose's sister unwittingly fulfills a prediction her brother had made: ". . . his sister, the virgin, kissed his hand as of a priest, and he smilingly said: Lo! as I told thee now thou kissest my hand as of a priest" (III.113). The action described is above all else the fulfillment of a prophecy; to narrate it in terms other than the ones used by Ambrose himself would be not simply different, but wrong. The essence of the action is its coincidence with the prediction.

I think it is easier for the modern reader to sense the rightness of the use of the same words by narrator and character in this sentence from the *Golden Legend* than to sense the rightness and force of confirmation in romances. We understand the metaphysical assumptions of the saint's life. Ambrose's words are correct because he is the spokesman for the God who creates the things being described. In the legend, in which we are constantly being shown that things do not just happen, in which almost every important event is "Goddes sonde," one man's interpretation of events, one man's name for them, is certainly not as good as another's—particularly if the other is God's spokesman. Responding to, feeling the imaginative truth of confirmation in other works of this period, we move in a world where descriptions and value judgments are as definitively right or wrong as in a saint's life, even if the metaphysical basis for those standards of correctness is not often in evidence.

Two minor devices fairly common in late medieval dialogue (but found to a lesser extent in later dialogue also) may be profitably considered along with confirmation. The first of these, the "I shall tell" formula, is used in replies to questions, and is simply an acknowledgment by the speaker that he is indeed giving the requested information:

> "For what cause is that boye Arthur made your kynge?"
> "Syres," said Merlyn, "I shalle telle yow the cause. . . ."
> [*Works*, 17]

"Now I pray you," said the kyng, "tell me howe ye escaped and howe ye were saved." "My fair sonne, I shall tell you. . . ." [*Ponthus*, 121]

Often, as in these examples, the "I shall tell you" formula of response occurs together with confirmation, and sometimes, as in the lines from *King Ponthus and the Fair Sidone*, "tell" is itself one of the confirmed elements. The two devices are finely harmonious, even though the "I shall tell you," simply by being an opening formula, marks off the speech it begins from what preceded it. The deeper harmony of this formula with confirmation is in the way these "I shall tell you" openings impress the continuity of different speeches upon the reader. They assure us that the attention of the answerer is focused on the same matter as the attention of the questioner, just as confirmation is an implicit assurance that the points of view of various speakers are in some way the same. The matters being discussed, facts, evaluations, remain, to use Ezra Pound's word, unwobbling.

The second device is the "it was so" summary: essentially a brief indication by the narrator that the commands or instructions of one character have been carried out by another:

"Now shall ye do by myne advice," seyde Merlyon unto the three kyngis, and seyde: "I wolde kynge Ban and Bors with hir felyship of ten thousand men were put in a woode here besyde in an inbusshemente and kept them prevy, and that they be leyde or the lyght of the day com, and that they stire nat tyll that ye and youre knyghtes a fought with hem longe. . . ." All the three kynges and the hole barownes seyde how Merlion devised passynge well, and so hit was done. [*Works*, 27; the ellipsis represents an omission of 55 words of further directions.]

"And so hit was done": the narrator's statement is a blanket one. An assurance of this kind suggests that the command as carried out exactly coincided with the command as given; to put this negatively, the device keeps us from looking for personal, idiosyncratic elements in the command as expressed. Rephrasing of the command as narrative, it is implied, is superfluous: the speaker has said what he wished, and what was done, in exactly the right way. Confirmation and the "it was so" summary use opposite means but work toward essentially the same effects.

Collective Discourse

Collective discourse, speech delivered by two or more characters in unison, is extremely common in medieval literature. It occurs seventy-eight times in the *Chanson de Roland*, for instance, and is also popular with the early French historians and in the prose romances.[10] This device works toward a merging of the personalities and visions of various characters parallel to the merging of the personalities and visions of narrator and character suggested by mixed forms of discourse and confirmation. Malory is particularly fond of this device; as he reshapes his source material he not only renders collective discourse by collective discourse, but frequently substitutes collective discourse for individual speech or narrative summary.[11]

One feels the otherness of medieval literature here, at times quite strongly. "*Les discours collectifs*," as Jean Frappier has well said, "constitutent le procédé le plus curieux, en tout cas le plus médiéval, car il est bien d'une époque où les formes de pensée et d'expression reflètent souvent un état d'esprit en quelque sorte unanimiste."[12] That "état d'esprit en quelque sorte unanimiste" is what I have been calling the spiritual etymon of our devices.

Now collective discourse can occasionally be found in realistic fiction, but there its uses and forms are far more restricted than they are in late medieval prose. The novelist is reasonably free to use collective discourse for very brief exclamations (e.g., "Help!"); his employment of this device to present more complex statements is

10. See Peter M. Schon, *Studien zum Stil der frühen Französichen Prose: Robert de Clari, Geoffroy de Villehardouin, Henri de Valenciennes* (Frankfurt am Main, 1959), p. 188 f.

11. Compare, for instance, *Works*, 99.17–21 and *Huth Merlin*, II.69; *Works*, 854.9–17 and *La Queste*, 2.21–29; *Works*, 964.28–31 and *La Queste*, 180.17–21; *Works*, 984.2–8 and *La Queste*, 200.5–14; *Works*, 1167.14–17, *La Mort*, 116.37–41 and *Stanzaic Morte*, 1836 ff.; *Works*, 1169.27–33 and *Stanzaic Morte*, 1892 ff.

12. "Les discours chez Villehardouin," *Etudes Romanes Dédiées à Mario Roques* (Paris, 1949), p. 50. Quoted in Beer, p. 86 n.

usually limited in two ways. First, collective discourse as a rule does not represent the speech of those characters who most interest us in a particular scene; it presents the reaction of supernumeraries rather than of protagonists. Second, when we do have a complex statement in collective discourse, it is always in indirect rather than direct form. ("All the neighbors said it was too bad the Smiths had to move just when the city was finally putting in a sewer line.") The indirect form is usefully ambiguous; the reader cannot be sure whether "all said " means that they all used the same words or that they all expressed similar sentiments in various ways. The first of these two limitations confines the device to characters about whom we know and care little; the second lets the novelist exploit the dramatic possibilities of unanimity without absolutely committing either himself or the reader to the idea that various characters all used exactly the same words.

In modern works the power of collective discourse rises from the very thing which makes its use risky: the assumption that speakers have individual views and voices; that "diverse folk diversely they demed" describes the normal state of things. The device suggests extraordinary unanimity, and the extraordinary can easily become the unbelievable. Collective discourse must be used discreetly: it should not occur too frequently. Indirect discourse should relieve the strain on the reader's credulity; the statement of the *vox populi* should not be *too* long, should not be *too* complex.

Now while some medieval uses of collective discourse would be more or less acceptable in realistic novels (e.g., "wherof the Frensshe men sayden al wyth one voys: 'A! saynt marye, what a stroke hath Olyuer gyuen to thys paynym!'")[13] a great many others would not. Quite often the medieval collective voice is the voice of participants rather than observers. The collective speeches run on to a fair length; more important, the speakers freely use first person plural verb and pronoun forms. The following passage is typical:

> "Ser," said the barounes all with oon voice, "we wot not wher to haue a bettre, if itt lyke hym, then Ponthus, for he is moste worthie to gouerne an empyre, as for bountie, beautie, of wytt

13. *Charles the Grete*, 4. This work was first published by Caxton in 1485.

& gouernaunce and gentylnes—as a kynges sone, and with the
beste begynnyng of his knyghthode that thys day is lyvying."
[*Ponthus*, 32]

Such "we" forms suggest that here collective discourse is not the
coincidence of a number of individual statements, as it is in modern
narrative, but a statement radically plural; each member of the
group not only spontaneously uses the same words as every other
member but spontaneously abandons individual identity for group
identity.

It is another indication of the difference between medieval and
modern attitudes toward collective discourse that the medieval
writer feels free to create dialogues between individual and group
voices, while the novelist does not. In Malory's last tale, for instance,
there is a scene in which Lancelot is speaking with 163 knights who
have sided with him (*Works*, 1170 ff.). Here we have direct discourse
by Lancelot (1170.30–1171.5, 1171.9–20); Bors (1171.21–33);
Lancelot (1172.1–5); a short exclamation by all the knights ("We
woll do as ye woll do"—1172.7); Lancelot again (1172.8–12); then
an eighty-six-word speech spoken by the knights "all at onys with
one voice" and using "we" throughout (1172.14–21); then speeches
by Lancelot (1172.23–33); Bors (1172.34–1173.11);[14] Lancelot
(1173.12–20); and finally, Bors again (1173.21–25). One cannot
imagine such a scene in a novel. For the modern writer there is
always something hyperbolic about collective discourse; he will not
force his audience (as this scene does) to put collective and individual speech on a single plane of reality. But the medieval writer
really does not regard one form of speech as more stylized than the
other.[15]

It is also significant that medieval writers will on occasion present
collective discourse by a group whose number is quite small and
whose members are individually major characters:

14. Notice that this speech is an answer by Bors to a question addressed by
Lancelot to "my fayre lordis" (1.23). Bors is not rudely answering a question put
to others; rather, a query to a group may be answered either by the group as a
whole or by just one of its members. One kind of speech is not more conventional,
and Malory moves with ease from one possibility to the other.

15. For other examples of this unselfconscious movement between collective
and individual speech, see *English Merlin*, II.260 and *Huth Merlin*, I.113.

And the kyng commaunded hym to harpe itt be-for hym and the quene; and they thoght itt mervellously goode, and said to their two doghters, "Truly, fair doghters, we wold that ye lernyd itt, for itt is ryght goode, and the knyght doos itt wonderly wele—and of all dyssportes and plays he canne enowe." [*Ponthus*, 74]

All three of the following speeches occur in the first two pages of Malory's last (and greatest) tale:

"So God me helpe," seyde sir Gaherys and sir Gareth, "we woll nat be knowyn of your dedis." [1161]

"That woll I nat," seyde sir Aggravayne and sir Mordred. [1162]

"Alas!" seyde sir Gawayne and sir Gareth, "now ys thys realme holy destroyed and myscheved, and the noble felyshyp of the Round Table shall be disparbeled." [1162]

I have already laid down several conditions for the acceptability of collective discourse in a modern work. These last passages, which strike us as especially "unrealistic," suggest two more rules: first, the clearer our previously formed idea of the individual characters, the more unwilling we will be to accept collective discourse from those characters. Second, it is easier for us to accept a chorus than a duet. We find it difficult to visualize or to think of the individual members of a large group while we are being invited to consider them as a group; on the other hand, it is hard for us *not* to see a group of two as two individuals. In medieval works characters need neither the anonymity conferred by a crowd nor the anonymity conferred by lack of prominence to engage in collective discourse.

Formality of Speech

There has recently been some scholarly disagreement about a rather odd passage in Malory's "Book of Sir Tristram." Sir Lamerak rides to a fountain:

. . . and he alyght and tyed his horse and sette hym downe by the brynke of the fountayne, and there he made grete langoure and dole. And so he made the dolefullyst complaynte of love that ever man herde, and all this whyle was he nat ware of kynge Marke. And this was a grete complaynte: he cryed and wepte and sayde,

"O thou fayre quene of Orkeney, kynge Lottys wyff and modir unto sir Gawayne and to sir Gaherys, and modir to many other, for thy love I am in grete paynys!" [579.16–25]

"And modir unto sir Gawayne and to sir Gaherys, and modir to many other": unless we see Lamerak as strongly oedipal, and for that matter even if we do, this is an extraordinary way for a lover to speak of his lady. Charles Moorman has said that this complaint "surely . . . is meant as a parody of *l'amour courtois*."[16] But P. J. C. Field dismisses Moorman's reading as "unlikely and unproved"; this is simply a case where Malory's "literary tact deserts him," and "that fatal 'many other' is the product of Malory's tendency to heighten everything."[17] It seems to me Field is more nearly right than Moorman. There is no compelling reason to see this complaint as parody; my own suspicion, in fact, is that Malory never wrote a line of parody in his life. No, if we twentieth-century readers smile at Lamerak's words we smile at and not with Malory. But the interesting thing here is this: whether or not we agree with Field in considering this passage a "mistake"—and I am not sure that we have to—it is hard to imagine a comparable "mistake" in a nineteenth- or twentieth-century work. The novelist understands that the attributes a lover thinks of first in referring to his mistress in a love complaint are those which relate to her as a love object: the lover does not see her first in terms of the king she married and the two great knights she bore, regardless of the importance of knightliness in the world. The lover sees as lover, sees her desirability or inaccessibility as the central fact about her, even if the objective narrator sees her in another way.

This is the essential thing: Malorian lovers speak correctly. Lamerak loves Morgawse, the Queen of Orkney. I turn to the "Index of Proper Names" in Vinaver's edition of the *Works* and look

16. Charles Moorman, *The Book of Kyng Arthur: The Unity of Malory's Morte Darthur* (Lexington, Kentucky, 1965), p. 27.
17. *Romance and Chronicle*, p. 197, n. 23, and p. 110.

up the first five passages in which Morgawse is mentioned, either by the narrator or by another character, and find that it is normal to refer to the queen's relatives when her name is reintroduced into the narrative. It is proper to touch on her knightly and royal lineage when speaking of her; these connections are (in a way Odysseus would have understood) the central fact about her. Malory's "mistake" is really that Sir Lamerak *doesn't* make a mistake; the lover's vision is not deflected. The use of the genealogical identi- fication by Lamerak as well as the narrator is essentially like the use of the same word by character and narrator in confirmation: neither individuality nor emotion interfere with accuracy of vision and of statement.

"Non-deflection" is of course the absence of change, and it is somewhat difficult to think of such absence as a stylistic device. Nevertheless, it seems to me that an omnipresent felt difference between medieval prose romances and novels is that in the earlier works the style of dialogue deviates far less from the style of nar- rative than it does in the later ones.

In Lamerak's complaint we find this "non-deviation" (which, from a novelistic point of view, is seen as "formality") strikingly exhibited in a choice of epithets. Quantitatively, however, the most significant kind of formality in late medieval prose dialogue is syn- tactical. On the whole, when we encounter a speech of any length in the prose of this age (and this is particularly true of fifteenth- century English narratives) it will be at least as complex in its syntax as the narrative prose in which it is embedded, and the character will appear at least as devoted as the narrator is to making cause and effect clear. Thus, for instance, this confession from *Paris and Vienne*:

And Vyenne ever thought in hyr self who myght he be that had goten the worshyp and prys of the Ioustes and sayd to ysabel/ Neuer truste me dere suster but þe kny3t to whom I haue yeuen the shelde of crystal and my garlond is he that so swetely sange for the loue of me tofore our chambre/ *for* myn herte gyueth it me/ and by my fayth syster he is ful noble and worthy/ & in alle hys dedes ryght curtoys and gentyl as we

myght haue seen whylere *wherfor* I say you my swete syster
that in hym I haue putte the rote of myn entyere herte/ my
wylle and al my loue/ nor neuer I shal haue playsyr ne Ioye
vnto þᵉ tyme that I knowe what he is/ *for* my loue is al hys/ &
of what so euer estate he be of I neuer shal take myn herte fro
hym/ [9–10]

Vienne is not, in fact, a master logician, but the pivotal "for,"
"wherefore," and "for" in her speech suggest that her thoughts,
even when their subject is her own feelings, follow a discernible
pattern of cause-and-effect. Vienne's syntax treats the urgings of her
heart in the same way it might treat an objective, demonstrably
valid argument for the preceding conclusion, or the way the narrator might treat an explanation of why a particular king happened
to need archers for a particular battle.

There is much the same employment of "for" and "wherefore"
in this fairly typical speech from *Ponthus and the Fair Sidone*:

". . . and fair doghtre," said the kyng, "ye aghte forto doo itt,
for he has doon you myche worship; *for* by his swerd he has
sent to your prisoune so mony goode knyghtes and lordes,
wherof grete worschip is comen to you and to youres and to all
our reaume; *wherfore* I am myche beholden to the blak knyght."
[56]

A moment of heroism in Caxton's *Charles the Grete* seems even
odder to the modern reader. Oliver has been carrying Fierabras
acorss the front of his saddle when he sees a pagan with an enven-
omed "faus dart"riding at him on a horse "as swift as a greyhound."
At this moment he says to Fierabras:

"Syr kyng, ye must needs descende; I may no ferther conduyte
you, *wherefore* I am meruayllously sory and dysplaysaunt. *For*
I knowe that I muste nedes be oppressyd; ye see it wel. And yf
they may attayne I shall be put to deth. And Charles shal
neuer see me whyche shall be to hym grete dyscomforte." [79]

That Oliver pauses to explain that Fierabras must dismount is, to
latter-day readers, an impressive courtesy; but the orderliness of the

explaining strikes us as preposterous. The impression of order is created not principally by the "wherefore" and "for" but by the pairing of phrases: "ye must needs descende; I may no ferther conduyte you"; "I must nedes be oppressyd; ye see it wel"; "I shall be put to deth. And Charles shal neuer see me." These pairs are generally similar in rhythm and in meaning also: in each of them Oliver sees one situation from two different points of view, his own and someone else's ("I must . . . ye see . . ."; "I shall . . . Charles shal . . ."). Now this is certainly grace under pressure; balanced, ordered language at this moment seems to us ideally—and improbably—heroic. But, as my other examples suggest, ordinarily the speaker's emotions do not affect the form of his speech even when he is not being markedly heroic. Except for oaths and interjections, it would be highly unusual for any character in Caxton to suggest love, fear, anger, weariness, or any other feeling by the rhythm or syntax of his speech.

The fundamental difference between the novelistic attitude toward dialogue and the attitude of the prose romancer is clear. In the realistic novel the individuality of the character's voice is basic. In the romance it is a sometime thing: the individual voice can merge into a chorus (or, indeed, a duet), "I" can be replaced by "we." In confirmation and in the usages discussed in this last section, narrative voice and character's voice are more closely parallel than is usual in modern works, while in mixed forms of discourse the voices weave in and out with one another and almost merge.

Certainly, fifteenth-century dialogue does not sound like an ideal medium for dramatizing faint nuances of character or hints of subconscious motivations and conflicts. On the other hand, it has obvious possibilities—obvious, that is, *after* we have read Malory— for thematic emphasis, for a presentation of reality not as a range of truths and possibilities, but as *a* truth, *a* possibility, for the celebration of one set of values as *the* set of values. It has great possibilities for a Hebraic but not a Hellenic vision.

NARRATION

In its potentials and limitations, fifteenth-century romance narration is of a piece with fifteenth-century dialogue. But our

reactions to the two are somewhat different. For the modern reader
this narration is not simply strange, but strange in two opposite
ways. On the one hand, this storytelling seems too subjective: the
narrators keep making value judgments and assuming our assent to
those judgments in a way that would scandalize any creative writing
teacher. On the other hand, it is too objective: why, for instance,
do we have those long, dull lists of participants in battles? One
wants to know not only what view of reality gave rise to a particular
device, but also what view of reality gave rise to the peculiar combination of devices which, so to speak, places the romance at once
to the right and to the left of the realistic novel.

I take my examples primarily from five English works: *Le Morte
Darthur, Charles the Grete,* the *English Merlin, Paris and Vienne,* and
King Ponthus and the Fair Sidone. Because style within genre matters
here I concentrate on romance, and I emphasize English material
because these prose romances (with the obvious exception of the
Morte) have been far less read and discussed than the French ones.
The quotations from Malory's sources later in this book will, I
hope, make the continuity of French and English style fairly clear.

Superlatives

The following description of Guinevere from the *English Merlin*
is wholly typical of its period and genre:

> And Arthur hir be-hielde full debonerly, and plesed hym wele
> that he saugh hir so nygh, ffor she was the feirest lady that was
> in all Breteigne in that tyme; and the mayden was fayre, and
> hadde on hir heede a riche chapelet of preciouse stones, and hir
> visage fressh and wele colowred, and so entermedled white and
> reade so naturally that it neded nother more ne lesse, and her
> shulderers streyghte and euen, and merveylously well shapen of
> body, for she was sklender a-boute the flankes and the haunche
> lowe and comly well sittynge, and of alle fetures the feirest
> shapen that myght be founde in eny londe; and yef she hadde
> grete bewte ther-to she hadde as moche bounte of valour, of
> curtesie, and nurture.

Whan Arthur saugh this mayden that hadde so grete bewte,

he be-heilde her with a gladde chere, and saugh her pappes
smale and rounde as two smale apelis that were harde; and her
flessh whitter than snowe, and was not to fatte ne to sklender;
and he covyted her gretly in his herte. . . . [II.227]

Perhaps the first thing one notices in this passage is the use of
superlatives: "the feirest lady that was in all Bretaigne in that tyme
. . . of alle fetures the feirest shapen that myght be founde in eny
londe." Now one encounters such superlatives frequently in medieval literature—for instance, they are quite common in Middle
English verse and in the thirteenth-century French historians[18]—
but they are particularly if not uniquely important in the prose
romances. We begin to sense something of that importance when we
look at two supporting phrases in the *Merlin* passage: "so enter-
medled . . . that it neded nothir more ne lesse"; "and was not to
fatte ne to sklender."Guinevere is not *sui generis*, but the best in a
category; the author describes her by holding her up to an implied
standard of ideal feminine beauty. Our modern irrelevant reaction
to "sklender a-boute the flankes . . . well sittynge," which makes
of Guinevere a prize heifer and potential roast, is in fact not wholly
irrelevant, even if the nuances of "flanks" and "haunch" have
changed since the fifteenth-century; like a prize heifer in a cattle
show, Guinevere is praised insofar as she conforms to a standard.

Of course not only fair women are described as best of class in the
prose romances. Superlatives are used for so many things that one
comes to feel there is a class and standard of judgment for every
object and phenomenon:

> . . . and certeyn the melodye of their songes and the sowne of
> theyr Instrument was so playsaunt & so swete that it passed al
> other melodye. [*Paris and Vienne*, 3]

> . . . Fyerabras the moost meruayllous geaunt that euer was
> seen borne of moder, for of the greteness and hugenes of hys
> body and also of his strengthe to hym was none like. [*Charles the
> Grete*, 40]

18. See Beer's discussion of hyperbole in *Villehardouin: Epic Historian*, p. 111 ff.

> Than thei set forth her wey thourgh the town, so fresch and
> richely armed that no people might be better. . . . [*English
> Merlin*, II.206]

> . . . thei were alle so well horsed that no men myght be better.
> . . . [Ibid., II.211]

In the following lines from "The Tale of King Arthur," Malory
manages to get three superlatives into a very few words:

> And as they stood and hoved, there cam by them the fayreste
> knyght and the semelyest man that ever they sawe, but he made
> the grettyst dole that ever man made. [164]

So heavily are superlatives used in late medieval prose narrative
that sometimes two or more persons must share a given uniqueness.
In the *English Merlin*, for instance, it is said that when Urien and
Bandemagnus surprised the Saxons "ther was grete slaughter of men
and of horse bothe, for neuer so small a peple made so grete occi-
sion" (II.239). Later we read in the account of another battle:
". . . and on tother side the kynge Ydiers faught at the end of the
cauchie so merveilously, that neuer of so few peple was done so
stronge bataile . . . " (II.279). Here the author does not intend a
distinction between how "strong" a battle is and how many of the
enemy are slain; when he comes to the later superlative he has simply forgotten the earlier one. On page 190 of *Charles the Grete* Caxton
says of a battle "there was neuer seen warre so mortal, for they that
were lyuyng were lette by them that were dede." The evidence of
superlativeness is not conclusive; there are other passages in *Charles
the Grete* where corpses are so numerous they impede movement—
including one on the very next page.

Superlatives imply standards. To describe something as the best
suggests that degrees of excellence in a particular category can be
measured. And frequent implied references to standards, together
with a wide range of things so referred, encourage the audience to
see the world of the romance as one in which values are fixed and
objective (there is no "in my opinion" attached to these superlatives)
and comparative worth can be determined with assurance. That
superlatives occasionally contradict one another suggests only the

obvious: they are used heavily, and the author isn't *really* keeping score in each of the categories whose existence we infer from his rhetoric. The important thing is that the rhetoric *suggests* he is keeping score—or that he might be.[19]

At the beginning of this chapter I said that Malory's stylistic originality lies primarily in his full exploitation of parts of the common inheritance. His use of superlatives is a good example of this full exploitation, for the world of the *Morte Darthur* is one in which values are fixed, and comparative worth is something at once determinable and immensely important.

Probably the best known use of superlatives in Malory is Ector's climactic threnody for Lancelot:

> "A, Launcelot!" he sayd, "thou were hede of al Crysten
> knyghtes! And now I dare say," sayd syr Ector, "thou sir Laun-
> celot, there thou lyest, that thou were never matched of erthely
> knyghtes hande. And thou were the curtest knyght that ever
> bare shelde! And thou were the truest frende to thy lovar that
> ever bestrade hors, and thou were the trewest lover, of a synful
> man, that ever loved woman, and thou were the kyndest man
> that ever strake wyth swerde. And thou were the godelyest
> persone that ever cam emonge prees of knyghtes, and thou
> was the mekest man and the jentyllest that ever ete in halle
> emonge ladyes, and thou were the sternest knyght to thy
> mortal foo that ever put spere in the reeste." [1259]

It is difficult to imagine a reading of *Le Morte Darthur* in which this passage would not be thematically central.[20] Lancelot matters,

19. In view of the heavy use of superlatives in these romances, it is interesting that "passing" is used so frequently as a synonym for "full" or "very." It is also worth noting that, as Field points out, Malory is very fond of the expression "out of measure" (*Romance and Chronicle*, p. 76). Though I suspect Malory's liking for the phrase is indirectly connected with the theme of *mesure* in courtly French literature, "out of measure" is a particularly appropriate kind of hyperbole in a work where, to a great extent, the audience sees the world in terms of standards, categories, and measures.

20. There is, by the way, a brief parody of Ector's speech in the "Oxen of the Sun" chapter of Joyce's *Ulysses:* "And sir Leopold that was the goodliest man that ever sat in scholars' hall and that was the meekest man and the kindest that ever

finally, not because he is interesting in himself, or nice, or good, or complex, but because he is the *best* of earthly knights. And in Malory supremacy is fact, not opinion. Notice how frequently the plot involves supernatural recognition of the worth of characters—and such recognition clearly makes rank a matter of fact. Only Galahad is able to draw the sword on whose pommel is written "NEVER SHALL MAN TAKE ME HENSE BUT ONLY HE BY WHOSE SYDE I OUGHT TO HONGE AND HE SHALL BE THE BESTE KNYGHT OF THE WORLDE" (856). In the "Healing of Sir Urry" section, Urry cannot be healed until the best knight in the world searches his wounds (1145). Examples could easily be multiplied, but the important point is this: enchanted wounds, swords in stones, perilous sieges, and boiling cauldrons do not make idiosyncratic judgments. Degrees of excellence are part of the objective reality of the Malorian world, and an important part of that reality: a number of the most memorable episodes in *Le Morte Darthur* turn on the discovery of who is the best in a particular category. The metaphysical ideas (or if not ideas, predispositions) implicit in this kind of plot are impressed upon us throughout *Le Morte Darthur* by the ranking which is a prominent feature of Malory's style.

Qualitative Descriptions

In his discussion of Coleridge in *The Uses of Poetry and the Use of Criticism*, T. S. Eliot has a shrewd note on the value to a poet of readings in the literature of travel and exploration:

> The circumstances of early exploration might well stimulate the imaginations of those who endeavoured to set down precisely what they had seen in such a way as to convey an accurate impression to Europeans who had no experience of anything similar. They would often, naturally, stimulate the imagination beyond the perception, but it is usually the accurate images, the fidelity of which may still be recognized, that are the most telling.[21]

laid husbandly hand under hen and that was the very truest knight of the world that ever did minion service to lady gentle pledged him courtly in the cup" (London, 1964, p. 506 f.).

21. *The Use of Poetry and the Use of Criticism: Studies in the Relation of Criticism to Poetry in England* (London, 1933), p. 78 n.

It is the natural task of travel writers to be exact in their descriptions of the exotic. But, as a typical passage from Hakluyt's *Voyages* (1589) suggests, qualitative descriptions—and especially qualitative modifiers—are ubiquitous in Tudor prose; and even the travel writer, with his desire for precision, does not stay away from them for long:

> The king did sit in a *very rich* pavillion, wrought with silke & golde, placed *very plesantly* upon a hill side, of sixteene fathom long, and six fathom broad, having before him a *goodly* fountaine of faire water: whereof he & his nobility did drinke, he being of a meane stature and of a *fierce* countenance, *richly* apparelled with long garments of silk, and cloth of gold, imbroidred with pearles and stone. . . .[22]

The sixteenth-century writer is much like his medieval forebear in his taste for qualitative modifiers: again and again in our romances, to describe is to evaluate. The superlative is only the most resounding judgment in a style where perception and evaluation go together.

The descriptive vocabularies of late medieval prose works tend to be small—in Villehardouin, perhaps an extreme example, Beer finds only one hundred different adjectives[23]—and descriptive passages usually emphasize evaluation at least as much as objective physical detail. The portrait of Guinevere I quoted at the beginning of the last section is typical of its period and genre not only in its use of superlatives, but in its heavy employment of evaluative modifiers: ". . . and the mayden was fayre, and hadde on hir heede a riche chapelet of preciouse stones, and hir visage fressh and wele colowred. . . ." To cite two more passages:

> . . . and thei weren alle *right wele* clothed and *richely* arrayed, and alle yonge bachelers at pryme barbe, excepte two kynges that yede be-fore, that somedell were in age, and thei were

22. Richard Hakluyt, *Voyages*, introduction by John Masefield, 8 vols. (London, 1907, reprinted 1962), 2: 14. This passage is from "The voyage of M. Anthony Jenkenson through Russia. . . ."

23. Beer, *Villehardouin*, pp. 100, 122 f. Beer's discussion of description in Villehardouin and other Old French writers (p. 100 ff.) is excellent.

feire knyghtes and *semely*, and thei were be-holden of grete and
smale of alle that were ther-Inne, ffor thei were of freissh aray
and *riche* atire. [*Charles the Grete*, 203]

. . . and ther thei fought to-geder *right harde;* ffor the kynge
Ydiers was a *full noble* knyght and a *sure*, and he dide ther *mer-
veilous* of armes, and he hadde many *good* knyghtes in his com-
panye, that hym *right wele* dide helpe, and thei foughten all the
day at the rewarde of the hoste, and were xxML. [*English
Merlin*, 278]

A comparatively small group of evaluative modifiers—including,
perhaps most prominently, "courteous," "fair," "rich," "false,"
"good," "goodly," "knightly," "marvellous," "mighty," "noble,"
"passing," "sad" (as in "many sad strokes"), and "worthy"—
occurs again and again in the English romances. The imaginative
world we enter in those works is one in which values and physical
attributes exist on a single plane of reality ("the metal was noble
and corrugated") or in which values sometimes seem the most
prominent occupants of the plane of reality closest to us ("the metal
was fair and noble"). To an imagist poet, let us say, the passages I
have quoted from Hakluyt, *Charles the Grete*, and the *English Merlin*
might seem merely lazy, but they are not. Worth, quality, and value
are part of the texture of these worlds; they are felt as things in the
scene described, rather than as a viewer's judgment of that scene.

Such "qualitative vision" is not the exclusive gift of narrator and
audience. In the romances, the character's vocabulary is very like
the author's, and virtually everywhere romance dialogue is as
thickly strewn with "fair's" and "goodly's" as the prose around it.
It is also instructive to consider point-of-view in such a description
as the following:

Than were they ware in the wynde where cam a *ryche* vessell
heled over with rede sylke, and the vessell londed faste by them.
Therewith sir Trystram alyght and his knyghtes, and so sir
Trystram wente afore and entird into that vessell. And whan
he cam in he saw a *fayre* bedde *rychely* coverde, and thereuppon
lay a *semely* dede knyght all armed sauff the hede, and was all

bloody with *dedly* woundys uppon hym, whych semed to be a
passynge good knyght. [*Works*, 700]

All of this is implicitly the scene as it appeared to Tristram. Yet the
descriptive vocabulary here is as heavily evaluative as in passages of
"pure" narrative description. Notice particularly the word "dedly."
What we observe is not the physical wounds (length, depth, etc.)
but the effect of the wounds upon the knight. Tristram sees—as we
see—the quality of the wounds, their severity, their mortal nature,
rather than the wounds as gashes, just as he sees the bed in terms of
its quality of fairness, the covering in terms of richness, the knight in
terms of seemliness, etc., rather than in terms of concrete physical
attributes.

One group of evaluative terms has a special resonance in *Le
Morte Darthur*: "courteous," "gentle," "knightly," and Malory's
favorite,[24] "noble"; the solemn vocabulary of knightliness. One of
the most moving lines in the narrative portion of the *Morte* is of a
kind that would be altogether silly in a novel. Malory describes
Arthur's conduct in the last, ruinous battle between the king's
forces and Mordred's; "But ever kynge Arthur rode thorowoute
the batayle of sir Mordred many tymes and ded full nobely, as a
noble kynge shulde do, and at all tymes he faynted never" (1236.1–
3). ". . . *kynge* Arthur . . . *ded* full *nobely*, as a *noble kynge* shulde
do": the chiasmus is artful, the tautology is magnificent. In the world
of *Le Morte Darthur* virtue consists essentially of living up to a code,
behaving in the manner characteristic of (or, as I suggested in the
last section, being the best individual according to the defining
standard of) one's category. What Malory tells us here is that
Arthur's actions were indeed those characteristic of his category.
There may be higher praise in *Le Morte Darthur*, but none nearer the
heart of Malorian reality, none which has more to do with the way
we've been made to look at events in the preceding 1200 pages.
The modifiers of the "noble" group help sustain this vision of reality.
The line about Arthur's last battle is splendidly tautological, but in
one sense there is a tautology almost every time such modifiers are

24. See Field, *Romance and Chronicle*, pp. 75, 82, and my discussion below, pp.
140–42.

used in *Le Morte Darthur*. Almost always they describe members, or the actions of members, of the social or political group indicated: the knightly deed is done by a knight, the courteous behavior is that of one whose base of operations is a court, etc. But literary tautologies are not mere tautologies: these modifiers keep us aware that the central fact about the event being described is that the action is characteristic of those in the actor's category. The heavy use of modifiers of the "noble" group tends to suggest that conformity or non-conformity to chivalric standards or norms is the important aspect of any event, the most "real" thing about it.

Heavy use of qualitative description is one of the characteristics of late medieval prose most likely to make that prose seem naive or careless to the modern reader. But in fact there is evidence the romancers relied on such description out of a sense of decorum, a sense that important information was conveyed by these modifiers, rather than because they lacked skill to do otherwise. In the *English Merlin* for instance, we find these sketches of Merlin disguised as an old man:

> . . . and Gawein hym cleped efte soones, and than he lefte vp his heed that was lothly and rivelid, and loked on high to hym with oon eye open and a-nother clos, and grennynge with his teth as a man that loked a-gein the sonne, and an-suerde, "What wilt thow?" [II.262]

> Whan Gawein vndirstode the wordes of this wise man he hym be-heilde and saugh that he was right olde and so croked that he merveilde that he myght holde hym on horsebakke, and saugh he hadde a grete beerde and a longe that couered all his breste and was all white, and a chapelet of coton vpon his hede, and clothed in a robe of blakke, and for age heilde hym by the sadill bowe. . . . [II.294]

The incisiveness of the final details in the two passages—the eyes, teeth, and especially the smile in the first, the mention of the sad-dlebow in the second—is delightful. The romancer doesn't use detail this way more often largely because he has no occasion to: both these passages come at moments of comic relief, in which the audience is to enjoy the grotesqueness of Merlin's disguise.[25] These are low moments, described with a low particularity. High events call for a grander mode of description.

Much of the description in *Reynard the Fox* supports the view that decorum rather than necessity produced the evaluative descriptions in the romances. This is Caxton telling about Bruyn the bear caught in a split tree:

> . . . he sawe wel that he begyled was he began to howle and to braye / and crutched wyth the hynder feet and made such a noyse and rumour that lantfert cam out hastely / and knewe nothyng what this myght be / and brought in his hand a sharpe hoke / bruyn the bere laye in the clyfte of the tree in grete fere and drede / and helde fast his heed and nyped both his fore feet /he wrange he wrastled / and cryed / and all was for nought / he wiste not how he myght gete out. . . .[15]

The quick successions of markedly active verbs describing Bruyn ("howle . . . braye . . . crutched; . . . nyped . . . wrange . . . wrastled . . . cryed . . .") contrast nicely with the quite ordinary (". . . cam . . . knewe . . . brought . . .") and less thickly clustered ones describing Lantfert's actions with the result that the panicked and useless activity of the bear is vividly conveyed. This is a tale of animals; only mock solemn, essentially low and comic. Such vividness would be unseemly in other contexts.

Catalogues

A heavy use of superlatives and qualitative modifiers suggests that in the romance world values are fixed and almost palpable. The romancer is more subjective than the novelist. He will not allow values to emerge from data; for him they are the data. But the same writers who see a world of fairness and goodness include long lists of names in their fictions; we are reading along, and suddenly the work takes on the objectivity of an almanac. What is the function of the romance list, and what is its connection with the subjective narrative devices? A bird's-eye view of the history of literary

25. Malory does not like the comic aspect of Merlin's disguises. See pp. 115–16.

catalogues (a very high flying bird, this one) will help place the kind of list we find in Malory and the *Charles the Grete*.

Omne tulit punctum qui miscuit utile dulci: the Horatian tag applies nicely to the oldest literary catalogues. As C. M. Bowra says, "In days when written history did not exist, one of its functions was taken by a versified list of names . . . . Being in verse it could be memorized and passed on to posterity with less danger of corruption than if it were in prose . . . . Into it accumulated tradition was crystallized, and it carried the weight of the inspired word."[26] Certainly early lists brought enjoyment as well as instruction—particularly those verse lists. In fact, this kind of usefulness must involve pleasure, since the same regularity of form which makes a mnemonic effective makes it satisfying; we like to say "Thirty days hath September."

Now when we look at the literature of later periods (such as the later Middle Ages) we find what is basically a division of catalogues into two kinds, one of which is *dulce* (at least in intention) and the other *utile*. The *dulce*, the literary catalogue, appears in the "atmospheric" lists of the French verse romances[27] and the thematically suggestive, epithet-laden bird and tree stanzas of the *Parliament of Fowls*. Such lists (and of course the later lists of Marlowe and Milton) may be delightful purely as sound, and may enrich the thematic patterns of the works in which they occur; but it is rarely their immediate purpose to help us deal with the world beyond the work: Chaucer is not interested in helping us remember bird names, nor Milton in helping us remember geographical ones.

The second, useful kind of list is typical of the chronicles. Here the lists are unadorned, and often run on to forbidding length. The following passages from the *Brut*, most popular of fifteenth-century English chronicles, have the texture of real history:

> And forthwith þe said King Henry dubbed al this knyghtes, whose names folowes, þat is to say: Richard, Duke of York, Also þe sone & heir of þe Duke of Northfolk, þerle of Oxen-

---

26. Sir C. M. Bowra, *Tradition and Design in the Iliad* (Oxford, 1930), p. 69.

27. See Charles Muscatine, *Chaucer and the French Tradition* (Berkeley and Los Angeles, 1957), p. 17.

forth, perle of Westmerland, þe sone & heir of perle of Nor-
thumbreland, þe sone & heir of perle of Wormond, þe lorde
Rose, Sir Iames Botler. . . . [The list continues for another
25 names.] [*Brut*, II.499]

And the whiles he purveid hys naves, and made his retenewe
in ENGLOND, in al þe hast he myght; of which þe namz of
the chef lordes and capteyns, with their retenewe and the
noumbre, folowith heraftir in this table, that is for to say:

PRYNCE EDWARD with xj banerettes, Ciiij knyghtes,
CClxiiij men of armes, CCCiiij^{xx} Archers on horsbak, iijix^{xx}
Archers on foote, vj C Walshmen, whereof on was a chapelyn
& anoþer a leche, and anoþer a crier. And in his retenewe was
xxvti vynteners, & iiij C & iiij footmen, & v standart berers.

HENRY, Erle of Lancastre, with an Erle, xj banerettes, C.
iiij^{xx} xiij knyghtes, c and xij men of Armes, and Clxj of
Archers on horsebak. . . . [II.538]^{28}

Now in the prose romances there is occasionally a "literary"
catalogue, more or less similar in function to the catalogues in contemporary verse.^{29} But more often romance lists are like those found
in the chronicles. This passage, typical of the entire genre, comes
from the *English Merlin*:

In this same wise swor sir Ewin, and Segramor, and Agrauain,
and Geheret, and Gaheries, and XXV of her felowes, and that
oon was Doo of Cardoell, and Sacren of the streite Marche,
and Taulus le rous, and Biloc de Cassell, and Caues de lille and
Amadas de la Crespe, and placidas li gais, and laudalus de la

28. This list of those going to Calais contains another 39 items, similar to the
two quoted here, though growing somewhat shorter as the chronicler comes to
lords and allies with retinues smaller than those of the prince and the Earl of
Lancaster. As we will see later, such lengthy catalogues are often found in the
romances also. One list in the *English Merlin* contains 43 names. (II. 212).

29. In the *English Merlin*, for instance, there is something of a virtuoso piece (II.
280–281) exhibiting the author's skill in solving a rhetorical problem; how to describe essentially the same act (the leading of groups of warriors) six times, keeping
to one basic sentence form, but differentiating the acts through changes in detail.

playne, and Aiglins des vaus, and Clealis lorfenyns, and
Grires de lamball, and kehedins li bens, and Caros de la broche,
and Segurades de la forest perilouse, and Purades de Car-
melide, and Carmeduk the blake. . . . [II.682]

Such a list is very like the first of the two catalogues quoted from the
Brut; other romance catalogues are more like the second. In this
passage from his first tale, for instance, Malory has the chronicler's
interest in the number of men in each division of a host:

. . . and than they made an othe. And the first that began the
othe was the deuke of Canbenet, that he wolde brynge with
hym fyve thousand men of armys, the which were redy on
horsebakke. Than swore kynge Brandegoris of Strangore that
he wolde brynge with hym fyve thousand men of armys on
horsebacke. Than swore kynge Clarivaus of Northumbirlonde
that he wolde brynge three thousand men of armys with hym.
Than swore the Kynge with the Hondred Knyghtes that was
a passynge good man and a yonge, that he wolde brynge
four thousand good men of armys on horsebacke. Than there
swore kynge Lott, a passynge good knyght and fadir unto sir
Gawayne, that he wolde brynge fyve thousand good men of
armys on horsebak. Also there swore kynge Uryens that was sir
Uwaynes fadir, of the londe of Goore, and he wolde brynge six
thousand men of armys on horsebak. Also there swore kynge
Idres of Cornuwaile that he wolde brynge fyve thousand men
of armys on horsebak. Also there swore kynge Cradilmans to
brynge fyve thousand men of armys on horsebak. Also there
swore kyng Angwysshauns of Irelonde to brynge fyve thousand
men of armys on horsebak. Also there swore kynge Nentres
to brynge fyve thousand men on horsebak. Also there swore
kynge Carados to brynge fyve thousand men of armys on
horsebak. [25–26]

Qui miscuit utile dulci. . . . Now such bare chronicle lists are not
delightful in themselves, and they are not *really* useful either. (We
know, for instance, that Malory was not scrupulously transmitting
older lists; he felt quite free to lengthen catalogues and sometimes

to make them up entirely.) What, then, are these unprepossessing lists for? I suspect the chronicle–lists are in the romances, and particularly in *Le Morte Darthur*, just because they do smack of the chronicle. The romancer wants us to regard his work somewhat the way we regard "real" history. By this I mean not that he necessarily wants us to think of his stories as literally true, but that he wants us to think of the actions described with the respect and earnestness with which we think of true historical events; or more accurately, he wants us to think that *he*, the narrator, brings this respect and earnestness to the task of telling these stories.[30] On this point the introduction to a catalogue in the *English Merlin* is illuminating:

> Ther dide the xlij felowes so well that it was spoken of longe tyme after her deth in that contry; and the storye seith thei mangled and slow so many, that by the traces oon myght haue sued half a day euery wey of the deed bodies and horse that thei hadde wounded, as thei that nought ne cessed ne rested; and therefore me semeth reson to reherse the names of tho worthi men. [II. 211–212]

The romancer introduces a catalogue not to entertain us, but to pay homage to the great men and events he is describing and to preserve information about those great events. He is performing an act of piety. The very dullness of the list impresses us with the sincerity of his devotion; the monotonousness reminds us that the audience's delight is not the author's first concern.

Once we notice the general similarity between prose romance lists and chronicle lists, a minor but very curious characteristic of prose romance narrative begins to make stylistic sense. This is what I shall call the "ragged edge" detail: that is, a complicating factor, a bit of information, an action, which is included in a catalogue but seems

---

30. Although he does not discuss catalogues in this connection, P. J. C. Field is very much concerned with the importance of chronicle usage in Malory, as the title of his book indicates. When considering the relation of prose romance catalogues to chronicle lists, we might recall Geoffrey of Monmouth's narrative style. Geoffrey also includes rather long, bare catalogues of names (e.g., *Historia Regum Britanniae*, IX, 12), and undoubtedly expects them to add to his book's plausibility as a serious historical work.

to contribute nothing to either plot or theme—an irrelevancy, in short. As this negative description suggests (I will attempt a positive one below) the modern reader, on encountering such details, will likely dismiss them with the reflection that Caxton, too, may nod, or, if he is of a scholarly turn of mind, will suspect that the seeming irrelevancy conceals a contemporary reference.[31] Here are two ragged edge details from *King Ponthus and the Fair Sidone*:

> This counsell was holden goode aboue all othir and was ful-fylled. And messyngers was sent throgh oute the contre to the Erle of Morteyne, to the Erle of Mayne, to the Lorde de La Vale, and of Sylle; and to the Duches of Aniou, for the Duke was deid; also he sent to the Lorde of Chasteaue Gouter, and to Guyllen de Roches, to Bortane de Doune, and to Landry de La Toure; into Petewe thei sent to the Erle of Peyters, bot he was goon to Rome, and thei sent vnto Geffrey de Lazenyen, to Lernell de La Mauelyon, and to Henri de La Marche: so thes knyghtes wer chosen for the best that was in thos dayes in thoos countrees aboute theym. . . . [74]

Why "and to the Duches of Aniou, for the Duke was deid" and "to the Erle of Peyters, bot he was goon to Rome"? These details have no obvious narrative purpose, and the characters referred to are unimportant in the story.

A second example, this time from the *EnglishMerlin*. The romancer lists those Christian rulers who meet at Salisbury to plan resistance to the Saxons:

> . . . after hym com the kynge Cleolas that after was cleped the firste conquered kynge, and in his company vj ML men, and he loigged next Aguygueron, the Seneschall of Clamedien. But this kynge Cleolas hadde but litill tyme be ther whan hym be-hoved to go thens for grete sekeness, and lefte his peple to Guyonce his Senescall that was a goode man and a noble knyght; after hym com. . . . [II. 578]

31. Which may be true in some cases. There can be little doubt, for instance, that *King Ponthus and the Fair Sidone* contains many oblique references and compliments to the Tour Landry family. (See Mather's "Introduction.") But a detail may be a veiled contemporary reference and have other functions as well.

According to the index of Wheatley's edition. Guyonce is never mentioned again, and Cleolas (or Cleoles) only once more.[32] At that final appearance (II. 600) Cleolas fights vigorously with the chief Saxon lord; his arm is broken in the fight, but we hear nothing of his earlier illness. It is entirely reasonable to suspect that the author has forgotten it by the time he writes the second passage.

I think that in both the *Ponthus* and *English Merlin* catalogues the function of the ragged edge detail is to enhance the chronicle-like appearance of the list by introducing a certain asymmetry: the one or two minor exceptions to the general pattern, the unimportant, incidental complications which one expects to find fairly often in real chronicles. The ragged edge detail, then, may be defined as mention and brief discussion of a minor exception to a pattern in a catalogue of those conforming to that pattern. Its function is to increase the resemblance between the romance catalogue in which it occurs and catalogues in true chronicles.

Romance historicism, the historicism of bare lists and ragged edge details,[33] is highly relevant to an esthetic question I briefly raised earlier in this chapter. A heavy use of evaluative modifiers is something a creative writing teacher will tell his students to avoid. It is sentimental; we should be shown, not told; when a penny is thrown into the street we "want to hear that penny *hopping and chinking.*"[34] If in the romances we have neither the thickness nor the synecdochal incisiveness of phenomenal particulars we find in the novel,[35] if romance descriptions tend to the evaluative rather than the concrete, how do they convince us? What makes us *feel* the worthiness, goodness, and fairness of a fictional world where things are endlessly described as worthy, good, and fair? The evidence of the superlative

32. The King Cleoles mentioned on II.595 is a Saxon, and appears to have no connection with the character we are discussing.

33. I employ the word "historicism" in referring to romance imitations of chronicle style because in one standard usage the word suggests that attitude of reverence for the past which, it seems to me, is conveyed by these imitations. I am not, of course, dealing with the theory of history known as historicism.

34. The last phrase is from Dostoevsky's correspondence, and is quoted from J. Middleton Murry, *The Problem of Style* (London, 1960, originally published 1922), p. 71.

35. On the thickness of particulars, see below, pp. 69 ff.

quality of characters and events in the best of these romances is not the concreteness of those characters and events, but the concrete manifestation of the romancer's respect for them. This is especially true of Malory: we believe in Lancelot's importance less because of what we see Lancelot do, than because of the narrator's attitude toward what Lancelot does. The creative writing teacher (or the imagist poet) isn't wrong in saying accurate detail must be there; but we must not draw the boundaries of "there" too quickly.

I have said historicism is particularly important in Malory. There must be few narratives in which our cumulative sense of the weight of what happens and the greatness of those involved so exceeds our episode-by-episode impression, and that sense of the weight of events depends to a great extent upon the historicism of the narrative. Our sense of that historicism and of the earnestness and reverence of the narrator rises from Malory's use of catalogues(particularly prominent, as I have said, in his two last tales) but of course from a number of other devices also. As P. J. C. Field points out, Malory's French sources display a "more accomplished, fluent, and varied subordination of clauses" than *Le Morte Darthur* and most other English works of the period. Malory's heavier use of parataxis makes his tales sound more like a chronicle than the French romances do.[36]

---

36. P. J. C. Field, *Romance and Chronicle*, p. 38. Field stresses the colloquial nature and unselfconsciousness of Malory's style, but here his argument seems to me based on far too restricted a conception of rhetoric, and his case for the unselfconsciousness of parataxis and other devices in the *Morte* inconclusive. "Rhetoric is a conscious art, and there are no signs that Malory was in any way a conscious stylist, and several indications that he was not" (p. 72). But the two May passages are the work of a conscious stylist, unless "conscious" must mean "well read in rhetorical treatises." It may seem natural to assume, as Field does (p. 45), that Malorian parataxis is a colloquial feature, but in fifteenth-century French prose parataxis may suggest dignity and solemnity rather than artlessness, and I believe it suggests those things in Malory also. (See Jens Rosmussen on the varied functions of polysyndeton in French narrative prose: *La Prose Narrative Française du XVe Siècle: Etude Esthetique et Stylistique* [Copenhagen, 1958], p. 73f.). Again, Field apparently assumes Malory's frequent "wyte you welle's" come from popular storytelling (p. 71)—but can we be sure of this? They correspond to the "sachiés que" and "bien sachiés que" of Malory's French sources, and according to Schon, "sachiés que" is a "lehrhafte" formula in the not very much earlier French of the historians (*Studien zum Stil der frühen französichen Prosa*, p. 161). I would speak of the sobriety

As I shall show in the next chapter, Malory presents his characters from the outside; the name of his hero is not Lancelot, but *Sir Lancelot*; the audience is invited to share the broodings and perplexities of the Arthurian company far less often in Malory than in the French. The narrative voice is that of the historian, not of the omniscient fictionalist: Malory never patronizes his heroes as narrators of French romances occasionally do; he respects them too much to be amused at their expense. Malory is constantly adding English place names to the narrative, which of course enhances the realism and matter-of-factness of the narrative by quite literally supplying a local habitation and a name. But it is especially important that he adds explanations, such as, "in the grettest chirch of London—whether it was Powlis or not the Frensshe booke maketh no mencyon" (12.26–27) or "Somme men say it was Anwyk, and somme men say it was Bamborow" (1257.27–28) which impress upon the normal reader, who is not comparing Malory with his sources, the scrupulous, painstaking nature of the narration. Such a narrator can be trusted; this does not sound like someone telling an old wives' tale. But this is also a man who respects his subject matter and believes finding the truth about these events important enough to point out where that truth is uncertain.

Conventional and Blueprint Details

I now come to two kinds of detail which are fairly common in the prose romances. One is the traditional, formulaic detail; the other what I shall call the blueprint detail—a stylistic feature which contributes to the historicism discussed in the last section. Here I will be looking mostly at descriptions of combat; for the sake of clarity it seems useful, when trying to discriminate between similar descriptive techniques, to limit the range of things described. In Malory, combat is an obvious choice; fighting is not the whole of the chivalric life, but it is central to it.

Combat is central to that life, but it should also be said that in

---

and dignity rather than the colloquial simplicity of Malory's style, but my point here is not that Malory is not colloquial but that it is more difficult than it seems to demonstrate that he is, and more difficult still to show that he is an unselfconscious stylist.

Le Morte Darthur (and to a lesser extent in the other romances) combat is really a manifestation of the hero's virtue and courage, not of his skill. As Field has pointed out, "None of Malory's battles is decided by the physical circumstances in which it takes place. We are not here in a world in which mechanics has a great deal to do with success."[37] In this world, where the inner quality of the combatants is more important than the physical circumstances of the combat, battle passages contain a good deal of qualitative description. But we also find a large number of concrete physical details, in both literal and metaphorical descriptions. It is this physical description I want to discuss. What is it, and what is its function in a world where mechanics has little to do with success?

First, the Malorian simile:

> And than they began to feauter theire spearys, and cam togydir as thundir. . . . [474.14–16]

> . . . and there he fared amonge the knyghtis as a grehounde amonge conyes. [525.30–31]

> And somtyme they russhed togydyrs with their shyldis lyke two boorys other rammys. . . . [641.2–4]

> Than they hurteled togedyrs as two wylde bullys, russhynge and laysshyng with hir shyldis and swerdys. . . . [267.11–12]

> Than sir Launcelot rode here and there as wode as a lyon that faughted hys fylle, because he had loste sir Trystram. . . . [527.18–20]

Needless to say, these similes of thunder and bellicose animals enjoy wide distribution in medieval narrative. Chaucer, for example, includes what may be called the lion's share of Malory's similes in five lines of the *Knight's Tale* (1655 ff.):

> Thou myghtest wene that this Palamon
> In his fightyng were a wood leon,
> And as a crueel tigre was Arcite;
> As wilde bores gonne they to smyte,
> That frothen whit as foom for ire wood.

Le Morte Darthur uses a very small number of these comparisons

37. Field, *Romance and Chronicle*, p. 93; "Description and Narration," p. 484.

again and again; and almost as important as the heavy repetition of a few similes is the rudimentary form in which those few nearly always occur. The Chaucerian boars, conventional as they are, "frothen whit as foom for ire wood." Malory gives us a similar (though less visual) elaboration in ". . . that faughted hys fylle," but this is exceptional; usually the second term in a Malorian simile is little more than a noun or adjective and noun.

Now, as I shall maintain later, every concrete object mentioned in a simile contributes something to the phenomenal density of a literary work; no physical detail is so worn down by repetition that it really becomes equivalent to an abstraction in effect. But clearly the Malorian lion, bull, and boar are not very vividly present. These are traditional comparisons; when Tarquin and Lancelot hurtle together like two boars the reader does not visualize those boars (and thus the boars do not help him visualize the knights) very distinctly, and the simile does not mark off the combat being described as different from other battles. Almost the reverse is true: "lyke two boorys" serves to link this combat with all the other boar- (and, I think, lion-, and bull-, and thunder-) like combats the audience has heard of in Malory and, indeed, in other romances. Almost as much as it suggests two boars fighting, the phrase "like two boars" suggests "in a knightly manner; in the manner of all the other heroes to whose combats this phrase has been applied." The standard comparison implies normative chivalry.

A number of other conventional, semiformulaic details of combat recur frequently in *Le Morte Darthur* and the other prose romances. Like the similes, these details convey at once something of the event's physical reality and of its normativeness. The battle of Palamon and Arcite in the *Knight's Tale* introduces us to one of the most popular of these semiformulaic details, as well as to the similes just discussed. The line immediately following those already quoted is "Up to the ancle foghte they in hir blood." In Malory this traditional motif is usually adapted to battle on horseback:

> So there com into the thycke of the prees Arthure, Ban, and Bors, and slew downeryght on bothe hondis, that his horses wente in blood up to the fittlockys. [36][38]

38. See F. N. Robinson's note to *Knight's Tale*, 1.1660, for some analogues to

Related motifs are the field running with blood and the field covered with bodies:

> And ther they slewe so many of theym within a whyle that all
> the felde ran of blode and lay full of deyd bodyes, that it was
> mervell to see. [*Ponthus*, 30]

> Ther was dolerouse fight, and the mortality so grete, that ther
> ran stremes of blode as a rennynge river thourgh the felde.
> [*English Merlin*, II.337]

> . . . but dide soche occision of peple that alle the felde was
> couered of deed peple and wounded. [*Ibid.*, II.398]

Other conventions of verbal form or content which are particularly
frequent in Malory's battle scenes are "horse and man," as in "and
smote hym downe horse and man"[39] and "on the right hand and on
the left hand," as in "and slew on the ryght honde and on the lyffte
honde." Both these phrases may be found in *Ponthus* also (29;84).
In the romances sparks are traditionally struck by galloping hooves
or by swords hitting helmets; the "many . . . many" form is
frequently employed (" . . . and many a grym worde was there
spokyn of aythir to othir, and many a dadely stroke . . .";
"Antyaume, the senescall, smote in to the bataile with as grete
randon as horse myght renne, and ther was many a spere spent, and
many a sore stroke . . ."); and, perhaps somewhat less frequently, the "might see" or "should have seen" formula ("Ther myghte
men here and see swordes breke and clatre on the helmetes of
stele . . ."; ". . . and then ye myght see English, Scottysch and
Iresch, men showte and cry strongly vpon theym and sloo theym
vpon euery side . . ."; "Ther sholde ye haue sein the baners and
fresh armes glyteringe in the wynde. . . .")[40]

---

the Chaucerian line, and also Field's list of typically Malorian "familiar stock
phrases," *Romance and Chronicle*, p. 59. Such analogues as those cited by Robinson
encourage me to regard many of the Malorian similies as in their effect ceremonial
and tradititonal rather than colloquial and unobtrusive.

39. A particular favorite of Malory's in his earlier tales. Between *Works*, 28.6
and 29.26 (in a context, it is true, where horses are particularly important) he
uses the "horse and man" (in one case "man and horse") formula twelve times.

40. *Works*, 1235.32–33; *English Merlin*, II. 401; *Ponthus*, 84; *Ponthus*, 85; *English
Merlin*, II.281.

Malorian descriptions of combat usually include and very often center around pairs (and sometimes larger groups) of gerunds: ". . . and lasshed togydyrs egerly with swerdys and myghtyly, now here now there, trasyng and traversynge on the ryght honde and on the lyffte honde more than two owres" (400.24–27); "And than sir Trystrames algyht and dressed hym unto batayle, and there they laysshed togedir strongely, rasynge, foynynge and daysshynge many sad strokes . . ." (409.12–14); "Than they russhed togydyrs lyke two borys, trasynge and traversynge myghtyly and wysely as two noble knyghtes . . ." (415.24–25). This is of course an ono-matopoeic device, the swing of the paired gerunds echoing the rapid give and take of combat. But when used as heavily as it is in *Le Morte Darthur*, it works not to distinguish a particular battle from other battles, but to link that one with the others. Like the other intrinsically vivid but clichéd details and verbal devices I have been discussing, it draws the reader's attention not to "*this* chivalric com-bat," but to "this *chivalric* combat."[41]

Malory's particular skill lies in having his heroes speak with great forcefulness, but yet speak in a correct rather than an indivi-dual way; there is no Lancelotian turn of phrase, there are only knightly turns of phrase. The similes and other devices I have been considering here do (or ought to do) with knightly action what Malory does with knightly speech: impress the reader with both vividness and normativeness. There is much the same aim in dia-logue and descriptions of fighting; the difference is in the writer's success. Malory is wonderfully good at making his dialogue both normative and vivid; in his descriptions of combat, the normative-ness is more impressive than the vividness.

The second stylistic feature I want to look at here, the blueprint detail, is common both in descriptions of battles and more pacific scenes. This kind of detail is specific, physical, and nonmetaphorical. It is unlike the physical and nonmetaphorical details I discussed earlier (e.g., the field running with blood) in three ways. First, it is not conventional: the blueprint detail does not testify to the tradi-tional nature or propriety of the thing described. Second, it tends

41. Compare the normatively heroic and spectacularly gruesome *chanson de geste* motif of splitting opponents in two.

to occur in a cluster with other blueprint details: it is not felt to be climactic or emphatic as are details of the other kind. Third and most important is the effect created by a cluster of blueprint details: such a group impresses us with the *variety* of its objective facts. We seem to be getting a number of different "hard" specific data as to what, when, where, and precisely how things occurred. They are such data as would be admissible in a court of law, or discussable with Mr. Gradgrind; things one could show on a blueprint.

An example from Malory:

> And whan kynge Arthure saw that kynge ryde on sir Ectors horse he was wrothe, and with hys swerde *he smote the kynge on the helme, that a quarter of the helme and shelde clave downe; and so the swerde carve downe unto the horse necke,* and so man and horse felle downe to the grounde. Than sir Kay com unto kynge Morganoure, senesciall with the Kynge of the Hondred Knyghtes, and smote hym downe horse and man, and ledde the horse unto hys fadir, sir Ector.
>
> Than sir Ector ran unto a knyght that hyght Lardans and smote horse and man downe, and lad the horse unto sir Brastias, that grete nede had of an horse and was gretly defoyled. Whan Brastias behelde Lucas the Butler that lay lyke a dede man undir the horse feete—and ever sir Gryflet dud mercyfully for to reskow hym, and there were allwayes fourtene knyghtes upon sir Lucas—and than sir Brastias *smote one of them on the helme, that hit wente unto his tethe;* and he rode unto another and *smote hym, that hys arme flow into the felde;* than he wente to the thirde and *smote hym on the shulder, that shuldir and arme flow unto the felde.* And whan Gryfflet saw rescowis he *smote a knyght on the templis, that hede and helme wente of to the erthe.* . . . [*Works*, 29–30]

There is a good deal of formulaic repetition just before this description and indeed even within it. Malory uses the traditional "horse and man" heavily in the preceding paragraphs, and in the quoted passage itself he keeps turning to "he smote hym, that. . . ." Such repetition should emphasize the similarity of all things described by the same formulation; but notice that Malory is almost clinically exact in differentiating the blows described by "smote . . . that

. . . ." These almost clinical observations are the blueprint details.

P. J. C. Field has acutely observed that "throughout the *Morte Darthur*, the general lack of sustenance for the visual imagination gives [Malory's] infrequent *aperçus* a startling force."[42] This same kind of contrast makes a cluster of blueprint details prominent against a background of evaluative modifiers and traditional formulas. But what makes the cluster quite different from the kind of *aperçus* Field refers to is that the blueprint details are not synecdochic flashes of insight into the reality of a situation, but somewhat miscellaneous observations; a magpie's collection of objects.

I reintroduce my creative writing teacher. This teacher will certainly tell Malory to prune. If the description is all conventional and evaluative, and Malory then says "he smote the kynge on the helme, that a quarter of the helme and shelde clave downe; and so the swerde carve downe unto the horse necke," Arthur's prowess takes on a special vividness and reality because of the (in context) extraordinary concreteness of the description. But because Malory includes five such descriptions, no one of them seems especially vivid simply because of its concreteness. At the same time, the five acts of prowess have a curious relation to one another. They are not all on the same level: in terms of both aim and prowess, lopping off an arm is less impressive than lopping off an arm and shoulder, and cutting through the helmet to the teeth is a more impressive feat than either. Yet the differences between these feats have no thematic or rhetorical meaning; we cannot see any significant pattern in the sequence of blows.[43]

A longer passage from *Le Morte Darthur*:

> Wyth that com in sir Launcelot, and he threste in with his spere in the thyckyst of the pres; and there he smote downe with one spere fyve knyghtes, and of four of them he brake their backys. And in that thrange he smote downe the kynge of

42. *Romance and Chronicle*, p. 98.

43. Another notable example here would be the two killings on II. 199 of the *English Merlin*. The first is a *chanson de geste* splitting, the second a two-stage killing of an opponent by two different heroes. The author seems to regard the first act as the really splendid one, but he arranges the two in an anticlimactic sequence, and devotes about as many words to the second as to the first.

North Galys, and brake his thygh in that falle. All this doynge
of sir Launcelot saw the three knyghtes of Arthurs, and seyde,
"Yondir is a shrewde geste, therefore have here ons at hym."
So they encountred, and sir Launcelot bare hym downe horse
and man so that his sholdir wente oute of joynte.

"Now hit befallyth me," seyde sir Mordred, "to stirre me, for
sir Mador hath a sore falle." And than sir Launcelot was ware
of hym, and gate a spere in his honde and mette with hym. And
sir Mordred brake his spere uppon hym; and sir Launcelot
gaff hym suche a buffette that the arson of the sadill brake,
and so he drove over the horse tayle, that his helme smote into
the erthe a foote and more, that nyghe his nek was broke, and
there he lay longe in a swowe.

Than com in sir Gahalantyne with a grete spere, and sir
Launcelot agaynste hym in all that they myght dryve, that
bothe hir sperys to-braste evyn to their hondys; and than they
flange oute with her swerdes and gaff many sore strokys. Than
was sir Launcelot wroth oute of mesure, and than he smote sir
Gahalantyne on the helme, that his nose, erys, and mowthe
braste oute on bloode; and therewith his hede hynge low, and
with that his horse ran away with hym, and he felle downe to
erthe.

Anone therewithall sir Launcelot gate a speare in his honde,
and or ever that speare brake he bare downe to the erthe
syxtene knyghtes, som horse and man and som the man and
not the horse; and there was none that he hitte surely but that
he bare none armys that day. And than he gate a spere and
smote downe twelve knyghtes, and the moste party of hem
never throoff aftir. [262–263]

The asymmetry here is deliberate: the backs of only four of the five
knights were broken; Lancelot "bears down" sixteen knights, "som
horse and man and som the man and not the horse"; "*the moste
party*" of the twelve knights never thrived afterwards; it is not
"none that he hitte but that he bare none armys that day," but
"none that he hitte *surely* but that he bare none armys that day."
This asymmetry, the exceptions to a general pattern are rather like

the ragged edge details in catalogues; and like those details, they suggest the untidiness of history and the scrupulousness of the historian.

Consider what happens to Lancelot's opponents in the encounters Malory singles out: one breaks his thigh, another has his shoulder thrown out of joint, a third has his helmet driven a foot and more into the ground, and the nose, ears and mouth of a fourth burst out bleeding. Any one of these details would be fair testimony to Lancelot's prowess, but the miscellaneousness of the assorted details serves not directly to testify to that prowess (it would be more impressive if Lancelot defeated all of his mounted opponents in exactly the same way, just as it would be more impressive if *none* of the twelve knights ever thrived afterwards, and if all sixteen knights were overthrown "horse and man") but to give an impression of careful, accurate record-keeping.

All of the clustered blueprint details I have so far considered work toward this effect. Individually such details may serve other literary ends as well; in a cluster they suggest scrupulous record-keeping by the author. The clustering itself, the frequent anticlimactic or nonclimactic sequences I have mentioned, contributes to the effect of data-gathering. In general function the blueprint cluster is like not only the ragged edge detail within the catalogue but the catalogue itself; all three devices impress upon us the importance of the thing described by convincing us that the writer believes in that importance.[44]

Not all blueprint details describe battles, and it is helpful to look at some uses more obliquely related to mayhem. The following is especially interesting because it comes from the "Gawain, Ywain and Marhalt" section of Malory's "Tale of King Arthur," a section which, with its symmetry of three maidens whose ages form a neat mathematical sequence (fifteen-thirty-sixty) and one knight for

44. The sort of cluster of details about victories in combat discussed in the last few pages seems to be, like the catalogue, a feature of at least some kinds of early, "record-keeping" poetry. The descriptions of woundings in *Iliad*, V.59–83, for instance, are rather like those I've quoted from Malory and the *English Merlin* in their clinical detail and miscellaneousness, though the Homeric "capsule biographies" give the epic passage a poignance alotgether lacking in the English ones.

each maiden, is far more *märchen*-like in atmosphere than most of
Le Morte Darthur:

> Now turne we unto sir Uwayne that rode westwarde with his
> damesell of three score wyntir of ayge. And there was a turne-
> mente nyghe the marche of Walys, and at that turnemente sir
> Uwayne smote doune thirty knyghtes. Therefore was gyffyn
> hym the pryce, and that was a jarfaucon and a whyght stede
> trapped with cloth of golde. So than sir Uwayne ded many
> strange adventures by the meanys of the olde damesel, and so
> she brought hym to a lady that was called the Lady of the
> Roch, the whyche was curtayse. [176–177]

There is no attempt here to narrate the tournament; it is simply
summarized, the score given. But while giving us that score Malory
tells us exactly what the prize was: a falcon of a particular kind and
a horse of a particular color with trappings of a particular kind.
Where the tournament was, how many knights were overthrown,
exactly what was given to the winner: we have not had mimesis of
the event, but we may feel that we have had anticipatory mimesis of
a sports record-book.

A second example. In the following passage Malory carefully
gives us the blueprint details of direction,[45] location, and date
before what is to be Arthur's final battle. Some of these details may
be symbolic; but even if they are these sentences impress the reader
primarily as a sober historian's attempt to set forth the data before
he recounts a most important event:

> And anone kynge Arthure drew hym wyth his oste downe by
> the seesyde westewarde, towarde Salusbyry. And there was a
> day assygned betwyxte kynge Arthur and sir Mordred, that
> they shulde mete uppon a downe besyde Salesbyry and nat
> farre frome the seesyde. And thys was assygned on Monday
> aftir Trynyté Sonday, whereof kynge Arthur was passyng glad
> that he myght be avenged uppon sir Mordred. [1232–1233][46]

45. This is a kind of blueprint detail Malory often adds to his descriptions. Cf.
Vinaver's note to *Works*, 118.9: "References to the points of the compass, frequent
in *M*, are characteristically absent from the French romances."
46. Although Malory himself dislikes long descriptions of setting, such descrip-

I have been speaking of blueprint clusters in romance. Let me return to the *Brut* for examples of the thing imitated. The real encounter described in the following passage ends more happily than the romance fights discussed, but the chronicler is like the romancer in attending to which blows are struck and how:

> And in this same yere was a batell doon, the XXXth of Ianuare, in Smythfeld, betwene .i j. worthy men, and bold in armes and fight: þat oon men called Sir Philipe Beef, a knyght of Cateloyne; and on þat oþer party, a Squyere of the Kynges of England, þat men called Iohn Astley. And at þe comyng to þe feld, eyþer of theym toke theire tent; and then was þe knyghtes son of Cateloyne brought to the Kyng, and the Kyng made hym knyght; and then he was brought ageyn to his faders tent. And then, within a while after, the heraudes of armes called theym bothe oute, to do their fight; and so þey come in bothe armed with all theire wepen about theym; bot the knyght come with his swerd drawe, and the Squyere with his spere. And the Squyer cast his spere to þe knyght; and the knyght avoyded it with the swerd, and cast it to the ground; and the Squyer hent his axe, and went to the knyght at onys,

tions are found in other prose romances and often contain a fair amount of blueprint detail. The passage on the Castle in the Morass in the *English Merlin* (II.604–05) is a good example. Though there are other kinds of blueprint details there, the numerical ones are particularly worth noticing: ". . . and this Castell was closed rounde with vij walles thikke and high, and feire enbateiled, and right deffensable; and with-ynne the baile were v. toures that were high and streight all rounde, and foure were mene, and the fifthe was gret and high. . . ." Such numerical specificity is characteristic of Malory as well. (Gawain's last letter is written "but two owrys and an halff" before his death [1232.6–7].) In fact, though it obviously works very well in a record-keeper's style, this device is by no means confined to prose romances and chronicles. It is found, for instance, in Old French epics and history. Beer points out that "the expression of a large, indefinite number by a misleadingly definite figure gave vividness and authenticity to the style of the *chanson de geste*," and that it is difficult to know how literally Villehardouin's definite figures are to be taken (*Villehardouin*, p. 109). One wonders how widespread this use of misleading definite figures was (might there, for instance, be a common tradition behind the *chanson de geste* usage and Chaucer's "Wel nyne and twenty in a compaignye"?) and about its connection not only with the use of numbers in our romances but with the use of other "asymmetrical" details.

and smote many strokes hard and sore vpon his Basenet and on
his hande, and made hym lese his axe. And it fell from hym
to þe grounde, and brast vp his vmbrere .iij. tymes, and kaught
his daggere, and wold haue smyten hym in the face forto haue
slayne hym in the feld. And then the Kyng cryed "hoo!" and
so they were departed; and eyþer of theym went hoom ageyn
to his tent. And then the Kyng sent for his squyere Iohn
Astley, and made hym to be dubbed knyght, for his worthy
and good Iourney þat he did and wrought at þat tyme on his
enemy in his noble presence. . . . [II.482]

The true chronicler is not only as interested as the romancer in
recording data, but also as willing to mix evaluative modifiers with
blueprint details. In fact, "betwene .ij. worthy men, and bold in
armes and fight," which is both qualitative and iambic, might sit
inconspicuously in a verse romance.

With the more pacific blueprint passages in romance, such as the
description of the prizes awarded to Uwayne, one might compare
an excerpt from the *Brut*'s extensive description of the devices set
up for Henry VI's entry into Paris for his coronation:

And at comyng to þe gate of Seint Denys of Parys, there was
afore the fronte of the gate þe armes of the towne in gowles,
a chieff of asure, with the flourdelice of gold in asure; and also
þer was a verrey shippe, with alle the appurtenaunceȝ þerto
belongyng, couered with siluer foyle, and certeyne persones
standing þerin. And at the Kynges comyng to the gate, they
henge ouer the shippe borde iij. blody hertys like vnto mennys
hertys, bot þey were gretter. And as the Kyng come to the gate,
these thre hertes opened; and oute of hem flewe white dovys
and oþer briddes, and certeyn scriptures made, shewyng vnto
the Kyng þat they receyued hym with alle hertys, and for theire
souereyn Lord and Kyng. And at the comying in of the gate
was ordeyned a clothe of gold, and vj men beryng it vpon vj.
spere-shaftes, and eche of the men bare heded; and on theire
hodes, garlaundes of gode foyle, and they clothed in blewe.
And in the same strete was a condit, and iij. meremaydes
swymmyng aboue on the water; and oute of the condite come

> rennyng dyuers wynes; oon ypocras; the second rede wyne, the thridde, with mylke. And euery Englissh man þat wold drynk ypocras, had ynough; and alwey men redy to serue theym with cuppes and pecis. And iij wodewoses playing vpon the toppe of þe condyte; and other wodewoses benethe, playing to kepe this condite. [II.459]

There are various kinds of significance here. There may be particular meanings in the heraldic details. There are thematic implications in the description as a whole (the glory of England reflected in the homage of the French to an English king; the apparent security of Henry's position at the beginning of his reign). And the chronicler, it seems safe to say, enjoys the ceremonial splendour. But one feels a sense of duty, albeit pleasant duty, behind this description also: beyond specific meanings understood by the writer is the sense that facts related to an important event should not be lost.

Chronicle usage seems to me most important for an understanding of blueprint clusters in the prose romances. But there is one other kind of writing which is relevant here. This is the saint's life. In the saint's life, more even than in Malorian romance, the focus is what is normative in the protagonist (i.e. saintly) rather than what is individual, and what is meaningful rather than what is "realistic" in episode and setting.[47] Yet in the legends there are passages where data are carefully presented. Consider this description from a life of Elizabeth of Spalbeck, who devoutly imitated Christ's sufferings:

> Also wee sawe blood sprynge oute often atte þe woundes of

47. Donald A. Stauffer's remarks on the saint's life are extremely interesting in the light of Malorian attitudes and the Malorian presentation of reality: "[The modern] eagerness for particulars would not have been easily understood by the early biographers. . . . In the common popular biographies the saints lose their individual characters and tend to merge into a single ideal figure. . . . Direct characterization is slight and is usually formal. . . . The life of a saint, to the orthodox mediaeval writer, could not be described by presenting his personal appearance, his thoughts, his peculiar bent of mind, the development of his opinions, his debt to society or his influence upon history. The life of a saint was a collection of his deeds" (*English Biography Before 1700* [Cambridge, Mass., 1930], p. 5).

hir handys and of hir feet and oute of hir syde on a fridaye atte
noon. Wee sawe blode not allynges rede, but as it were mengyd
wiþ water, rennynge oute þorowe an hool of hir coot, made
aboute þe pappe; and þe wollen cloth þat satte next hir flesche,
was defuyled wiþ þe same blode, and also a party of hir syde
aboute þe wounde. And wee sawe not alloonly þe vtter cloþe
þat toucheþ maydens flesche, þat is to saye handes, feet and
syde, sprenkelyd and dyed with blood, but also hir pappys
were all defuyled wiþ blode rennynge fro hir eyȝen. And
also oþere-while blode ronne oute at hir fynger endys, bytwix
þe nayles and the flesche. . . . [*Prose Legends*, 114]

There is of course one major difference between the details in this
passage and most blueprint details in romance or history. The significance of most of the data here is evident: these details are symbolic, even though the author of that symbolism is God rather than
the writer. But what matters here is that in religious as in historical
writing, the fifteenth-century reader was accustomed to blueprint
details in descriptions of important things by sober, conscientious
writers who respected the men and women whose deeds they re-
corded.[48]

Clearly the romancer does not achieve simple realism when he
uses blueprint details; or at least does not achieve it in any very
important way. To be realistic in the modern sense a work has to
have a fairly even distribution of phenominal particulars, a norm of
sensory detail. Blueprint details are very unevenly distributed in the
romances, tending, as I have said, to occur in clusters. Realistic

48. In saints' lives we find blueprint details not only in descriptions of such events
as miracles, the appearance of stigmata (as here) and martyrdoms—climactic
events *within* the narrative—but in reference to relics-to-be and the places where
those relics will eventually be kept. (See, e.g., the passage on the arms of St. Alban,
Golden Legend, III.238.) Blueprint details about relics are particularly understand-
able to us. A relic may help us; we want to know where to look for it and how to
recognize it. But what is most significant here is not the possible utility of relics,
but the attitude which underlies belief in that utility: the feeling, as I have said,
that anything associated with an important figure, an important event, is or may
be charged with meaning, even if we do not now understand that meaning. In this
sense, the blueprint detail is to the historian (and to the hagiographer as historian)
what the relic is to the worshipper.

details work by making us suspend our disbelief in the events being narrated; blueprint details work by making us suspend our disbelief in the narrator's belief in the events being narrated. They persuade us of his belief and, more important, of his reverence.

The continuity of dialogue style and narrative style in our romances is quite clear. Fifteenth-century dialogue is a medium suited to presenting a reality in which there are central, normative truths. Such devices of romance prose narration as superlatives, qualitative details and conventional details also build a world with standards, norms, fixed values; a world in which *notatio* deals with things as objectively real and considerably more important than those dealt with by *effictio*. The common etymon of most of the devices I have described is a vision of reality in which what is most real, most matters, is the relation of the individual character or incident to normative values and standards; the common function of most of these devices is to project that vision.

This is the common function of most of these devices, but not all. What such "objective" devices as bare catalogues, ragged edge and blueprint details contribute to the prose romances (or can contribute) is a narrator who both believes in and reveres the value-centered world portrayed by the other devices. And because he believes in it, and cares about it, we do also.

Contribute, or *can* contribute. . . . As I said earlier, it is in *Le Morte Darthur* that these various devices are most effectively used because it is Malory who cuts away the underbrush, cuts back things which in the other romances choke off or (to change the image) at least dissipate the expressive potential of those devices. My next chapter is about that cutting back.

2

Reduced into English: Malorian Style

Malory's art is an impure, inconsistent one: he is sometimes more the translator, even the puzzled, vaguely disapproving translator, and sometimes more the original artist. And often Malory's artistry, just when he is being most original, consists more of leaving out than of putting in; it is rather like the art of a movie director cutting the scene he wants out of the day's takes. To study the making of Malory's prose, then, we must have both large minds free of hobgoblins and also some interest in cutting rooms. But even for those of us who meet these requirements it is very helpful to have a clear idea of what Malory is moving towards as he cuts the paragraphs of *Le Morte Darthur* out of the pages of the French romances. I want to begin this chapter, therefore, by looking closely at one of those parts of Malory's book where his art is most powerful and most itself, and style, plot, theme, and characterization work together fully and hauntingly. I have selected the "Healing of Sir Urry" episode, the story Malory tells just before he moves to the final disintegration of Arthurian society.

"The Healing of Sir Urry" is, I would say, the most purely Malorian episode in *Le Morte Darthur*. It is a celebration of knightliness, a vision of chivalric fellowship and excellence as the center of reality, revered and served by both characters and author. Reading along, we find that we too share in the celebration; when Lancelot weeps, and Arthur and the others praise God, we are startled to find how deeply we have been moved. The episode is our most intense experience of the reality reflected in and shaped by Malory's style.

The story of "Sir Urry" can be summarized very quickly. A Hungarian knight is wounded while fighting in a tournament with a Spanish knight whom he then kills. The mother of that Spanish knight is a sorceress, and she casts a spell by which Urry's wounds will not be healed until they have been "searched" by the best knight in the world. Urry is brought to Arthur's court where King Arthur and other kings, dukes, earls, and knights try to heal him but fail; the list of those who tried, with various explanatory digressions, makes up about a third of the whole episode. Lancelot comes, Arthur insists that he also try searching Urry's wounds, Lancelot secretly prays to God that he be allowed to heal this knight so that his "simple worship and honesty" may be saved, he does cure Urry's wounds, and Arthur and the others thank God and the Virgin while Lancelot weeps. Urry becomes a knight of the Round Table, and one of Lancelot's followers. This episode has no known source, but one is tempted to say that what is really original here is not the plot Malory invented but Malory's discovery that he didn't need to invent more of a plot than this.

If "The Healing of Sir Urry" has no one source, it certainly has many analogues, including a good many earlier parts of *Le Morte Darthur*.[1] This kind of plot in which there is a supernatural confirmation of supremacy, appeals to Malory's instinctive antinominalism: it focuses the story upon the objective existence and measurability of knightliness; the thing emphasized on the stylistic level by the various devices discussed in the last chapter.

The story turns upon the measurability of knightliness, and here, as elsewhere in *Le Morte Darthur* we are interested in characters as vessels of knightliness rather than as individuals who happen to be knights. It is, I think, because of Malory's concentration on the normative rather than the unique, that he introduces a new character, Urry, here, where he could presumably have had one of the Round Table knights suffer the enchanted wounds. We have no previous associations with Urry or his kin, and thus Malory can present him quite simply as the positive of which Lancelot is the superlative. This, in any case, is what he does. The story opens with a description of this knight:

> . . . there was a good knyght in the londe of Hungré whos name was sir Urré. And he was an adventurys knyght, and in

1. See, e.g., the various episodes referred to in my discussion of superlatives, and, of course, the Grail quest as a whole.

all placis where he myght here ony adventures dedis and of
worshyp there wold he be. [1145]

Urry is a *good* knight, the episode turns upon the identity of the *best*
knight; the adventurous knight goes off seeking "*adventures* dedis and
of worshyp;" Lancelot is the last to search Urry's wounds because
when the others try he is away "uppon hys *adventures*" (1148.6);
when Lancelot prays, he prays that his "symple *worshyp* and honesté
be saved" (1152.21–22). Sir Urry is a knight rather than a man who
happens to be a knight; he does not exist except in relation to chivalric activities. Wounded in a tournament, he is healed by contact
with the best knight in the world. His cure, his recovered wholeness,
is both proved and celebrated by participation in a joust:

> Than kynge Arthur asked sir Urré how he felte hymselff. "A!
> my good and gracious lorde, I felte myselffe never so lusty."
> "Than woll ye juste and do ony armys?" seyd kynge Arthur.
> "Sir, and I had all that longed unto justis, I wolde be sone
> redy." Than kynge Arthur made a party of a hondred knyghtes
> to be ayenste an hondred, and so uppon the morn they justed
> for a dyamounde, but there justed none of the daungerous
> knyghtes. And so, for to shortyn this tale, sir Urré and sir
> Lavayne justed beste that day, for there was none of them but
> he overthrew and pulled down a thirty knight. [1153]

Now this Malorian emphasis on knight as knight is associated
with two things both in "The Healing of Sir Urry" and in *Le Morte
Darthur* as a whole. One is the kind of qualitative vision and comparative judgment which is, as we have seen, found in the central
motif of this episode. If what is important about all knights is the
quality they share, then it is meaningful to rank them, to be concerned about who has more and who has less of this quality. The
second thing is a sense of fellowship. If what is most central in a
character's being is what he has in common with other characters
rather than what distinguishes him from those others, the character's group-loyalty and group-identity can be enormously strong.
Hence the theme of the Round Table fellowship: for Cicero friend-
ship is one soul in two bodies; for Malory knightliness is one soul

in one hundred and forty bodies. (We might say that the use of superlatives is the stylistic correlative of the first of these associations of knightliness, and collective discourse the stylistic correlative of the second.)

If we think about the matter abstractly, we realize that these two things might easily be in conflict: ranking suggests a movement toward distinction from the group, and that sense of fellowship a movement toward coherence with the group. But in *Le Morte Darthur* (at least the parts of it which come before "Sir Urry"), there really is no such discord: the best knight is *primus inter pares*, loving both worship and the goodly company. In this episode, however, Malory raises the possibility of just such a conflict; but he raises it in order to deny it, and by denying it to underscore the sense of fellowship and coherence in the company.

Here I must draw back for a moment. That possible conflict between the movement toward distinction and the movement toward fellowship in the Round Table society is associated in the episode as a whole with the conflict between pride and humility, and it is well to come to Malory's presentation of distinction/fellowship by way of his presentation of pride/humility. The theme of Pride, then, is introduced in the first two pages. The enchantress who prevents Urry's wounds from healing boasts of what she has done:

> And thus she [the sorceress] *made her avaunte*, wherethorow hit was knowyn that this sir Urry sholde never be hole.
>
> [1145.20–22]

> And thus she tolde the kynge, and where he was wounded and with whom, and how hys modir *discoverde hit in her pryde* how she had worought by enchantemente that he sholde never be hole untyll the beste knyght of the worlde had serched hys woundis.
>
> [1146][2]

There is a fine economy in this. The enchantress undoes herself through pride: the possibility and conditions of Urry's cure would presumably never have become known if she had not boasted. (We

2. See also 1147.11–12.

may recall Chauntecleer's escape in the *Nun's Priest's Tale*.) At the
same time Urry's affliction has now been associated with pride, and
thus we will expect the cure to be associated with humility.

Our expectations are met. Just before Lancelot heals these
wounds, he does show the humility which is the proper *remedium
contra peccatum Superbie*. To Urry he says, "I shame sore with myselff
that I shulde be thus requyred, for never was I able in worthynes to
do so hyghe a thynge" (1152.23–25);[3] he prays to the Trinity that
his simple worship and honesty be saved: "Thou mayste yeff me
power to hele thys syke knyght by the grete vertu and grace of The,
but Good Lorde, never of myselff" (1152.23–25). But here we may
return from pride and humility to distinction and fellowship: for
between the enchantress's boasting and Lancelot's prayer a very
Malorian context has been created for humility, so that we associate
the cure of the disease not simply with denigration of self, but with
an emphasis upon the communal order, the chivalric fellowship of
which one is a part, rather than upon one's individuality. Arthur's
conversations with Urry's mother and with Lancelot establish this
context. The king explains to Urry's mother that he will search her
son's wounds literally *pour encourager les autres*, and his speech is
lovely in its combination of personal humility and great pride in the
assembled company:

> . . . And wyte you welle, here shall youre son be healed and
> ever ony Crystyn man may heale hym. And for to gyff othir
> men off worshyp a currayge, I myselff woll asay to handyll
> your sonne, and so shall all the kynges, dukis and erlis that ben
> here presente at thys tyme, *nat presumyng uppon me* that I am so
> worthy to heale youre son be my dedis, but I woll corrayge
> othir men of worshyp to do as I woll do. [1146]

The antithesis of the enchantress's individual pride is not simply
individual humility but individual humility and pride in the group.
Arthur's expression "nat presumyng uppon me," and his emphasis
upon the fellowship rather than the self, are confirmed in his later
conversation with Lancelot:

3. The *never* is important. Lancelot is not thinking about the resumed adultery
or about any *loss* of worthiness.

Than seyde kynge Arthur unto sir Launcelot, "Sir, *ye muste do as we have done*," and tolde hym what they had done and shewed hym them all that had serched hym.

"Jesu defende me," seyde sir Launcelot, "whyle so many noble kyngis and knyghtes have fayled, that I shulde *presume uppon me* to enchyve that all ye, my lordis, myght nat enchyve."

"Ye shall nat chose," seyde kynge Arthur, "for I commaunde you to do *as we all have done*."

"My moste renowmed lorde," seyde sir Launcelot, "I know well I dare nat, nor may nat, disobey you. But and I myght or durste, wyte you well I wolde nat take uppon me to towche that wounded knyght in that entent that I shulde passe all othir knyghtes. Jesu deffende me frome that shame!"

"Sir, ye take hit wronge," seyde kynge Arthur, "for ye shall nat do hit for no *presumpcion*, but for to bear us felyshyp, insomuche as ye be a felow of the Rounde Table. And wyte you well," seyde kynge Arthur, "and ye prevayle nat and heale hym, I dare sey there ys no knyght in thys londe that may hele hym. And therefore I pray you do *as we have done*." [1151–1152]

"For to bear us fellowship, insomuch as ye be a felow of the Round Table": here is the element of conflict in the episode, the tension between the communal theme and the evaluative motif. The King commands Lancelot to make the attempt so that he will continue to act as a knight of the Round Table; Lancelot is reluctant to make the attempt lest he appear to set himself above and apart from his fellows.

This humility, then, is a very Malorian one, a sense of belonging to the fellowship of the Round Table and ultimately to the order of knightliness itself. One acts for and takes pride in the order. And here is where narrative style, the use of the devices I discussed in my first chapter, is important: Malory serves the order as record-keeper, Arthur serves the order as king.

Stylistically, the most remarkable thing in "The Healing of Sir Urry" is that catalogue of knights which occupies about one third of the episode. This seems at first to put an extraordinary strain upon the reader's good will, but it works, emphasizing the fellowship theme quite powerfully. It is of course Lancelot who is the best knight in the world, the one who must search Urry's wounds; but the reader experiences the cure (as Lancelot would wish him to) as the work of the company, with the searching by Lancelot as that work's culmination. The first part of the cure which will return the knight to knightliness is, in terms of the story, the attempts of the various knights present to search Urry's wounds; in terms of the reader's experience of the work, this first stage is the catalogue: almost a ritual recitation of Arthurian adventures.

The form of the catalogue as well as its content is meaningful here. All the knights participate in the curing "for no presumpcion," but to do as the others have done. Implicitly, the writer also works for the order, recording the names of those who were present, supplying brief explanations "just for the record"; "ich dien" could be the motto of both characters and the author. "Sir Urry," in fact, is virtually a thesaurus of bookkeeping rhetoric: pains are being taken. The treatment of combat is remarkably abstract, all notation of result and circumstance, no mimesis of action. Malory does not describe Urry's fight with Alpheus, but we are given the blueprint detail of the result: "seven grete woundis, three on the hede and three on hys body, and one uppon hys lyffte honde" (1145.13–14). Arthur, as I have said, is eager to have Urry participate in the jousting once he is cured; but we are not shown any of these encounters, though we are told that the prize was a diamond, that there were one hundred knights on each side, that none of the "dangerous knights" fought and that Urry and Lavayne each "overthrew and pulled down a thirty knyght" (1153.19). The catalogue of knights is full of the record-keeping of past encounters (e.g., ". . . sir Belyaunce le Orgulus that the good knyght sir Lamorak wan in playne batayle, sir Neroveus and sir Plenoryus, two good knyghtes that sir Launcelot wanne . . ." [1150.8–10]) but the only fighting at all particularized in the episode is particularized because it is contemptably unknightly: "that traytoure kynge slew the noble knyght sir Trystram as he sate harpynge afore hys lady, La Beall Isode, with a trenchaunte glayve . . ." (1149. 28–29). That "trenchaunte glayve" is the only weapon mentioned in "The Healing of Sir Urry."[4]

4. In the more pacific sections of "Sir Urry" there are a few "realistic" partic-

The author and the characters serve the fellowship and see a reality centered around knightliness. I said before that the newness of Urry in *Le Morte Darthur* is useful to Malory in that it allows this knight to be purely an image of knightliness, the positive to which Lancelot is the superlative. Here I would suggest that Urry is not simply an image of knightliness, but of the Round Table fellowship itself.[5] The patient mirrors the physician in a way that makes "The Healing of Sir Urry" the furthest development of Malory's stylistic emphasis on Round Table knightliness as the one thing needful, and also makes this episode the most moving in *Le Morte Darthur*.

There is a kind of pun underlying "The Healing of Sir Urry," though I don't know whether one should say the pun is *in* the episode or that it associated various motifs in Malory's mind—perhaps without his full awareness of the verbal link. The pun is on the word "whole." This word is not the one most frequently used in connection with the healing of Sir Urry, but it is employed several times here[6] and, what is more significant, it receives a strong initial emphasis in the phrase *sholde* (or *might*) *never be hole*:

> . . .and she, for the despyte of hir sunnes deth, wrought by her suttyle craufftis that sir Urry *shulde never be hole*, but ever his woundis shulde one tyme fester and another tyme blede, so that he *shulde never be hole* untyll the beste knyght of the worlde had serched hys woundis. And thus she made her avaunte,

ulars—the arrangements for transporting Urry after he is wounded (1147.23–27), the gold cushion for Arthur to kneel on (1147.6–9)—but here too one is most impressed by the record-keeping circumstantiality. After going through many lands Urry is brought into Malorian territory: "unto Scotlonde and into the bondes of Inglonde" (1145.30–31); at this time Arthur is holding his court at Carlisle (1146.1); this is (perhaps conventionally) at Pentecost (1145.31–32); "at that tyme there were but an hundred and ten of the Round Table, for forty knyghtes were that tyme away" (1146.33–1147.1); Urry's sister is named Fyleloly (1145.26); the French book, Malory's ostensible source, is mentioned twice on the first page and twice on the last page; the circumstantiality of the curing itself (1152.26–32) is rather like the circumstantiality of accounts of miracles in some saints' lives. (See above, pp. 53–54.)

5. His participation in jousting, as I said, both proves and celebrates Urry's recovery. But here we should recall that there is a stage in Urry's healing even beyond the jousting: his entry into that Round Table fellowship which brought him back to health (1153.20–24).

6. 1145.17; 1145.19; 1145.22; 1146.8; 1146.12; 1147.6; 1152.29.

wherethorow hit was knowyn that this sir Urry *sholde never be hole.* [1145][7]

Now "hole" is of course a word frequently used to describe individuals in *Le Morte Darthur*, but it is also, together with the adverb "holé," employed by Malory to refer to the Round Table fellowship. In the sixth book, for instance, Arthur requests what is essentially an earlier "curtain call,"[8] a foreshadowing of the present last gathering of the chivalric company:

> "Now," seyde the kynge, "I am sure at this quest of the Sank-greall shall all ye of the Rownde Table departe, and nevyr shall I se you agayne holé togydirs, therefore ones shall I se you togydir in the medow, all holé togydirs! Therefore I wol se you all holé togydir in the medow of Camelot, to juste and to tur-ney, that aftir youre dethe men may speke of hit that such good knyghtes were here, such a day, holé togydirs." [864]

This is a tale of fellowship: the individual's restoration to wholeness brings him into the larger whole of the Round Table; the best knight cures him "for no presumpcion, but for to bear . . . fely-shyp"; as Arthur and Lancelot act with Malorian humility in think-ing of the Round Table whole, so Malory himself pays Arthurian civilization the chronicler's homage of earnest record-keeping.

But there is finally a difference between the wholeness of Urry and the wholeness of the fellowship; and here we come to the most mov-ing line in the entire episode, the splendid "And ever sir Launcelot wepte, as he had bene a chylde that had bene betayn" (1152.35–36). Where does the power of this lie? C. S. Lewis says "Here Lancelot is proved by infallible signs to be in one sense (he knows too well in what and how limited a sense) the best knight of the world. Hence, while all praise him to the skies, he can only weep like a beaten child."[9] Lewis is right in pointing to the contrast between failure in

---

7. See the next two occurrences also.

8. Edmund Reiss's phrase for the "Healing of Sir Urry." See his *Sir Thomas Malory*, p. 170. For other uses of "hole" and "holé" in connection with the Round Table fellowship, see, e.g., 1201.20–22 and 1260.16–19.

9. "The English Prose *Morte*," *Essays on Malory*, 7–28, p. 20.

the Grail quest and success here[10] but more than this is involved. Urry's wholeness is an image of Round Table wholeness: and the Round Table is doomed. In that last catalogue of Round Table knights and achievements we have reminders of death and treachery—including the "treson" of Gawain and his brothers (1149.34–35). At the end of the episode Malory turns from Urry and Lavayne to Aggravain lying in wait (1153.32–34). We know what must soon follow. The Round Table is whole, and wholeness cures into wholeness, but this is true for the last time: Urry is an image of the order which is about to end. Lancelot weeps because of the contrast between this success and his earlier failure; but for the reader these are the *lacrimae rerum,* tears for the fall of the Arthurian world, sorrow at the contrast between this moment of integration and the disintegration to come.

One of the oldest ways to regard style—and still the common sense way—is to think of it as the outer covering of a work; suitable to the essence of the thing, sometimes beautifully and ingeniously so, but nonetheless not the thing itself. With the "Healing of Sir Urry" I suspect just the opposite is true. The style came first, it is the heart, or better, the deepest level of the work, while plot, characterization, structure, etc. came later, following the contour of the stylistic level. Essentially, Malory's style in "Urry" is what it almost always tends toward being; but here the other levels of the work are joined more surely to that style, flow more eloquently and meaningfully with it than anywhere else. Malory's style is constantly evaluating and serving the Arthurian world, and here both activities are important on those other levels also. Language in *Le Morte Darthur* suggests a monocentric reality, and finally the one fully worthy recipient of Round Table knightliness—the one beneficiary who matters as much as the giver—is what we sense the recipient to be in "Sir Urry": that Round Table knightliness itself.

10. Though Lewis is curiously wrong about what the other characters are doing. No one, in fact, praises Lancelot at all; in keeping with Malory's emphasis on the fellowship, Arthur, the kings and the knights respond by giving *thanks* and loving unto God and unto His Blessed Mother. They respond as recipients, not as observers.

It is of course possible that there is or was an Ur-Urry somewhere, but the episode *feels* original, seems to grow vigorously and purely out of those attitudes and meanings which elsewhere Malory half perceives in older works and half creates.

Half perceives and half creates . . . but occasionally doesn't bother with at all. I come now to Malory's work-a-day style, to what he actually did to "the noble hystoryes of kynge Arthur and of certayn of this knyghtes" when, in the words of Caxton's "Preface," he took a copy of those histories "out of certeyn bookes of Frensshe and reduced it into English." Consistency, as I have said, is not a Malorian virtue; one of the preliminary questions about this work-a-day style is whether it exists or not.

In the French prose romances and the English poems which he drew upon in writing *Le Morte Darthur*, Malory found characters referred to both by name alone and by title and name, i.e., both "Arthore wolde no lenger a-byde . . ."; "Quant Boorz voit que Lancelos se retret . . ."; and also "Sir Kayous knewe wele . . ."; "Cele nuit pensa li rois Artus. . . ."[11] The proportion of one kind of naming to the other varies from work to work and often from character to character within a work; in the French romances, for instance, Gawain is usually named with his title, Lancelot without his. Malory follows period usage in the earliest parts of *Le Morte Darthur*, "The Noble Tale of King Arthur and the Emperor Lucius" and "The Tale of King Arthur," and names characters either with or without their titles. For instance, on one page of Vinaver's edition (p. 194), we find "And so Lucius com unto Cullayne . . ." (1.6); "And thus Lucius within a whyle . . ."(1.7); "So thus Lucius . . ." (1.10); and also "Now leve we sir Lucius" (1.15). But in his later works Malory almost always names characters with their titles.[12]

---

11. *Stanzaic Morte*, 2086; *La Mort*, 152.1; *Alliterative Morte*, 2177; *Stanzaic Morte*, 1991; *La Mort*, 7.1.

12. I have counted authorial namings without titles of kings, queens, and knights in several sections of the *Works*. In the 16 pages of the "Arthur and Accolon," name without title is used 68 times. (In addition, Arthur is referred to as "sir Arthur" rather than "king Arthur" 14 times.) In "The Noble Tale of Sir Launcelot du

It is revealing that the mature Malory thinks of his hero as "Sir Lancelot" rather than as "Lancelot." His "Sir Lancelot" is essentially a knight rather than a man who happens to be a knight. We will be invited less often to share the private doubts and perplexities of Malory's character than of the *Vulgate* Lancelot. Malory's use of titles makes sense as one in a cluster of stylistic devices; it works together with those other devices to suggest a particular view of reality.

I describe this difference between Malory's later and his earlier, more conventional practice as revealing. But for the student of prose style it is much more than that. It is a glint of ore; nice, clear, compact evidence that Malory does indeed have a style. The Malorian singleness of vision makes *Le Morte Darthur* quite unlike the French prose romances; but it is rarely by consistent formal singularities that Malory achieves his singleness of vision. I assume, as I have said before, that period usage is not stylistically neutral, not something we subtract from a writer's gross style to find his net

---

Lake" (35 pages) characters are named without their titles eight times. In the 17 pages of the "Sir Palomides" section of the "Tristram," there are four uses of "La Beall Isode" but no other namings without titles. In the "Bors" section of the "Quest" (21 pages) there are no namings without titles; in the 35 pages of the "Fair Maid of Astolat" there are four. The page references to namings without title are:

"Arthur and Accolon": 137.1, 137.21, 138.21, 139.16, 139.18, 139.22, 139.24, 139.27, 139.37, 140.5, 140.10, 140.33, 141.1, 141.8, 141.9, 141.13, 141.22, 141.23, 141.36, 142.7, 142.10, 142.23, 142.26, 142.27, 142.28, 142.30, 142.34, 142.35, 142.36, 143.1 (twice), 143.3, 143.16, 143.17, 143.19, 143.26 (twice), 143.27, 143.29, 144.12, 144.14, 144.15, 144.16, 144.19, 144.25, 144.29, 145.8, 145.12, 145.17, 145.21, 145.29, 146.4, 146.7, 146.8, 146.30, 147.6, 148.15, 148.16, 148.20, 148.28, 149.32, 149.35, 150.3, 150.23, 150.33, 151.9, 151.28, 152.24, ("sir Arthur": 141.32, 142.3, 142.8–9, 142.28, 143.6–7, 143.10, 143.14, 144.4, 144.16, 144.26, 145.4, 145.15, 148.5, 148.18).

"Sir Launcelot du Lake": 255.29, 261.13, 265.11, 265.29, 268.21 (twice), 286.23.
"Sir Palomides": 779.8–9, 779.17, 780.2, 780.16.
"The Fair Maid of Astolat": 1069.21, 1070.4, 1072.20, 1080.6.

The idiosyncrasy of Malory's namings is only apparent in the Winchester text. Caxton apparently omitted "sirs" at his convenience, and his edition of *Le Morte Darthur* contains throughout a normal period mixture of namings with and namings without titles. In his Book X, chapters 82–88, for instance, corresponding to the "Sir Palomides" section of the "Tristram," there are 49 namings without title.

style. Malory becomes an original stylist, not by inventing, but by intensifying; and usually he intensifies by cutting rather than by adding. It is in his tendency to prune, above all in his tendency to be less specific than his sources in rendering things, actions, and psychological processes that Malory the stylist is most importantly seen. But this is indeed a *tendency* to prune: tabulations based on random samplings are helpful when we look at Malory's titles and a few other things, but much of the time they are not useful at all— or at least not convenient. With style as with structural interlacing, we must look for the things which distinguish the Malorian version from its source when there *are* differences, rather than for consistency throughout the book. There is Malorian style and vision, but not every paragraph of *Le Morte Darthur* unmistakably proclaims its author.

Throughout this chapter, but especially in the first sections of it, I will be discussing or citing a fairly large number of passages in order to make what are really just a few points about Malory's style as a presentation of reality. There are three reasons for this multiplication of examples. First, the hope of giving some sense of how numerous these changes are, how much they *are* a work-a-day part of "Englishing" for Malory rather than special effects occasionally sought. Second, since we possess neither Malory's autograph manuscript nor (as far as we know) the copies of the French romances he actually used, close verbal comparisons of Malory and his sources are meaningful only in groups. In most cases, we may assume, the original change was the one we can study by comparing the extant versions of *Le Morte Darthur* and its sources; but we would not want too much of our interpretation of Malory to depend on any single difference between the extant versions. Third, there is the ale-and-roast-beef hypothesis; that is, the idea that Malory, as a good English writer, is more realistic, practical, and down-to-earth than comparable French writers. As evidence of his realism critics have cited changes by which Malory makes his version of some action or episode more particularized and concrete than the French one. Such changes do exist, of course; but they are the exception rather than the rule in *Le Morte Darthur*, and I can best indicate the exceptional nature of these changes by suggesting the frequency of the other kind of change.[13]

PARTICULARITY AND NARRATIVE STYLE

The realistic novel is particular in setting and characterization, and we tend to think of particularity as essentially novelistic. Ian Watt, for instance, discusses this particularity in terms of historical change:

> Much else besides the plot had to be changed in the tradition of fiction before the novel could embody the individual apprehension of reality as freely as the method of Descartes and Locke allowed their thought to spring from the immediate facts of consciousness. To begin with, the actors in the plot and the scene of their actions had to be placed in a new literary perspective: the plot had to be acted out by particular people in particular circumstances, rather than, as had been common in the past, by general human types against a background primarily determined by the appropriate literary convention.[14]

F. W. Bateson calls "non-functional details"—details of setting which add nothing to our understanding of plot, characterization, or the story's meaning but are simply "there"—"the mark of the realistic convention."[15] A bit of quibbling may be in order here.

13. In the following sections I am of course concerned with those areas of style where a text written in one language can be compared with a text written in another language. In Marie Borroff's terms, my interest is in "formulation" and still "more abstractive" levels of form; I have comparatively little to say about "verbalization." See "Words, Language, and Form," *Literary Theory and Structure: Essays in Honor of William K. Wimsatt,* ed. Frank Brady, John Palmer, and Martin Price (New Haven, 1973), pp. 63–79.

14. Ian Watt, *The Rise of the Novel: Studies in Defoe, Richardson and Fielding* (Berkeley and Los Angeles, 1967), p. 15.

15. F. W. Bateson, "A Sort of Answer," *Essays in Criticism,* 21 (1962), 349. Quoted in David Lodge, *Language of Fiction: Essays in Criticism and Verbal Analysis of the English Novel* (New York and London, 1966), p. 44. The example Bateson focuses on is the greenness of a chair in Katherine Mansfield's "The Fly." I should point out that when he says "non-functional," Bateson does not mean *completely* without function. For Bateson, in Lodge's words, "the particularity of realistic

Watt and Bateson correctly point out a connection between particularity and novelistic fiction, but there is something hyperbolic in the way they discuss this connection; in both statements there is—despite the "primarily" in Watt's last sentence—a misleading absolutism: a quantitative distinction is treated as qualitative. In some periods writers have indeed aimed at presenting "general human types," but this is an ideal, not an attainable goal; at least it is hard to think of any *perfectly* generalized narratives of any period—of any narratives, that is, in which *every* detail of characterization is typical and *no* detail of setting aconventional or "non-functional." Bateson considers ". . . the plethora of concrete detail (the convention of phenomenal particularity) . . . "[16] the mark of the realistic convention, but though the frequency of phenomenal particulars will clearly show a greater similarity between *Sister Carrie* and *Maggie: a Girl of the Streets* than between either of these and Gascoigne's *The Adventures of Master F. J.*, there will also be different densities of particularity in the Dreiser and Crane novels: some plethoras are more plethoric than others. Particularity really is not one of "prose fiction's equivalents of meter, etc. . . . "[17] A work of fiction is not either particular or nonparticular in the way a poem either is or is not in iambic pentameter couplets. It seems to me better to compare phenomenal particularity with enjambment in verse or doublets in prose. Enjambment and doublets are used more heavily in some periods than in others, but no two writers use either with precisely the same frequency, and it would be difficult to find any sizable verse composition wholly without the one or any sizable prose composition wholly without the other. Though of great importance for studies of form and genre, phenomenal particularity is itself a stylistic trait rather than a formal or generic one.

The density of particulars in narrative prose, like the temperature of water, can vary a great deal. Although I have been taking them rather narrowly at their word, I suspect Watt and Bateson would, after all, assent to this proposition. Where I think we would disagree

prose fiction is functional only *en masse* as a means of obtaining suspension of disbelief."

16. F. W. Bateson, 347, quoted in Lodge, p. 44.
17. Ibid.

is on the usefulness of distinguishing certain densities of particulars. Ice and cold water are very different things, and one is no better off skating on water that is 33° F. than on water that is 76° F. In this chapter I will assume that there is no freezing point for particularity, and that it does matter that one medieval romance is thicker with detail than another, even if the romances all seem very watery when compared to *Sister Carrie* and similar works.

There is another assumption I make here, which I have touched on before. Except for ironic effects, there are no rosy-fingered dawns in realistic or naturalistic novels. There are no standard or traditional phenomena; details of action and setting all exist on one plane of reality. Obviously this is not true of the romances. When in Malory a knight strikes "on the right hand and on the left hand," as many a Malorian knight has done before him, we have a much weaker sense of *thisness* than we have when told that Gawain "loved well all maner of fruyte, and in especiall appyls and pearys" (1048.-31–32). But I take it to be just as obvious that "he struck on the right hand and on the left hand" nonetheless *is* a particular, that it has a kind of texture and weight which makes it different from "he struck a great deal" or "he struck in a proper, knightly manner." When the author of *La Queste del Saint Graal* says Perceval prayed all night, waiting until the sun had circled the firmament and reappeared to the earth, ". . . and when the sun had risen fair and clear, and had dried the dew somewhat, then Perceval looked all around him . . . " (93.9–13), he is being quite conventional,[18] but nonetheless gives us more sense of a physical world than does Malory, whose adaptation of this description is simply "And so he prayde all that nyght tylle on the morne that hit was day, and anone he saw . . ." (912.14–15).

Let us consider now how a number of Malory's changes in particularity affect one episode as a whole. The adventure of Perceval on the Island (912–914)—from which, in fact, my last quotation came—is useful here; it is short enough to be examined in some detail (though I will certainly not try to deal with every change

18. On this see Paul Imbs's "La Journée dans la Queste del Saint Graal et La Mort le Roi Artu," in *Mélanges de Philologie Romane et de Littérature Médievale offerts a Ernest Hoepffner . . . par ses Elèves et ses Amis* (Paris, 1949), p. 281 ff.

Malory makes in these two pages) and it comes from "The Quest of the Sankgreal," which lends itself well to stylistic investigation, since in it Malory keeps fairly close to his source.

Given the usual assumptions about Malorian concreteness, it is useful to approach the Perceval episode through a passage in Vinaver's Commentary. After speaking of the jejune symbolic description in the French version, Vinaver says:

> The fact that for this method of expression Malory substitutes one which can in a very real sense be described as imaginative constitutes his main claim to originality. When he finds a conventional simile such as *comme une mote de terre* he replaces it by the remark: "he myght nat stonde nothir stirre no membir that he had." The lion following Perceval does not merely, as in the French version, "make great joy": he goes "allwey about hym, fawnynge as a spaynell." The long-winded and amorphous phraseology of the French *Queste* is thus transformed into crisp and spontaneous idiom.[19]

Strictly speaking Vinaver is discussing only phrasing and idiom here, but in the context of his previous remarks on description in the French romance, the specific examples he gives rather suggest that the Malorian version is more concrete as well as crisper than the French one, and that we see Perceval's lion, for instance, more clearly in Malory than in *La Queste del Saint Graal*. A comparison of the references to this lion between the killing of the serpent and Perceval's dream in the two works shows that in fact we do not. These are the relevant passages:

> Quant li lyons se voit delivrez dou serpent par l'aide dou chevalier, si ne fait pas semblant que il ait talent de combatre a lui, ainz vient devant lui et besse la teste et li fet la greignor joie que il puet, si que Perceval aperçoit bien que il n'a talent de lui mal fere. [94]

> [When the lion sees it is rescued from the serpent by the knight's help, it makes no semblant that it has any desire to fight with

19. "Commentary," *Works*, p. 1540.

him, but comes before him and abases its head and makes him as great joy as it can, so that Perceval perceives well it has no desire to harm him.]

Whan the lyon saw that, he made no sembelaunte to fyght with hym but made hym all the chere that a beest myghte make a man. [912.28–30]

Et li lyons aloit adés apres lui coetant et fesant grant joie. Et quant il voit ce, si li comence a aplanier le col et la teste et les espaules. . . . Et li lyons li fet si grant joie come beste mue puet fere a home, et tout le jor demora o lui jusqu'a hore de none. Mes si tost come hore de none fu passee, si s'en vint aval la roche et emporta le lyoncel a son col a son repaire. [95]

[And ever the lion went after him wagging its tail and making great joy. And when he sees this, he begins to stroke it on the neck and the head and the shoulders. . . . And the lion makes him as great joy as dumb beast may make a man, and all day it stayed with him until the hour of nones. But as soon as the hour of nones was past, it went down the rock and bore the lion cub by the neck to its den.]

. . . and the lyon wente allwey aboute hym fawnynge as a spaynell, and than he stroked hym on the necke and on the sholdirs and thanked God of the feliship of that beste. And aboute noone the lyon toke hys lityll whelpe and trussed hym and bare hym there he com fro. [912–913]

Quant Perceval ot ce dit, si voit vers lui venir le lyon por qui il s'estoit combatuz au serpent; mes il ne fet mie semblant qu'il li violle maufere, ainz vient vers lui fesant joie. Et quant Perceval voit ce, si l'apele et il vet a lui maintenant et li aplanie le col et la teste. Et li lyons se colche devant lui ausi com se ce fust la plus privee beste del monde. Et il s'acoste delez lui et met sa teste sor s'espaule; si atent tant que la nuiz fu venue oscure et noire; si s'endort erranment delez le lyon. [*La Queste*, 96]

[When Perceval had said this, he sees coming toward him the lion for which he had fought with the serpent; yet it makes no semblant that it will harm him, but comes toward him making joy. And when Perceval sees this, he calls to it, and he goes to it at once and strokes it on the neck and the head. And the lion couches before him as if it were the tamest beast in the world. And he leans against it and puts his head on its shoulder; so he waits until night had come dark and black; so he falls asleep at once beside the lion.]

Thus whan sir Percyvale had preyde he saw the lyon com towarde hym and cowched downe at his feet. And so all that nyght the lyon and he slepte togydirs. [913.13–15]

La Queste del Saint Graal is certainly long-winded, and "fawnynge as a spaynell" is perhaps better than any phrase in the French. But the verbiage of the original is not all generalized and nonphysical. In dealing with the first passage quoted Malory translates "et li fet la greignor joie que il puet," but he leaves out "et besse la teste"; Malory's lion "trusses" its whelp where the *Queste* lion "emporta la lyoncel *a son col*"; only in the French does Perceval rest his head on the lion's shoulder. Even the repetition of the stroking motif in the third passage, even "beste *mue*" and "la teste" in "le col et la teste et les espaules" make their contribution to the particularity of the lion and of the scene. The only comparable detail Malory adds to his version is "at his feet." The *Queste*'s lion is of course symbolic and the French author does not have Malory's talent for singling out the *détail juste*. But there is a greater thickness of physical detail in the French than in the English passages. I would agree with Vinaver that Malory's version of this episode is better than the original; but it is also less concrete than the original. And there is, I should stress, no reason to believe Malory *wants* a more concrete or down-to-earth account than he finds in his source; when he comes upon ". . . et besse la teste et li fet la greignor joie que il puet . . ." Malory translates the abstract phrase and omits the concrete one: he has chosen to be concise and general rather than concise and specific.

Just as we are more aware of the physical presence of the lion in the French version of this episode than in the English one, we are more aware of landscape and setting.[20] Neither author gives us every stripe of the tulip; but the French author thinks of Perceval's adventure as being in a particular place (or at least a particular kind of place) and Malory does not. First, a detail Malory adds to his version. The following is his only description of the landscape from the time Perceval discovers he is on the mountain-island to the time he goes to the boat (912.14–914.24):

> . . . he saw he was in a wylde mounteyne whych was closed with the se nyghe all aboute, that he myght se no londe aboute hym whych myghte releve hym, but wylde bestes. And than he wente downe into a valey, and there he saw a serpente brynge a yonge lyon by the necke. . . . [912]

It is the valley Malory has added to this account, and as Vinaver points out, this valley "seems out of place here." Its very incongruity suggests in fact that Malory is not really interested in this landscape: he either does not see or does not care that the valley destroys the effect of entrapment. Malory adds this valley to his episode not because he likes valleys but because he dislikes mountains. He prefers a neutral background—the equivalent of "A Street" or "Another Part of the Forest" in eighteenth-century editions of Shakespeare—to one that calls attention to itself.

Now in itself the passage Malory was working from in describing the mountain-island (*La Queste*, 93.12–21) is neither particularly good nor particularly detailed. The mountain there is "large and marvellous and terribly wild," enclosed on every side by unbroken sea. There are no buildings; Perceval is alone except for "savage beasts, bears and lions and leopards and flying serpents." It is not as evident here as it was in the two descriptions of the lion, that the original has a greater thickness of particulars than the adaptation. But the French passage is only a first description; the

20. Here I might point to the difference between "si atent tant que la nuiz fu venue oscure et noire" and "so all that nyght." The first is clichéd, but does mark the transition from day to night, while Malory "syncopates": in one of the English sentences it is presumably day, in the next it is night. See my discussion of such syncopation below.

clear difference in phenomenal thickness is found not in these
initial accounts of landscape but in the pages which follow. There,
although the French writer does not tell us much that we have not
already heard about the mountain, he keeps us aware of the things
we do know, and makes us visualize the action in its setting with the
following phrases, which have no equivalents in the Malorian version: "et voit en mi l'isle une mout haute roche et mout merveil-
leuse" (93.31–32); "et s'asist ou sommet de la montaigne" (94.3);
"contremont la montaigne" (94.8); "si tost come il fu amont venuz
en la roche" (94.11); "si s'en vint aval la roche" (95.8); "en la
roche soutive et haute a merveilles" (95.10–11); "en la roche"
(95.23); "jusqu'a cest montaigne" (97.28); "jusqu'a ceste roche"
(97.29);[21] "cele roche ou il est" (98.29); "au pié de la roche"
(99.5); "qui ert en la roche amont" (99.6); "si descent de la roche"
(99.9). In the French we can never forget "montaigne" and "roche"
for long; in Malory mountain and valley are mentioned initially
and then (one suspects) forgotten.

At the end of the island adventures we have a French passage and
a Malorian adaptation of it which illustrate in another way the
different feelings for landscape in the two works:

> En ce que Perceval pensoit a ceste chose, si esgarda en la mer
> mout loign; et voit une nef qui acoroit le voile tendu et venoit
> droit au leu ou Perceval atendoit por savoir se Diex li donast
> aventure qui li pleust. Et la nef coroit mout tost, car ele avoit
> le vent derriere qui la hastoit; et ele vient vers lui le droit cors
> et arriva au pié de la roche. Et quant Perceval, qui ert en la
> roche amont, vit ce, si ot mout grant joie, car il cuide bien que
> il ait dedenz plenté de gent; et por ce se drece il en estant et
> prent ses armes. Et quant il est armez, si descent de la roche
> come cil qui voudra savoir quel gent il a dedenz la nef. Et
> quant il vient pres, si voit que la nef est encortinee et par
> dedanz et par defors de blans samiz, si qu'il n'i pert se blanches
> choses non. Et quant il vient au bort, si troeve un home revestu
> de sorpeliz et d'aube en semblance de prestre, et en son chief
> avoit une coronne de blanc samit ausi lee come vos deus doiz,

21. The preceding two phrases occur in dialogue.

et en cele coronne avoit letres escrites en quoi li haut nom
Nostre Seignor estoient saintefié. Et quant Perceval le voit,
si s'en merveille; et se triat pres de lui et le salue et li dit: "Sire,
bien soiez vos venuz!" Diex vos ameint!" [*La Queste*, 98–99]

[While Perceval thought of this thing he peered very far into
the sea, and he sees a ship which hasted with spread sail and
came straight to the place where Perceval waited to know if
God would give him a pleasing adventure. And the ship sped
very fast, for it had the wind behind which hastened it; and it
comes toward him on a straight course and arrived at the foot
of the rock. And when Perceval who was on the rock above saw
this, he had very great joy, for well him seems there should be
many people within; and therefore he rises at once and puts on
his arms. And when he is armed he descends from the rock like
one who wishes to know what people are in the ship. And when
he comes near he sees the ship is curtained both within and
without with white samite, so that nothing appears save white
things. And when he comes to the side he finds a man arrayed
in surplice and alb in likeness of a priest, and on his head he
had a crown of white samite as broad as your two fingers, and
in that crown were written letters in which the high names of
Our Lord were sanctified. And when Perceval sees him, he
marvels; and draws near him and greets him and says, "Sir,
you are welcome; God guide you."]

Than was sir Percivale ware in the see where com a shippe
saylyng toward hym, and sir Percivale wente unto the ship
and founde hit coverde within and without with whyght
samyte. And at the helme[22] stoode an olde man clothed in a
surplyse, in lyknes of a pryste. "Sir," seyde sir Percivale, "ye
be welcom." [914]

We are much more aware of space in the original. In part, the difference in awareness is related to the different lengths of the two passages; in the French but not in Malory an impression of a physical
expanse is created by the duration of the description of motion.

22. "At the helm" is a problematic reading. See Vinaver's note to *Works*, 914.23.

In the *Queste*, that is, we have a humbler version of the effect in Milton's description of Mulciber:

> From morn
> To noon he fell, from noon to dewy eve,
> A summer's day.

In the romance passage there is not that superb use of long syllables which allows Milton to suggest an expanse of space in relatively few words. Instead, the French writer achieves his effect by describing the ship's approach with verbs of rapid motion ("acoroit," "coroit," "hastoit")[23] while separating the first sighting of the ship from its arrival with a fairly large number of words. Thus as readers we experience the distance the ship sails as we do not in Malory's "Than was sir Percivale ware in the see where com a shippe saylyng toward hym, and sir Percivale wente unto the ship and found it."

The second difference between the versions also has to do with the sense of space in the two works. In the French there are indications of *degrees* of closeness as Perceval draws toward the ship: "Et quant il vient pres. . . . Et quant il vient au bort . . . et se trait pres de lui. . . ." Malory does not give us this kind of perspective; in his version separation and proximity seem absolute rather than relative.

The difference between the vision of the French episode and the English one is epitomized in the change from "venoit au *leu* ou Perceval atendoit" to "saylyng toward *hym*." The author of *La Queste del Saint Graal*, whatever his limitations as a landscapist, thinks of the ship, the lion and the knight as objects in a physical setting in a way (or to a degree) that Malory does not.

LANDSCAPE AND SETTING

Although, as we shall see later in this chapter, Malory modifies and stylizes action in his adaptations of the French romances, he basically prefers action to description, deeds to setting.[24] His reduc-

23. Quantity matters here. Malory has only "*com* saylying," while in the original we find *venoit*, *vient*, and *arriva* as well as the three more colorful verbs.

24. See M. C. Bradbrook on tournaments in *Le Morte Darthur* (*Sir Thomas Malory* [London, 1958], pp. 22–23).

tion of landscape, as a study of the two "Perceval on the Island" episodes would lead one to expect, is especially striking, but it is also more varied in its techniques, less purely negative than that one adaptation would suggest.

Occasionally in the French romances we find set piece descriptions, moments where the author devotes a page or so to the features of a new and interesting landscape. Such set pieces, which tend to interrupt the sequence of chivalric actions, are not to Malory's taste, as we can see by comparing the description of Ector's arrival at Tarquin's fountain in the *Vulgate Lancelot* with the interesting reshaping of it in "The Noble Tale of Sir Launcelot du Lake":

Si a tant ale quil vint el tertre & y troua vne tor qui estoit close de bons murs tot entour & de haus. Et par dehors la porte a mains dune archie auoit vne fontaine qui sourgoit par . i . tuiel dargent qui cheoit sour vn perron de marbre. Et du perron aloit en . i . vaissel de plom . si pooit bien estre aussi grant comme vne tonne.

Deles la fontaine auoit trois pins et estoient li vns les lautre . et estoient si grant et si haut que des branches & des fuelles estoit la fontaine toute couerte . Si y pendoient par lez guiches .lx. escus & .lx. heaumes & .lx. espees . il regarde lez escus & les heaumes & les espees et sest moult esmeruellies porcoi on les y auoit mises . puis regarde lez escus. Si y connoist lescu agloual & lescu saigremor le desree & lescu keu le senescal & le Gosenain destrangort & le brandelis . mais de tous lez autres nen puet il puis connoistre . Lors sen uait deuers la fontaine & trueue lettres escriptes qui disoient chi sont il non de ceuls qui laiens sont en prison . Et uees la lor armeures . Et il lez commence a lire . Et trueue lettres qui dient el vintetroisime an en apres la coronemente le roy artu . a conquis terican de la forest desuoiable tous lez cheualiers dont li non sont chi escrit. Et il commence a lire lez nons . Si connut de telz en y a . et de teuls y a que il ne connut mie . ensi comme il estoient la uenu destranges terres . Si y trueue iusques a . xxiiij . cheualiers de la maison le roy artu . sans lez compaignons qui estoient de la queste et sans lyonel. Et quant il voit cest escrit si sen e

esmerueille plus que de riens quil eust onques mais veu.. Si ne
croit mie que ce soit voirs . que vns seuls cheualiers peust tant
de preudommes auoir conquis se il ni auoit traison.

   Lors retorne a la fontaine pour faire boire son cheual qui
moult grant mestier en avoit. . . . [89–90]

[Thus he went so far that he came to the hill and there he found
a tower that was closed all about with good walls and high.
And outside of the gate, less than a bowshot away, was a
fountain which rose through a silver pipe and fell upon a
marble stone. And from the stone it went into a leaden vessel
which might well be as large as a tun. Beyond the fountain
were three pines and they were one beside the other and they
were so great and so high that all the fountain was covered by
branches and leaves. So there hung by their straps sixty shields
and sixty helms and sixty swords. He looks at the shields and
the helms and the swords and marvels greatly that they have
been put there. Then he looks at the shields. So he knows the
shield of Agloval le Desree and the shield of Kay the Senescal
and Gosenain D'estrangort and Brandelis. But of all the rest,
no other does he know. Then he goes toward the fountain and
finds letters written which said "These are the names of those
imprisoned within. Behold their armor there." And he begins
to read and he finds letters which say "In the three-and-
twentieth year after the crowning of King Arthur Terican de la
Forest Desvoiable overcame all the knights whose names are
written here." And he begins to read their names. So he knew
of some of those there, and of others he knew not at all, for they
were come there from foreign lands. So he finds full four-and-
twenty knights of King Arthur's house there, without the
fellows who were on the quest and without Lionel. And when
he sees this writing he marvelled more than at anything he had
ever seen. So he does not at all believe a single knight could
have overcome so many heroes unless there were treason.
Then he returns to the fountain to let his horse drink, which
had great need of it.]

   "Sir," seyde the foster, "this countrye know I well. And

hereby within this myle is a strong maner and well dyked, and by that maner on the lyffte honde there is a fayre fourde for horse to drynke off, and over that fourde there growys a fayre tre. And thereon hongyth many fayre shyldys that welded somtyme good knyghtes, and at the bole of the tre hongys a basyn of couper and latyne. And stryke uppon that basyn with the butte of thy spere three tymes, and sone aftir thou shalt hyre new tydynges; and ellys haste thou the fayreste grace that ever had knyghte this many yeres that passed thorow this foreste."

"Gramercy," seyde sir Ector and departed. And com unto this tre and saw many fayre shyldys, and amonge them all he sawe hys brothirs shylde, sir Lyonell, and many mo that he knew that were of his felowys of the Rounde Table, the whyche greved his herte, and promysed to revenge his brother. Than anone sir Ector bete on the basyn as he were woode, and than he gaff his horse drynke at the fourde. [255]

Two changes here are especially notable. First, Malory adds and devotes a fair amount of space to the motif of striking the basin: a passage which in the French was basically a description of things[25] becomes a description of action (although in this case action set in the future). Second, in a characteristic rearrangement,[26] Malory substitutes dialogue for authorial narrative. This change makes the description itself an action.

With this recasting of the description comes the typical simplification. The "vaissel de plom" becomes a "basyn of couper and latyne," but almost all the other changes in particularity go the other way: branches, leaves, marble, silver pipe, etc. are omitted in the English version. To some extent Malory simplifies by viewing individual objects less minutely as well as by seeing fewer objects: not only do we have "shyldys" in place of "escus . . . heaumes . . . espees," but "hongyth" in place of "pendoient par lez guiches." Malory's fondness for the general, abstract, and evaluative is also evident here: he uses "tre" in place of "pins"[27] and "fayre"

25. Although it does, of course, describe Hector seeing those things.
26. See, e.g., Vinaver's note to *Works*, 853.1–7.
27. *Works*, 255.5—*Vulgate Lancelot*, V.90.1. Other such changes: *un petit arbrissiel*

four times (and "fayreste" once) in close succession. The sensibility behind these wordings is the sensibility behind "made hym all the chere that a beest myghte make a man" as a rendering of "et besse la teste et li fet la greignor joie que il puet" in the story of Perceval and the lion.

As Malory does his cutting, he clearly knows what he likes as well as what he doesn't like. In this Englishing of a passage from *La Queste*, for instance, there is a rather elegant economy:

> Einsi chevauchierent uit jorz qu'il ne troverent aventure nule; si lor en poise moult. Un jor lor avint qu'il chevauchierent *parmi une forest grant et estrange*, ou il ne troverent home ne fame. Au soir lor avint qu'il troverent *entre deus roches, en une montaigne*, une chapele vielle et anciane qui tant ert gaste par semblant qu'il n'i reperoit ame. [148.25–30]

> [Thus they rode eight days during which they found no adventure at all; so this grieves them greatly. One day it happened that they rode *through a great forest and a strange*, where they found neither man nor woman. In the evening it happened that they found *between two rocks, in a mountain*, an old chapel and an ancient, which seemed so wasted that not a soul thither repaired.]

> Thus sir Ector and sir Gawayne rode more than eyght dayes. And on a Satirday they founde an auncyant chapell which was wasted, that there semed no man nor woman thydir repayred. [941.26–31]

Malory wants the loneliness suggested by the French but not the complex landscape. Therefore he keeps the emphatic *home ne fame* from the description of the forest while omitting the forest itself.

Malory's domestic settings, as we might expect, are as frequently

---

—*a tre* (*Huth Merlin* I. 181—*Works*, 47.21); *si atachierent lor chevax a deus chesnes—there they tyed their horses* (*La Queste*, 154.24—*Works*, 945.21–22); *vn paueillon tendu deuant .i. grant orme—a pavylyon of rede sendele* (*Vulgate Lancelot*, V.96.3—*Works*, 259.22 [Malory's *rede sendele*, I should point out, apparently was suggested by *samit porpre* at V.66.5]). The English Lancelot, like the French one, sleeps beneath an apple tree (*Works*, 253.28 ff.) but it is Malory's general practice to omit or generalize references to kinds of trees.

stylized as his landscapes. In the *Vulgate Lancelot*, for instance, we find:

> Et Gaheries est entres en la tour terriquen . et trueue vn uarlet qui tenoit les cles en ses mains . *si se seoit en vne caiere deles vn piler de marbre* . et il entre laiens tous armes & salue le uarlet. . . .[207.40–208.1]

> [And Gaheries has entered Tarquin's tower, and finds a groom who holds the keys in his hands. *So he sits in a chair beside a marble piller*. And he enters there all armed and greets the groom. . . .]

This Malory renders:

> . . . and Gaherys yode into the maner, and there he founde a yoman porter kepyng many keyes. Than sir Gaherys threw the porter unto the grounde. . . .[268.21–24]

The degree of selectivity here is the degree of selectivity in the last adaptation I quoted: the keys (one of which is essential to the action of freeing prisoners), but not the chair or the marble pillar; the chapel (where important visions are to occur) but not the forest or mountain; this is one of the most frequent thicknesses of detail in *Le Morte Darthur*.[28] The episode continues:

> Than sir Gaherys threw the porter unto the grounde and toke the keyes frome hym; and hastely he opynde the preson dore, and there he lette all the presoners oute, and every man lowsed other of their bondys. . . .[268.23–26]

Here Malory has added to the action—"every man lowsed other of their bondys" is original—but once more reduced the particularity of setting: in the French we are told that the prison is a ground level hall with more than sixty iron windows opening onto a garden (208.9–13).[29]

---

28. "Kepyng many keyes" is an interesting version of *qui tenoit les cles en ses mains*. The particularity of *en ses mains* is gone, and "kepying" suggests the porter's responsibility, more than his physical grasp in a way that "holding," for instance, would not.

29. In the eight lines which separate this *Vulgate* passage from the one quoted

We might compare the retentions (keys and prison door) and exclusions (details of pillar, windows, and garden) in the passage above with Malory's retention, in the "Quest" section, of the silk cloth which covers the inscription on the Seige Perilous and his omission of the less "functional" tablecloths:

> . . . si font aporter un drap de soie et le metent ou siege por covrir les lettres[30] . . . Et li rois comande que les napes soient mises, car il est tens de mengier, ce li est avis. [*La Queste*, 4.20–5.1]

> [. . . so they lette bring a cloth of silk and place it on the siege to cover the letters . . . And the king commands that the cloths be spread, for it is time to eat, as he thinks.]

> Than made they to ordayne a cloth of sylke for to cover thes lettirs in the Syege Perelous. Than the kynge bade haste unto dyner. [855.25–27]

The author of *La Queste del Saint Graal* is very fond of the semi-traditional spreading and removal of tablecloths, almost the same way he is fond of the more poetic coming of the dawn formula. But Malory does not share this fondness:

> Quant cil de laienz orent mengié et *les napes furent levees*, il se drecierent et alerent *as fenestres dou palés*; si s'assist Boorz delez la dame.
> En ci qu'il parloient einsi entra laienz un vaslez qui dist a la dame. . . .[168–169]

> [When those within had eaten *and the cloths were removed*, they rose and went *to the windows of the hall*; so Bors sat next to the lady.
> While they were speaking thus a squire entered who said to the lady. . . .]

> Than aftir supper they spake of one thynge and of othir. So with that there cam a squyre and seyde. . . .[956.31–33]

---

above Gaheries intimidates the porter. Malory omits these lines because his hero uses different methods.

30. I have omitted eleven lines here, as has Malory.

By omitting the tablecloths and the windows, Malory has reduced this brief passage almost to pure action without setting.[31]

It is clear from the various changes we have examined here that there is both a certain range and a certain flexibility to Malory's adaptations of setting and landscape; he has other gardening tools besides the machete—or at least he wields the machete with a certain delicacy. But finally what is most important about Malory's landscaping, and what most makes the texture of the physical world in *Le Morte Darthur* different from the texture of the physical world in the French romances, is simply the reduced quantity of details.[32] *Fors de la chité par un jardin qui d'encoste sa chambre estoit . . . as fenestres dou palés . . . a la mer auques près . . . hors des murs . . . sous cest arbre . . . en la roche:* the ghosts of such phrases haunt almost every page of *Le Morte Darthur*. Such phrases, such details are neither intrinsically interesting (as are, let us say, the details of Tarquin's fountain in the *Vulgate* description) nor "needful to be understood." But neither are they in Malory's sources because the French authors did not know their business. Such details are "non-functional" or, as I would now prefer to call them, sustaining. They are there because the image or model of reality each author maintains in his work requires that things happen in a landscape of a certain thickness of specificity. These details do not so much enrich our understanding as sustain that thickness of particularity which in the given work is the texture of reality. To suggest an analogy: a novelist may feel it necessary to give a name to a minor character not because a certain name is meaningful (perhaps it's chosen from the phone book at random, or added to the work only at the last minute) but because it would violate the image of reality in the book if that character were *not* named. And much as the thickness of detail varies from work to work, so the use of names varies from novel to novel. How minor need a character be to go without a name?

---

31. P. J. C. Field points out Malory's omission of a "Quant les napes furent levees . . . " in his version of a *Mort Artu* passage. (*Romance and Chronicle*, p. 89.)

32. A garland of typical cuttings would be: *Huth Merlin* I. 185—*Works*, 48.28–34; *Huth Merlin* I.196—*Works*, 52.4–5; *Huth Merlin* I. 196–197—*Works*, 52.13–16; *Vulgate Lancelot*, V.210.25–36—*Works*, 269.19–20; *La Queste*, 151.29–152.4—*Works*, 943.25–30; *La Queste*, 172.20–29—*Works*, 959.5–7.

How often will a given character be referred to as "Mr. Jones," how often as "Johnny," "the fat man," "the lawyer," etc.? To such questions each novelist intuits his own answers, and every good novelist's answers are meaningful, reflecting or consistent with his vision of reality.

The difference between a *Huth Merlin* passage and Malory's adaptation of it usually suggests that physical setting is a less important part of the reality of *Le Morte Darthur* than it is of the reality of *Huth Merlin*. The point is not that Malory is a better writer than the author of the *Merlin,* but that he is less Antaean.

SYNCOPE AND THE DESCRIPTION OF ACTION

Malory, as M. C. Bradbrook has observed, much prefers action to setting. But the difference between action in Malory and in the French romances is not merely one of proportion. When we look closely at descriptions of action in *Le Morte Darthur,* and compare them with their sources, we notice that Malory has a tendency to modify them in a particular way. This tendency is toward what I shall call "syncope."

I am using the word "syncope" in an extension of its grammatical sense; that is, "the shortening of a word by the omission of a sound, letter or syllable from the middle of the word."[33] Here I will use the term to refer to the omission of minor actions in a narrative.

In the last section I discussed details of setting in terms of *degrees* of thickness rather than of the absolute presence or absence of realistic particularity. Here I will speak of details of action in much the same way. I assume an author does not make an either/or choice between summarizing and narrating any more than he does between non-particularity and particularity in describing. The writer finds his individual normative thickness of detail somewhere between "veni, vidi, vici" (or just "vici") and an account of the conquest which mentions every neural impulse in every soldier. "Syncopation," then, will be a movement in the direction of "veni, vidi, vici."

I should say one thing more before turning to the actual changes

33. *American Heritage Dictionary of the English Language*, s.v., 1.

we find in the *Morte*. It is convenient to distinguish between details
of setting and details of action, but the two are of course closely
related. If Malory omits a moment in which a character sits in a
chair, he omits a detail of action with respect to the sitting, of setting
with respect to the chair. In such cases the reasons for and the wisdom of my decision to discuss a particular instance in this section
rather than the last will not always be apparent. But the division of
this topic into two parts should be more often useful than confusing.

The "Tale of King Arthur" provides a simple, representative
example of Malorian syncopation:

> A l'endemain un poi devant la grant messe vint a la court tous
> montés li rois Pellinor, et descendi, et ala en une des chambres
> de laiens, puis revint el palais viestus moult biel et moult
> richement. . . . [*Huth Merlin*, II.74]

> [On the morn a little before high mass King Pellinor came all
> mounted to the court, and he alighted, and went into one of the
> chambers within, then came back into the hall very fairly and
> very richly clothed.]

> So on the morne kynge Pellynor com to the courte of kyng
> Arthure. [101.28–29]

Malory has a narrower interest in the major event which will take
place when Pellinor is in Arthur's court (Pellinor's meeting with his
son Torre) than does the French author. For Malory it is necessary
to know *that* Pellinor arrived, but there is no reason to know how, or
to visualize the entrance. For the French writer such things as "et
descendi, et ala en une des chambres de laiens, puis revint el
palais . . ." are part of the narrative not because they are intrinsically interesting, but because, like such indications of setting as *en
une montaigne*, they sustain a certain normative thickness of detail—
in the one case of action, in the other of setting—which is the texture
of reality in that work.[34]

34. Some other characteristic syncopations are: *Huth Merlin*, II.174—*Works*,
137.23; *La Queste*, 27.1–12—*Works*, 877.6–11; *La Queste*, 72.4–7—*Works*, 905.6–7;
La Queste, 148.30–149.3—*Works*, 941.29–31; *La Queste*, 168.33–169.2—*Works*,
956.31–32.

It is noteworthy that Malory tends to syncopate when he comes upon the quotidian actions of chivalric life. Arrival, departure, arming, unarming, mounting, dismounting, caring for one's horse, going to sleep and waking up—the things done in more or less the same way by good knights and mediocre knights, on important days and on uneventful days—are omitted or simplified:

> Si sen part atant . et sen issi par .i. uergier & puis entre en vne praerie . Et lors troua .i. estroit sentier qui le mena droit a vne forest . ou il auoit vn paueillon tendu deuant .i. grant orme . Il torna maintenant cele part por ce que gent y quida trouuer . Si descent a lentree et voit dedens .ij. cierges ardans. Et il voit .i. grant lit covert dun samit porpre . Il uait au lit errannment mes il ni trueue homme ne femme . ne el paueillon aussi. Et quant il voit ce si uait a son cheual & li oste le frain & la sele . puis le maine paistre . et apres se desarme & met sespee au cheuech del lit quil auoit troue el paueillon . puis se despoille & dist quil se couchera dedens puis quil ni trueue nullui Si estaint lez cierges pour la clarte que mal ne li feist . si se couche et sendort tout maintenant. . . . [*Vulgate Lancelot*, V. 96]
>
> [So thereon he leaves and he issues out through an orchard, and then enters into a meadow and so found a narrow path which led him straight to a forest where a pavilion was pight before a great elm. He turned that way now for he thought to find people there. So he alights at the door and sees therein two candles burning, and he sees a great bed covered with red samite. He goes to the bed quickly but finds neither man nor woman, nor in the pavilion either. And when he sees this he goes to his horse and does off its bridle and saddle and puts it to pasture, and after he unarms himself and puts his sword at the head of the bed which he had found in the pavilion. Then he unclothes himself and said he would lie therein since he found no one there. So he quenches the candles lest the brightness trouble him. So he lies down and falls asleep at once.]

And so he rode into a grete foreste all that day, and never

coude fynde no hygheway. And so the nyght fell on hym, and
than was he ware in a slade of a pavylyon of rede sendele. "Be
my feyth," seyde sir Launcelot, "in that pavylyon woll I
lodge all this nyght." And so he there alyght downe, and tyed
his horse to the pavylyon, and there he unarmed hym. And
there he founde a bed, and layde hym therein, and felle on
slepe sadly. [259.20–26][35]

In the source passage Lancelot dismounts, investigates the pavilion,
and returns to his horse. Malory leaves out that return; when his
Lancelot dismounts he attends to his horse immediately. Malory's
hero simply "tyed his horse to the pavylyon," where the French
knight "li oste le frain & le sele . pues le main paistre." The two
unarming and going to bed sequences are: ". . . unarmed hym
. . . founde a bed . . . layde hym therein . . ."; ". . . il voit
.i. grant lit[36]. . . se desarme & met sespee au cheuech del lit
. . . se despoille . . . estaint lez cierges . . . se couche."

When, in the last book of *Le Morte Darthur*, we come to the knights
who join Lancelot in the religious life, we are told "and soo their
horses wente where they wolde, for they toke no regarde of no
worldly rychesses . . ." (1255.8–9). As Vinaver says, "this remark,
absent from *M*'s sources, seems to reflect the attitude of a man who
knows from experience the value of a horse to a knight-warrior. The
underlying thought is that the moment a knight has ceased to take
care of his horse his worldly life is ended." This detail does mark the
end of worldly chivalry, and marks it poignantly; but it is characteristic of Malory that while Arthurian knighthood flourishes we pay
less attention to horses and armour than we do in the French romances. Malory knows the value of a sword, a horse, a shield; the
sentence I have quoted shows that he understands how much they
can be worth to a knight-artist as well as to a knight-warrior. But
for him these objects finally are far less important constituents of
reality than knightliness, and he will not clutter his narrative with
the small attentions these objects require. "We are not . . . in a

---

35. "Sadly" may be the result of Malory's reading *maintenant* as *malvaisement*.
See Vinaver's note.

36. Earlier in the passage.

world where mechanics has a great deal to do with success."[37] In fact when (to adapt Boswell's phrase) our minds are impregnated with the Malorian ether, we come to suspect that Malory found many of the details in the French romances faintly vulgar. In the *Vulgate Lancelot,* for instance, we're told of the hero just before he goes to fight Tarquin "lors regarde a son cheual que riens ni faille . et quil soit bien enfrenes" (205.36–37). The Malorian knight does nothing of the kind (265), and we feel that he *should not* do anything of the kind, that for Malory such actions would be bathetic. When most truly himself, a Malorian hero may wonder whether his equipment will reveal his identity, but not whether that equipment is in good working order. Malorian combats are won by the better knight, and Malory usually does not think of the better knight as the better craftsman.

If Malory is not very interested in the mechanics of knightly success, he is still less concerned with actions (and reactions) merely human, not specifically knightly.

> Au quart ior li auint quil se herberga chies vn forestier qui manoit a lentree dune forest . Apres souper mena li ostes lancelot couchier . Et quant il fu couchies & il se quida reposer si ne pot quar trop faisoit chaut . Et quant il uit quil ne dormiroit mie si prist sa chemise et sez braies & puis sen uint a vne fenestre de fer pour le uent recueillir . Et ensi quil demoroit illuec pour refroidier si uoit uenir en la cort vn cheualier arme & commence a crier oures oures. . . . [*Vulgate Lancelot,* V.306.25–31]

> [On the fourth day it happened that he lodged with a forester who dwelled at the entry of a forest. After supper the host brought Lancelot to lie down, and when he had lain down and thought to repose himself he could not for the heat. And when he saw that he would not sleep at all he did on his shirt and his breeches and then he went to an iron window to take the wind. And thus as he remained there to cool himself he sees an armed knight come into the yard and begins to cry "open, open!"]

37. Field, "Description and Narration," p. 484.

And at the laste by fortune hym happynd ayenste nyght to come to a fayre courtelage, and therein he founde an olde jantylwoman that lodged hym with goode wyll; and there he had good chere for hym and his horse. And when tyme was his oste brought hym into a garret over the gate to his bedde. There sir Launcelot unarmed hym and set his harneyse by hym and wente to bedde, and anone he felle on slepe.

So aftir there com one on horsebak and knokked at the gate in grete haste. Whan sir Launcelot herde this he arose up and loked oute at the wyndowe, and sygh by the moonelyght three knyghtes com rydynge aftir that one man, and all three laysshynge on him at onys with swerdys. . . . [272–273]

In this adaptation Malory is not merely compressing: he adds as well as leaves out details of setting. But he does simplify the action in one important way: he focuses our attention on knight as knight. The Malorian hero rises in response to the signal for help. He is not incidentally awake because of the heat, and he certainly does not go to the window in search of comfort. Lancelot is affected by the minor discomforts which trouble clown as well as emperor: Sir Lancelot is not.

Time impinges upon Malorian knighthood no more than climate. Characteristically Malory omits the sleepless (k)night: the night in which, for one reason or another, the hero can do nothing but wait for the dawn:

. . . li rois Artus pensa moult au chevalier la nuit. Et se il peust aler a lui si couvertement que si homme ne le seussent, volontiers le fesist; *et tant fu li rois pensis cele nuit, si dormi peu et pensa moult. Et un peu devant chou qu'il deuust ajorner,* il apiela un sien cambrelent qui moult estoit ses privés, se li dist. . . . [*Huth Merlin,* I.184–185]

[That night King Arthur thought much about the knight. And could he have gone to him so privily that men would not have known of it, gladly would he have done so; *and the king was so troubled that night he slept little and thought much. And a little before daybreak* he called a chamberlain of his whom he trusted well, and he said to him. . . .]

> But the kynge was passyngly wrothe for the hurte of sir Gryfflet
> and so he commaunded a prevy man of hys chambir that or hit
> were day his beste horse and armoure "and all that longith to
> my person be withoute the cité *or to-morow day*." Ryght so he
> mette with his man and his horse. . . .[38] [48.28–32]

Malorian syncopation is basically a reduction of the number of
details which are unrelated or tenuously related to the essential
knightliness of the event being described. The ordinary, the mechanical, time and weather, the merely human: such things have more
to do with Lancelot's reality than with Sir Lancelot's reality.

PSYCHOLOGY AND CHARACTERIZATION

All noble knights, like all happy families, are alike. Place, time,
weather, quotidian activities are peripheral to the reality of *Le
Morte Darthur*, and Malory does not want our eyes drawn away
from the center. Individuality is also peripheral; with men as with
things what matters is the relation to a norm. Such a description
of Malorian characterization as Robert H. Wilson's is essentially
accurate:

> In general Malory shows less concern with individuality of
> character than with motivation and consistency. If a character
> possesses a name, if he possesses the broad typical traits of a
> good knight, or a hermit, or of a king, that must usually be
> sufficient, in the *Morte Darthur*, to mark him off from his fel-
> lows. Minor personal peculiarities, such as Gareth's size and
> Gawain's taste for apples and pears, are unimportant rarities.[39]

But "must usually be sufficient" misplaces the emphasis. Malory is
not making do; he is stylizing his characterization in the same way
he stylizes his settings: in the world of *Le Morte Darthur*, the most
important, the most real thing about any knight is his possession or
non-possession of typical chivalric traits. Personality traits which

---

38. Compare also, e.g., *La Queste*, 151.18–28 and *Works*, 943.19–24; *La Queste*,
172.3–10 and *Works*, 958.29–33.

39. *Characterization in Malory: A Comparison with his Sources* (Chicago, 1934), pp.
120–21.

have no bearing on a character's knightliness are fundamentally trivial.

Eighty years ago, when everyone knew what a novel was, J. J. Jusserand explained why *Le Morte Darthur* was something else. "Everything. . . .," he said, "is in Malory's book; everything, except those marks of character which transform traditional types into living personalities; everything, except those analyses of feeling which are for us the primary *raison d'être* of the modern novel and its chief attraction."[40] To appreciate the originality of *Le Morte Darthur,* however, we must remember that literary "analyses of feeling" do not begin with the novel. One of the most notable stylistic features of the French and German *roman courtois* of the twelfth and thirteenth centuries is the extended passage which analyzes conflicting impulses. For instance, when Gottfried's Isolde discovers that Tristan, now in her power, is the killer of Morold:

> Those two conflicting qualities, those warring contradictions, womanhood and anger, which accord so ill together, fought a hard battle in her breast. When anger in Isolde's breast was about to slay her enemy, sweet womanhood intervened. "No, don't!" it softly whispered. Thus her heart was divided in purpose—a single heart was at one and the same time both good and evil. The lovely girl threw down the sword and immediately picked it up again. Faced with good and evil she did not know which to choose. She wanted and yet she did not want, she wished both to do and to refrain. Thus uncertainty raged within her, till at last sweet womanhood triumphed over anger, with the result that her enemy lived, and Morold was not avenged.[41]

It is true that usch passages usually are neither as elaborate nor as frequent in the French prose romances as they are in the earlier verse narratives, but in Malory there is still less detailed treatment

40. *The English Novel in the Time of Shakespeare,* trans. Elizabeth Lee, revised and enlarged by the author (New York, 1890), p. 56. Jusserand does go on to except Book 18, Chapter 25 from his stricture.

41. Gottfried von Strassburg, *Tristan,* trans. A. T. Hatto (Baltimore, 1965), pp. 176–77.

of emotion than in those prose romances. *Le Morte Darthur* is strikingly apsychological compared to what came before as well as to what came after: to say that Malory is uninterested in "analyses of feeling" is not to say that he is merely a man of his age or a writer born too soon.

With psychology, as with physical detail, it will be useful to begin looking at the texture of Malory's narration by examining one episode closely. The adventure of the "Castle Charyot" in Book III is both representative and convenient to discuss: here Malory does not greatly alter the structure of his original or suggest a radically different moral judgment of the characters but does change the way we look at those characters and their mental processes.

Malory's episode, we may recall, begins when four queens find Lancelot sleeping fully armed under an apple tree. Morgan le Fay, who is one of the queens, casts a spell upon Lancelot and he is carried to the Castle Charyot. This, then, is Malory's account of Lancelot's imprisonment and awakening; the knight is brought

> . . . unto the Castell Charyot; and there they leyde him in a chambir colde, and at nyght they sente unto hym a fayre dameselle with his souper redy idyght. Be that the enchauntement was paste.
>
> And whan she com she salewed hym and asked hym what chere.
>
> "I can not sey, fayre damesel," seyde sir Launcelot, "for I wote not how I com into this castell but hit be by inchauntemente."
>
> "Sir," seyde she, "ye muste make good chere; and yf ye be suche a knyght as is seyde ye be, I shall telle you more to-morn be pryme of the day."
>
> "Gramercy, fayre damesel," seyde sir Launcelot, "of your good wylle."
>
> And so she departed, and there he laye all that nyght withoute ony comforte. And on the morne erly com thes four queyns. . . . [257]

The feeling of the source passage is quite different:

Et quant il orent lancelot descendu . si le firent metre vne
cambre . ou il nauoit que vn huis & .ij. fenestres de fer. Et lors
desfirent lor enchantement . et il sesueilla tantost & regarda
tout entor lui si vit grant plente de candeilles si se commencha
a seignier & dist a soi meisme . sainte marie dame ou sui iou .
Iou me coulchai orendroit dormir desouz lombre dun pomier .
et or me sui troues iou ne sai ou en chastel . ou en forteresce .
ne ni voi homme ne femme . par foy ou iou sui enfantosmes .
ou iou ne sai que dire de moi meismes . Lors li souient de son
cheual quil auoit laissie deles lui . Si regarde tout entor lui
por sauoir se il le uerroit . Et quant il voit quil ni est mie si
est tant dolans quil ne set quil doie dire & dist que dyables lont
la aporte . Apres ce ne demora gaires quil uit luis de la cambre
ourir . Si entra laiens vne damoisele qui li aporta a mangier a
grant plente . Il le salue quant il le voit uenir . Et elle lui
autresi . Damoisele fait il par la riens el monde que vous plus
ames dites moi ou iou sui . Sire fet elle vous estes el chastel
de la charrete . qui siet en la terre de gorre . Et il se seigne de
la merueille quil en a . Sainte maire fet il qui mi a amene .
Sire fet elle ce ne vous dirai iou pas . mes mengies & vous
enforcies . & gisies sil vous plaist en cel lit qui asses est biaus
& riches Et de lyonel damoisele fait il quar men dites noueles .
se vous le saues . Si mait diex fait elle iou ne sai qui cils lyoniaus
est ne onques nen oy parler a mon escient . Ne iou ne vous en
sai a dire ne uoir me menchoigne Et quant il oit toutes uoies
quil est ensi desuoies . si ne set que dire . mais toutes voies
mangue & saaise comme cil qui nauoit toute ior mangie . si
mangue si dolans & si coroucies que nul plus . Et puis quant il ot
mangie si vint vns ualles laiens qui le descaucha . Et il se coucha
maintenant en vn lit qui estoit fais en mi la cambre . si a dormi
maluaisement toute la nuit . quar il ne fina de penser a soi & a
lyonel. [*Vulgate Lancelot,* 92–93]

[And when they had set Lancelot down they put him in a
chamber in which was but one door and two iron windows.
And then they undid their enchantment and at once he awoke
and looked all about him. So he saw full many candles and

began to bless him and said to himself: "Saint Mary, madam, where am I? But now I lay down to sleep in the shade of an apple-tree and now I have found myself I know not where, in castle or in fortress. Nor do I see man nor woman there. In faith, I am bewitched or I know not what to say of myself." Then he remembers his horse which he had left beside him. So he looks all about him to know if he could see it. And when he sees it is not there, he is so hevy he knows not what to say, and said that devils had borne it off. Then it was not long until he saw the door of the chamber open. So a damsel entered who brought him much mete. He greets her when he sees her come in, and she him again. "Damsel," he says, "by that you love best in the world, tell me where I am." "Sir," she says, "you are in the Castle Chariot which is in the land of Gorre." And he blesses himself for the marvel of this. "Saint Mary," he says, "who has brought me here?" "Sir," she says, "as for that, I will not say, but eat and refresh you and lie if you will in this bed which is fair enough and rich." He says, "I wish you would tell me tidings of Lionel, damsel, if you know any." "So God me speed," she says, "I know not who this Lionel is, nor to my witting have I ever heard speak of him, nor do I know anything to tell you of him, neither truth nor lie." And when he hears ever that he is so far astray he knows not what to think, but ever he eats and takes his ease like one who had not eaten all day. So he eats as hevy and wroth as might be. And then when he had eaten there comes in a groom who unshoed him. And he couched him in a bed which was made in midst of the chamber. So he slept but badly all night, for he ceased not to think of himself and Lionel.]

Malory's compression has virtually eliminated that direct expression of Lancelot's inner life we have in the French. His distress *is* indicated in the English, but both the mode of expression and the nature of the distress itself have changed; we see Malory's hero encountering not his own bewilderment, but external, objective difficulties. Characteristically, Malory includes fewer details of setting than does his source, but he also changes the nature of the details retained. Instead of the food "a grant plente" we have the neutral "souper redy idyght"; more important, instead of the not disagreeable appointments of the French chamber we have "a chambir colde."[42] *Cel lit qui asses est biaus & riches:* the maiden is not being ironic; the bewilderment and mental suffering are in contrast with the surroundings and with the service, and the reader is expected to enjoy the contrasting textures of imprisonment as physical fact and as psychological fact. But Malory does not care about such contrasts. His Lancelot simply encounters objective, ph, sical difficulties, and being Malory's Lancelot, encounters them taciturnly. We are not invited to share his private thoughts; indeed, we are not encouraged to suppose he has any.

When the Malorian hero speaks, his brief sentences are courteous and factual. His first words are in response to a question, while in the *Vulgate* a more anxious, less self-sufficient knight gives the first greeting and asks the first question. Malory's Lancelot begins his speech by confirming the narrator's terms "enchauntemente" and "fayre damesel"; in the French the narrator's term was "enchante- ment" and the character's "enfantosmes." Such confirmation, as I said in the previous chapter, tends to suggest objectivity and accuracy in speech. In Malory we are very far from the "par la reins el monde que vous plus ames" and "Sainte Marie" of the *Vulgate*.

That "Sainte Marie" warrants a short digression. Lancelot calls on Mary twice in the comparatively short *Vulgate* passage. Malory omits both these references, and in fact he seems to mention the Virgin remarkably little in *Le Morte Darthur* as a whole. Undoubt- edly the most important reference to her is the "thankynges and lovynge unto God and unto Hys Blyssed Modir" given by the Round Table knights at the climactic moment of "The Healing of Sir Urry," and the extreme rareness of such prayers underscores the climax. Elsewhere, according to the "Index of Proper Names" in Vinaver's edition of the *Works*, Mary is named only five times. In "King Arthur and the Emperor Lucius," Arthur makes a vow rather inappropriately "unto mylde Mary and unto Jesu Cryste"

42. See Vinaver's note.

that he will be avenged upon the Romans (188.20–22); toward the
end of the "Tristram" Palomydes says that although he cannot yet
be christened he has long believed in "Jesu Cryste and hys mylde
modir Mary" (842.3–6); in the "Grail" section there are two
references to Mary in doctrinal passages (991.26–29 and 999.29–
32) and, quite interestingly, a passage in which Bors sees a maiden
in distress who cries "Seynte Mary, succour your mayde!" (961.4).
Bors, who must choose between helping Lionel and helping the
maiden, says "Fayre swete Lorde Jesus Cryst, whos creature I am,
kepe me sir Lyonell, my brothir, that thes knyghtes sle hym nat,
and for pite of you and for mylde Maryes sake, I shall succour thys
mayde" (961.18–22). The passage in Malory's source is much the
same, except there Bors does not mention Mary—only the maiden
does.[43] Characteristically, then, Malory's heroes do not invoke
Mary's aid. The Arthurian knights believe in, make a vow to, and
do good for the sake of Mary, but they seek supernatural help and
comfort from God or Christ. This is quite in keeping with Malory's
general conception of his heroes and the masculine values of his
world. Mary the *mylde*, the intercessor for wretched, confused
humanity, may normally be invoked by Lancelot, but not by Sir
Lancelot. The wonderful moment in "Sir Urry" when she is invoked
is the moment when Lancelot weeps "as he had bene a chylde that
had bene beatyn."

To return to the Castle Charyot adventure: we have seen that
Malory's hero is more close-mouthed than the *Vulgate* one; the same
is true of his interlocutor. In neither version of this episode does the
maiden wish to reveal more than she must; yet the French maiden,
when compared with the English one, is almost chatty. The style of
the one is "mes mengies & vous enforces & gieses sil vous plaist en
cel lit qui asses est biaus & riches" and that of the other in "ye muste
make good chere." Tacuit et fecit" might be the motto of Arthur's
knights in Malory,[44] but it might be the motto of most of the minor
characters as well.

Earlier in this episode there is another very interesting reworking

43. See *La Queste*, 175.13–176.3 and Vinaver's note to *Works*, 961.20–21.
44. See Bradbrook, *Sir Thomas Malory*, p. 28.

of minor characters. In the *Vulgate* text the queen and her companions (who will become Malory's four queens) are introduced in this
passage:

Che dist li contes que quant lancelot fu remes dormant apres
ce que lyoniaus sen fu ales. il ne demora gaires que par illuec
passa vne Royne qui estoit roine de la terre de sorestan qui
marchissoit a norgales par deuers sorelois . si uenoient auec li
plus de .lx. cheualiers tous armes . si portoient par dessus li
quatre uallet .i. paile a cheual sor .iiij. lances . Et elle regarda le cheual lancelot qui paissoit de lerbe . Si pensa que la
se dormoit aucuns cheualiers pour soi reposer Si quide bien
que che soit des cheualiers errans de la maison le roy artu . Si
apela .ij. dames dont li vne /auoit a non Morgue la fee . &
lautre sebile lenchanteresce . Et ce estoient les .ij. femmes del
monde qui plus sauoient denchantemens sans la dame del lac.
Et la royne dist que elle veult aler ueoir qui cils cheuals est.
si vait cele part tout a cheual & trueue lancelot qui encore
dormoit . & la royne dist a ses compaignes que vous onques
mais ne ueistes nulle si bele cose si mait diex a mon auis .
Moult se deuroit priser la dame qui de tel homme auroit la
seingnorie . & pleust ore a dieu quil maimast ore autretant .
comme nul cheualier ama onques nulle dame . si mait diex ie
me tendroie a plus riche dame . que se il auoie tote la terre del
monde en ma baille. . . . [91–92]

[Here the tale says that when Lancelot was left sleeping after
Lionel had gone it was not long before a queen passed by who
was queen of the land of Sorestan which marched with Norgales
in the direction of Sorelois. So there came with her more than
sixty knights all armed. So four yeomen bore over her a riding
pall upon four spears. And she looked at Lancelot's horse which
pastured upon the grass. So she thought that some knight slept
there to repose him. So well she supposed it should be an errant
knight of King Arthur's house. So she called two ladies, of
which one was named Morgan la Fee and the other Sebile the
Enchantress (and these were the two ladies in the world who

most knew of enchantments, besides the lady of the lake). And
the queen said she would know what the horse was. So she goes
there all mounted and finds Lancelot still sleeping. And the
queen said to her fellows that "So help me God, methinks you
never saw a thing so fair. Much pride should that lady feel who
had the seigniory of such a man. And now would that it pleased
God he should now love me again more than ever knight
loved lady. So help me God, I would hold myself a richer lady
than if I had all the world's land in my power."]

We focus on the queen of Sorestan before we see the other ladies.
As we entered Lancelot's mind in the French imprisonment scene,
so here we watch the queen thinking ("Si pensa que la se dormoit
aucuns cheualiers pour soi reposer Si quide bien que che soit des
cheualiers errans de la maison le roy artu") as well as speaking at
some length. Now the other ladies, already distinguished by name,
are further individuated in a *débat*:

Ha . dame fet morgain moult seroit ore mieuz enploie en moi .
que en uous . quar ie sui de meilleur gent . & de plus haut
lignage que uus niestes . encore soiez uous roingne . & por ce
me tendroit il plus chiere & plus mameroit que vos . En non
dieu fet lautre dame qui auoit non sebile . encore le deuroie
ie auoir mieuz que vous . quar ie sui plus bele & plus ione &
plus enuoise de uos .ii. si le sauorie mieuz seruir a sa uolente
& por ce me semble il . que uous uos en deuez bien tere del
parler Or vous dirai que nous ferons fait la royne . esueillons
le & nos offrons totes a son seruise . Et telle quil uoudra
detenir remaigne o lui. Enon dieu fait morgains . ensi ne le
ferons nous mie . mais ie vous dirai que on en face . Faisons
faire vne biere cheualeresce . . . & le portons al chastel de la
charete . Par foy font elles vous dites bien . [92]

["Ah madam," says Morgan, "he would be much better busied
with me than with you, for I am of better kin and of higher
blood than you, queen though you be. And therefore he would
cherish me and love me more than you." "In God's name,"
says the other lady, who was named Sebile, "I ought to have

him rather than you, for I am fairer and younger and fresher than you two. So I would know better how to serve his pleasure, and therefore it seems to me you should cease to speak." "Now I shall tell you what we shall do," says the queen. "Let us wake him and all offer us to his service. And whoever he will detain will remain in the place." "In God's name," says Morgan, "we shall not do so by any means . But I shall tell you what is to be done. Let us let make a horse litter . . . and bear him to Castle Chariot." "In faith," say they, "you say well."]

This whole sequence is drastically simplified in *Le Morte Darthur*:

Now leve we thes knyghtes presoners, and speke we of sir Launcelot de Lake that lyeth undir the appil-tre slepynge. About the none so there com by hym four queenys of a grete astate: and for the hete sholde nat nyghe hem, there rode four knyghtes aboute hem and bare a cloth of grene sylke on four sperys betwyxte hem and the sonne. And the quenys rode on four whyghte mules.[45]

Thus as they rode they herde a grete horse besyde them grymly nyghe. Than they loked and were ware of a slepynge knyght lay all armed undir an appil-tre. And anone as they loked on his face they knew well hit was sir Launcelot, and began to stryve for that knyght, and every of hem seyde they wolde have hym to hir love.

"We shall nat stryve," seyde Morgan le Fay, that was kyng Arthurs sister. "I shall put an inchauntement uppon hym that he shall nat awake of all this seven owres, and than I woll lede hym away unto my castell. And whan he is surely within my

45. Malory has added some physical details to this scene: ". . . *of grene sylke . . . betwyxte hem and the sonne . . . whyghte mules.*" I wonder if these are not intended to suggest a certain decadence—especially the green silk which as a sun shade contrasts very nicely with the shade of the apple tree sought out by Lancelot. We may also notice that Lancelot is not said to be *all armed* in the original: Malory seems to be appropriating for his hero the *tous armes*, which in the *Vulgate* describes the forty knights. This appropriation reinforces the contrast between the Arthurian knight and his less martial discoverers.

holde, I shall take the inchauntement frome hym, and than
lette hym chose whych of us he woll have unto peramour."
[256]

By giving all four ladies the same rank Malory emphasizes what they
have in common rather than the differences between them; we also
observe that Malory's Lancelot is discovered by the queens in a
group, and that it is not until a page later, after Lancelot's interview
with the maiden, that we learn the names of all four of the queens.
Their miniature *débat* no longer exists: in the *Morte* we are not interested in why each thinks she has the strongest claim to Lancelot,
but simply in the fact that all four claim him. Here Morgan is the
only one who stands out from the group, but even her coryphaeus-
like individuality is not very distinct; it is characteristic that in
the longest of the queens' three speeches,[46] the collective voice and
the individual voice blur.

Malory's stylizing of narration has its usual effect here; it is
knightliness we focus on in this scene, where characterization is
flattened, individuality reduced. In *Le Morte Darthur* the four queens
desire Sir Lancelot precisely because he *is* Sir Lancelot: "And anone
as they loked on his face they knew well hit was sir Launcelot, and
began to stryve for that knyght, and every of hem seyde they wolde
have hym to hir love"; ". . . because that we undirstonde youre
worthynesse, that thou art the noblest knyght lyvyng . . . " (257.
25–26). "For the renowne and bounté that they here of you," as
the fair maiden explains to the hero, "they woll have your love"
(258.23–4). The *Vulgate* gave Malory the hint from which he devel-
oped a virtual equation between knightliness and erotic desirability;
in that episode, as we have seen, the queen of Sorestan thinks an
Arthurian knight may be about. But this is no more than a hint.
"La royne dist a ses compaignes que vous onques mais ne ueistes
nulle si bele cose si mait diex a mon auis." It is not worship that
makes Lancelot attractive here.

Courtly literature focuses on delicate discriminations of motive
and feeling, and the *Vulgate* episode is essentially courtly. The *débat*

46. 257.22–34. The speech in the passage quoted above is by Morgan, and the
third by the queens collectively.

itself is frequently a courtly motif; the queen speaks of "la seingn-
oirie"; Lancelot's possible refusal of all four of them is described
almost as a crime against the courtly code deserving punishment:
". . . et se vous ce ne uoles faire *que vous soies si orgueilleus* que nulle
de nous ne vous plaise . vraiement sachies que voux nisterois iamais
de prison ." [93.12–14]. (There is also a certain coyness in the
queen's voice: "Sire cheualiers vous estes en nostre prison . mais
de tant vous est il bien auennu que la raencon en sera legiere."
[93.8–10].) The French writer, the courtly writer, is willing to play
with different attitudes, is interested in character and attitude per
se in a way that Malory is not. As much as he can, Malory binds his
stories to the idea of knightliness; his Lancelot is not interesting in
this episode because he is a bewildered and anxious man, but
because he is encountering in a proper, knightly way—laconically
—proper knightly hardships—physical ones. Malory's ladies are
not a queen and two enchantresses all more or less distinct, but four
queen-enchantresses (258.3,.20–22), who naturally find the worthi-
est and noblest of knights a most desirable love. One of these four
ladies is distinguished as *prima inter pares*, and distinguished in this
way—so Malory might put it—"as reason is"; she is not higher in
rank than the others, but she is, as Malory but not the *Vulgate* reminds us here, Arthur's sister (256.30–31).

In *Le Morte Darthur* the thing that wommen moost desiren is
a verray, parfit gentil knyght. We perceive this in the Castle
Charyot episode but perhaps the tone of Malory's equation between
a man's knightliness and his erotic desirability is heard most clearly
in the Fair Maid of Astolat story. The important section here is the
conversation between Elaine and Gawain after he, having seen the
shield of the knight she loves, realizes that that knight is Lancelot:

> "A, Jesu mercy!" seyde sir Gawayne, "now ys my herte more
> hevyar than ever hit was tofore."
> "Why?" seyde thys mayde Elayne.
> "For I have a grete cause," seyde sir Gawayne. "Ys that
> knyght that owyth thys shylde youre love?"
> "Yee truly," she sayde, "my love ys he. God wolde that I
> were hys love!"

"So God me spede," seyde sir Gawayne, "fayre damesell,
ye have ryght, for and he be youre love, ye love the moste
honorabelyst knyght of the worlde and the man of moste
worship."

"So methought ever," seyde the damesell, "for never ar that
tyme no knyght that ever I saw loved I never none arste."

[1078–1079]

Elaine's last remark is quintessential Malory.[47] Castiglione or
Spenser might have drawn Platonic arabesques on Elaine's *for*,
but in Malory her inference is really just common sense: if a
noble maiden who has never loved other knights feels love now for
a certain knight, then surely the knight she loves is "of more worship," is more knightly, than the others. The values in Malory's
world have only one center.[48] The heart has its reasons which
reason understands very well.

Malory's minor characters deserve some attention here. As Vinaver pointed out in 1929, the abundance of these characters in the
French romances frequently causes the story to wander from its
point and fall into digressions. "Malory resists this, but on a large
scale lacks the power to carry out his design. He never goes so far as
to leave out a knight of the Round Table or any person of consequence, but confines himself to reducing slightly the number of less
conspicuous personages who are mostly anonymous: the knights
and damsels who act as messengers, or as guardians of castles and
towers, or again as hosts offering hospitality to knights-errant."[49]

47. There is no explicit cause and effect relationship between knightly worship
and love in the corresponding section of either *La Mort* or the stanzaic poem.

48. One other moment in "The Fair Maid of Astolat" deserves mention here.
In Malory (but not in his sources [see Vinaver's note to *Works*, 1089.9–1092.8])
Lavayne and his father are present at Elaine's last interview with Launcelot:
" 'Fadir,' seyde sir Lavayne, 'I dare make good she ys a clene maydyn as for my
lorde sir Launcelot; but she doth as I do, for sythen I saw first my lorde sir Launcelot I cowde never departe frome hym, nother nought I woll, and I may follow
hym' " (1091.11–15). Malory insists on the parallel reactions of brother and sister:
a young man responds to a knight of great worship by following him into adventures, a young lady by falling in love with him.

49. *Malory* (Oxford, 1929,) p. 35.

But equally as significant as the number of minor characters simply excluded from *Le Morte Darthur* is the stylized, externalized presentation of the ones who remain. We do not enter the minds of such characters, do not care about their motives. It is, for instance, typical of *Le Morte Darthur* that when Torre enters a pavilion and finds a brachet and a sleeping lady inside, we are told only that "the whyght brachett . . . bayed at hym faste" (110.31), while the *Huth Merlin* explains that the dog barks "por chou que il ne connissoit pas le chevalier" (II.105).

In the French romances a minor character may be very excited by the news he brings. A squire in the *Queste del Saint Graal* enters and tells the king he brings marvellous tidings. The king wants to be told quickly what those tidings are. "Sire," says the squire, "down below your palace there is a great stone I have seen float upon the water. Come see it," he adds, "for I know well this is a marvellous adventure" (5.11–17). But in *Le Morte Darthur* a *nuncius* does not become excited to the point of giving his superiors orders:

> So as they stood spekynge, in com a squyre that seyde unto the kynge,
>
> "Sir, I brynge unto you mervaylous tydynges."
>
> "What be they?" seyde the kynge.
>
> "Sir, there ys here bynethe at the ryver a grete stone whych I saw fleete abovyn the watir, and therein I saw stykynge a swerde."
>
> Than the kynge seyde, "I woll se that marvayle."
>
> [855.36–856.6]

When presenting his major characters, Malory again and again makes the kind of change we saw in the episode of Lancelot's imprisonment: he is far less willing than are his sources to give us a knight who is at once perplexed and heroic or even frightened and sympathetic. His "Quest of the Holy Grail" is especially interesting in this connection, because there Malorian characterization has a very peculiar effect. In the "Sir Bors" section, for instance, a "good man" appears to Bors in a dream and instructs him. The vision ends:

> "Now kepe the," seyde the good man, "that thou never se such adventure befalle the."

> Than he awaked and made a sygne of the crosse in myddys of the forehede, and so he arose and clothed hym. [958.27–30]

In the original, after the good man's teachings conclude, we are told "thus that night these two visions came to Bors which made him marvel greatly, for he could not at all think what this might be. And so greatly did they grieve him in his sleep that he woke and made the sign of the cross on his forehead; and much he commended himself to Our Lord; and waited until it was day." (171.29–172.5). Now in the English version Bors' sign of the cross may suggest the uneasiness which motivated it in *La Queste del Saint Graal*, but more likely it will not. Malory presents the gesture as one of a series of quite ordinary actions: Bors awakes, makes the sign, rises, dresses. Because we are not told Bors is troubled, and because the sign is in this series of normal getting-up-to-meet-the-world activities, that sign is more likely to suggest an affirmation of allegiance (perhaps even a mark of gratitude for the vision) than a call for help. Certainly we are shown Bors's bewilderment far less clearly in Malory than in the French, and we are likely to feel we have not been shown bewilderment at all. Our eye is on the act rather than the emotion.[50]

50. The beginning of the Perceval on the Island narration is relevant here. Notice that there is far more emphasis on the hero's reactions to his strange surroundings in *La Queste*, 93.9–30 than in *Works*, 912.14–18. A comparison of the two versions of the immediately preceding episode is also instructive. The *Queste del Saint Graal* has this description of Perceval mounting the infernal horse: "Quant Perceval voit le cheval, si le resgarde et l'en prent hisdor; et neporec il est bien tant hardiz que il monte sus, come cil qui ne se prent garde de la agait a l'anemi" (*La Queste*, 92.7–9). ["When Perceval sees the horse he looks at it and is frightened by it. And nonetheless he is so hardy that he mounts upon it, like one who takes no care of the fiend's ambush."] In Malory this becomes: "Whan sir Percyvale behylde that horse that he was so grete and so well apparayled. And natforthan he was so hardy he lepte uppon hym and toke none hede off hymself" (911.31–34). Vinaver comments: "*F* has warned the reader that the lady who brought the horse was the fiend *(li anemis)*. Having omitted the warning *M* has to substitute *he mervaylde, &c.*, for *si li en prent grant hideur* (Ms. cit., f. 536v, col. 2)" (Note to *Works*, 911.31–33). But it is the reader, not Perceval who is warned, and one wonders why Malory, who usually anticipates his sources in identifying characters, here omits the early identification. I would reverse Vinaver's cause and effect. Malory does not like the idea of Perceval being afraid of the horse any more than he likes Perceval fearing savage beasts in the following episode. The identifica-

Malory's characterization has a peculiar effect on the Grail narrative. There has been, we may recall, considerable disagreement about the "Quest" among Malory's critics. Vinaver describes his version as ". . . a beautiful parade of symbols and bright visions . . . deprived of its spiritual foundation, of its doctrine, and of its direct object."[51] Charles Moorman takes issue with this description: "Malory's changes do not . . . stem from his not understanding the religious tone of the French *Queste*; he always preserves the core of the French book's doctrinal statements, no matter how great his deletions."[52] Now what Moorman claims here is basically true but yet one *does* feel there is something wrong in Malory's "Quest." I think our uneasiness has less to do with the quality of Malory's understanding of religious doctrine than with his reluctance to take us into the minds of his heroes and show us their fears and perplexities. The real trouble is that Malory's presentation of his heroes as (in E. K. Chamber's phrase) "men of their hands"[53] and his tendency to cut away passages of psychological analysis work against that sense of inner reality, the constant awareness that mind has mountains, which is basic to *La Queste del Saint Graal*. Because in the French we experience and believe in the perplexities of the knights we are ready to believe that earthly chivalry is not enough. We feel that these heroes are not self-sufficient, and thus that their order cannot be made self-sufficient. In the French the presentation of the characters' emotions makes us experience the necessity for the symbols, things symbolized, and explanations, while the Malorian presentation does not.[54] The symbols have less literary impact in

---

tion of the lady is omitted because if we know this is the devil our judgment of Perceval's act is changed. In Malory we have the heroic *and toke none hede of hymself*, in the French *come cil qui ne se prent garde de la agait a l'anemi*, which is certainly not exemplary behavior. Malory would no doubt agree that one should fear the devil's snares, but he does not like situations in which being afraid of horses is a good thing.

51. *Malory*, p. 84.

52. " 'The Tale of the Sankgreall': Human Frailty," *Malory's Originality*, p. 187.

53. "Sir Thomas Malory," in *Sir Thomas Wyatt and Some Collected Studies* (London, 1933), p. 33.

54. Reading a bit further in the original Bors episodes we find that the knight sets out on his travels and rides in a forest "pensant a ce qu'il avoit veu en dormant: car mout desirroit que Diex le menast en tel leu ou il en poist oïr le sene-

Malory than in the French not because of their content but because
of their psychological context.

Throughout *Le Morte Darthur* Malorian heroes are more narrowly
heroic than their originals. Lionel decides to pursue an adventure
by himself and leaves Lancelot sleeping. In the *Vulgate* we are told
he does not wake him because he is afraid of being thought a coward
(88.36–38); Malory's knight simply and typically "thought nat for
to awake sir Launcelot" (254.18). Two pages later Ector is taken
prisoner. "Si en a si grant doel quil volsist bien estre mor," says the
original (90.34–35). Malory omits the despair; the only indication
of Ector's feelings are his refusal to be sworn Tarquin's "trew
presoner" and his promise to "do myn advauntage" (256.1–2).
But fairly often indications of reactions seem to be omitted not
because they refer to feelings which are obviously unheroic, but
simply because they do draw our attention to some kind of reaction.
We may recall the episode of Perceval and the ship. I pointed out
before that motion is more real in the French version of that scene
than in the Malorian one in part because of the length at which the
French author describes Perceval and the approaching vessel. Here
it is useful to look a little more closely at the phrases which contribute to that lengthiness: ". . . au leu ou Perceval atendoit por
savoir se Diex li donast aventure qui li pleust . . . si ot mout grant
joie, car il cuide bien que il ait dedenz plenté de gent . . . come cil
qui voudra savoir quel gent il a dedanz la nef . . . si s'en merveille."
It would not be improper for Malory's knight to have such thoughts
and emotions, but Malory avoids telling us that he does. In the
"Arthur and Accolon" section of Malory's first tale, Sir Outlake and
Arthur are pursuing Morgan le Fay and her company (151). The
Huth Merlin, which is Malory's source here, says "Et neporquant il le

---

fiance" (*La Queste*, 174.29–175.2). ["Thinking of what he had seen in his sleep: for
much he wished God to lead him to a place where he might hear its meaning."]
In Malory, from the time Bors makes the sign of the cross at 958.30 to the time he
asks for an explanation of his dream at 963.21, there is no indication that he thinks
about the vision at all, let alone wants to be led by God to a place where the vision
will be interpreted. The artistic consequence of this silence, and of like silences
between vision and explication in other parts of Malory's "Quest," is that we are
far less aware of the need for ecclesiastical instruction in the English than in the
French.

cuide erraument, mais che l'esmaie durement qu'il voit la forest si
prè d'eus, car il set bien que la se quatiront il se reponront, se il
pueent riens savior de sa venue" (II.222). There is nothing unheroic
about such thoughts at such a moment, but neither do they have
any effect upon the action of the adventure, and Malory omits them.
A page later Arthur finds Morgan and her followers turned to stone,
but he cannot find the scabbard Morgan had stolen from him. In
the *Huth Merlin* Arthur is "moult iriés de chou qu'il avoit pierdu le
fuerre" (II.222); Malory says only "And than he loked for the
scawberde, but hit wold nat be founde; and so he turned to the
abbey there she come fro" (151.26–27).[55] Malory allows us to observe the minds of his characters less frequently and more briefly
than do his sources.

Malory as narrator reveres his material and his heroes; implicitly
he shares their values. His reluctance to dwell on the emotions of his
characters, and his emphasis upon deeds, are very much in harmony
with the characters's own attitudes, particularly as those attitudes
are manifested in typical knightly speech.

It is worth pausing here to consider the special qualities of Malorian dialogue. If there is one thing virtually all Malory's critics agree
on it is the vividness of speech in *Le Morte Darthur*. Yet this vividness
should puzzle us; one's usual expectation is that vivid dialogue is
individual—a particular speech sounds like one character and not
others—and psychologically revealing: but neither of these things is
true in the *Morte*. What is it that makes a normative style vivid?

There are two things I would point to here. The first is Malory's
fondness for what the philosopher J. L. Austin calls "performative
utterances." Austin presents this term in the first lecture of his *How
to Do Things with Words* (ed. J.O. Urmson, New York, 1955), but
here it is sufficient to quote the concise explanation by Carol Chomsky:

Austin distinguishes between 'statements' and 'performative

55. It seems best not to discuss Arthur's remarks on Morgan in the lines immediately preceding these since, as Vinaver suggests in his note to *Works*, 151.24–
25, the change there in the tone of Arthur's comments may not be intentional, but
the result of a misreading. For another eliminated reaction in Malory's first tale,
see *Huth Merlin* II.102 and *Works*, 109.7–11.

utterances,' pointing out that whereas many sentences that a
speaker utters state a fact or report something, in other
sentences the speaker is actually doing an action by uttering the
sentence. That is, the speaker is not just saying something about
an action, but is actually performing the action by uttering the
sentence. Example of such sentences from Austin (1962) are:

> I bet you it will rain tomorrow.
> I apologize for the error.
> I deny having been there.
> I promise you to try harder.

The act of betting, apologizing, denying and promising is
performed by the very utterances of the sentences.[56]

A sentence which is an action rather than a statement about an
action obviously has particular dramatic force, a special vividness,
but in itself need not individualize the speaker. Such performative
utterances tend to occur fairly frequently in most late medieval
fiction (the equivalents of "bet," "apologize," etc. being such verbs
as "grant," "require," "beseech," "charge," "pray") and with
striking frequency in some parts of *Le Morte Darthur*.[57] In the last

56. *The Acquisition of Syntax in Children from 5 to 10* (Cambridge, Mass., 1969),
p. 13. I have expanded Chomsky's abbreviations.

57. I have counted performative utterances (strictly speaking, present indicative
active uses of explicit performative verbs) in four sections of *Le Morte Darthur* and
for purposes of comparison in about half of Caxton's *Reynard the Fox*, Sand's edition of which (*The History of Reynard the Fox, Translated and Printed by William
Caxton*, ed. Donald B. Sands, Cambridge, 1960) has pages of roughly the same size
as *Works*. Dividing the number of occurrences by the number of pages, I arrive at
the figures .32 for Caxton's *Reynard*, and .57 for Malory's "Noble Tale of Sir
Launcelot du Lake," but then .88 for the first forty pages of "The Tale of Sir
Gareth of Orkney," .89 for the "Poisoned Apple" section of the seventh tale, and
.79 for the "Fair Maid of Astolot" section of that seventh tale.

The occurrences are: *Reynard the Fox*, pp. 103–73 (chapters 21–39): pp. 103; 107;
108; 110(2X); 112; 118(2X); 122(2X); 134; 136(2X); 153; 155; 156; 157; 160;
161; 162; 166; 167; 168; 169.

"Sir Launcelot du Lake": 258.20; 259.10; 260.22; 264.3; 265.15–16; 265.30;
266.29; 267.7; 267.33; 268.3; 268.15; 272.10; 272.23; 273.29; 276.31; 278.10;
279.15; 281.4; 281.14; 284.35.

"Sir Gareth of Orkney" (pp. 293–332): 296.27; 297.4; 297.18; 299.11–12;
299.19; 299.25; 304.2; 304.31; 304.33; 305.19(2X); 307.1; 307.18; 308.17; 310.25

tale, for instance, "The Death of Arthur," they add special emphasis
to a number of the key speeches:

"My kynge, my lorde, and myne uncle," seyde sir Gawayne,
"wyte you well, now I shall make you a promyse whych I shall
holde be my knyghthode, that frome thys day forewarde I shall
never fayle sir Launcelot untyll that one of us have slayne that
othir. And therefore *I requyre you*, my lorde and kynge, dresse
you unto the warres, for wyte you well, I woll be revenged
uppon sir Launcelot; and therefore, as ye woll have my servyse
and my love, now haste you thereto and assay youre frendis.
For *I promyse unto God*," seyde sir Gawayn, "for the deth of my
brothir, sir Gareth, I shall seke sir Launcelot thorowoute seven
kynges realmys, but I shall sle hym, other ellis he shall sle me."
[1186]

". . . And therefore, sir Launcelot, *I requyre the and beseche the
hartily*, for all the love that ever was betwyxt us, that thou
never se me no more in the visayge. *And I commaunde the*, on
Goddis behalff, that thou forsake my company. And to thy
kyngedom loke thou turne agayne, and kepe well thy realme
frome warre and wrake, for as well as I have loved the heretofore, myne harte woll nat serve now to se the; for thorow the
and me ys the floure of kyngis and knyghtes destroyed. And
therefore go thou to thy realme, and there take ye a wyff, and
lyff with hir wyth joy and blys. *And I pray the* hartely to pray for
me to the Everlastynge Lorde that I may amende my mysselyvyng." [1252]

The performative utterance is not only vivid in Malorian dialogue,

---

311.2; 311.5; 312.12; 312.19; 313.10; 313.15; 314.35; 315.11; 316.12; 316.36;
317.1; 321.35–36; 321.36; 324.26; 329.12–13; 329.15; 329.29–30; 330.7; 331.1–2;
331.3.

"The Poisoned Apple": 1046.5; 1047.6–7; 1047.8; 1050.20; 1050.31; 1050.32;
1052.16; 1052.28; 1054.15; 1054.18; 1055.2; 1056.15; 1056.17; 1056.20; 1058.4–5.

"The Fair Maid of Astolat": 1066.5–6; 1067.17; 1067.22; 1067.27; 1073.17;
1073.23; 1074.7; 1077.33; 1078.11; 1079.28; 1079.32; 1080.31; 1081.2; 1081.16;
1083.7–8; 1083.23; 1083.30–31; 1087.11; 1089.17; 1091.1; 1091.4; 1093.9;
1093.12; 1093.16; 1095.3; 1096.31; 1096.33–34. (Notice that 1090–1095 are not
full pages of text; my figure of .79 occurrences per page is therefore somewhat low.)

but also particularly appropriate: the heroes of *Le Morte Darthur* are "men of their hands" and prefer actions to speech; when they do speak, it is fitting that they be fond of speeches which *are* actions.[58]

"Men of their hands" brings me to the second and more important thing I want to point out about speech in the *Morte*. The paragraph in which E. K. Chambers uses this phrase nicely describes what he calls "a trick of dialogue":

> Malory can be rhetorical, when a dramatic need calls for it. But for the most part the knights are of brief speech. They are men of their hands. . . . "They could no counsel give, but said they were big enough." Could a war debate among English lords be better or more briefly rendered? But a windbag will get his answer. "As for that threatening, said Sir Gringamore, be it as it may, we will go to dinner" . . . The phrasing may shape itself in gnomic homespun. "What, nephew, said the king, is the wind in that door?" When Launcelot's time of trouble comes, his fellowship recall that they have had much weal with him and much worship. "And therefore, sir Launcelot, said they, we will take the woe with the weal." These brevities of speech are Malory's nearest approach to humor.[59]

The vigor of this dialogue is in its brevity; the character says less than we might have expected. Malory's heroes speak straight to the matter at hand, give what information is required, prefer suggesting a course of action to describing their own feelings. If they do describe their feelings, they do it succinctly, with dignity and seeming objectivity: " 'I shall telle the,' said the kynge. 'I am seke for angre and for love of fayre Igrayne, that I may not be hool.' " Unlike the heroes of the French romances, Malorian knights rarely

58. In discussing period style one might also consider performative utterances together with the use of prefatory remarks such as "I shall tell you" and, adapting Austin's terminology, say that in Malorian and other late medieval dialogue speakers tend to label important illocutionary acts explicitly (that is, to specify what illocutionary act is involved), and that this labeling occurs either as a preliminary to ("I shall *tell* you") or simultaneously with (performative utterance) the illocutionary act itself. (Austin, I should say, would find the use of "label" here at least infelicitous.)

59. "Sir Thomas Malory," p. 30.

descant upon their emotions, either in dialogue or in interior monologue. They refuse the bait; we admire their speech, find it witty, when they say less than, given the particular situation, we thought they would. The quintessential heroic comment is "as for that, be as be may".[60]—or perhaps just the ubiquitous "well. . . ." With the attitude implicit in this heroic laconism, Malory's narrative technique harmonizes completely. Malory does not talk about his characters' feelings at length, does not take us inside their minds frequently, as the French romancers do. Deeds, not feelings: Malory respects not only his characters, but his characters' privacy.

It is perhaps in the handling of play that we see the difference between the French attitudes toward character and the Malorian one most strikingly exhibited. If the frightened or perplexed hero is being unknightly, the playful one is, we might say, being aknightly. Play is at best irrelevant to knightliness and at worst breaks the solemnity of the narrative. As we might expect, then, Malorian heroes are less given to japing than their French counterparts. When for instance, in the *Huth Merlin* Uther asks Igrayne about her pregnancy, the king is engaged in a cat and mouse game, and is as interested in enjoying her mental discomfort as in testing her truthfulness (I. 120). In *Le Morte Darthur* the episode is simply a moral test: a test of loyalty ("he asked hir by the feith she ought to hym") but even more of truthfulness, as emphasized by the confirmation of *trothe* at the beginning of each of the speeches: " 'Desmaye you not,' said the kyng, 'but telle me the trouthe. . . .' 'Sire,' saide she, 'I shalle telle you the trouthe. . . .' 'That is trouthe,' saide the kynge, 'as ye saye . . .' " (10.15–28). It is appropriate that the French king introduces the subject of pregnancy by placing his hand on Igrayne's belly, and that the English king does not.

At one point in Malory's third Tale, Kay and Lancelot have spent the night in the same place. Lancelot rises early, dresses himself in Kay's armor, takes Kay's shield and horse, and rides away. Kay now wakes up, sees what has happened, and says:

> Now, be my fayth, I know welle that he woll greve som of the courte of kyng Arthure, for on hym knyghtes woll be bolde and

60. See *Works*, 73.21; 276.34; 294.22; 312.22; 329.34; 421.35; 564.3; 1251.25.

deme that hit is I, and that woll begyle them. And bycause of his armoure and shylde I am sure I shall ryde in pease." [275]

In the *Vulgate*, as Vinaver points out, Lancelot originally takes Kay's armor by mistake. Here Malory seems to give us two new explanations of Lancelot's action. First, Kay, left with Lancelot's armor, will be able to travel unmolested; thus Lancelot, who was Kay's protector in the episode immediately preceding this one, continues to arrange for his safety. Second, with the seneschal's armor Lancelot can "beguile" Arthurian knights who would certainly not challenge him if they knew who he was. Now it is not at all surprising that Malory would rather show Lancelot performing an exemplary act of protection than making a trivial mistake; but what about that "beguilement"? It sounds rather frivolous, but in the Malorian ether it becomes a solemn, straight-faced thing, quite different from the beguilement of the *Vulgate*. There Lancelot first realizes he has put on the wrong armor when his host points it out to him just before his departure; Lancelot laughs: he does not want to arm again, and says that Kay may take his armor.[61] By itself, Lancelot's laughter here might seem no more than amusement at his own mistake, but one suspects, in light of his amusement later in the episode, that he has already seen possibilities latent in that mistake. Soon Lancelot passes some knights who are discussing the contemptible Kay they take him to be. He understands what they are saying, and laughs; he does not greatly mind being thought the seneschal and rides by without saying a word. A few lines later he is challenged as Kay, and smiles at his challenger's mistake (308.5–8). The *Vulgate* Lancelot is *eques ludens*; he enjoys the mistakes about his identity. Malory's knight is observed from the outside and, as I have said, there is very little evidence here, particularly in the early part of the episode, that he enjoys his "beguilement." It is not he who explains the switched armor at the beginning of the episode; we have only the imperfect Kay's surmise to guide us—and it is worth observing that, though we may discuss Kay's speech as an explana-

---

61. *Vulgate Lancelot*, V.307.30–32. The Malorian host makes no comment about the armor. Hosts, like squires, servants, and other minor characters do not ordinarily point out mistakes to the heroes of *Le Morte Darthur*.

tion of Lancelot's motives, it is in form a statement about the probable consequences of, not the motives for the switch. As the adventure begins we may think we can infer Lancelot's motives, but we do not feel we know his thoughts or mood.

Malory changes the subsequent action by having Lancelot pass the three knights *before* they make their comments about the "proude sir Kay" (275.15–21); his Lancelot presumably does not hear their remarks and thus cannot be amused by them. In the Malorian version of the challenge and combat (275.22–29) Lancelot is seen entirely from the outside: this is prowess and knightliness, not a jape. When the English hero is asked his name ("for welle we know ye ar not sir Kay") and answers

> "As for that, be as be may. For ye shal yelde you unto dame Gwenyvere, and loke that ye be there on Whytsonday and yelde you unto hir as presoners, and sey that sir Kay sente you unto hir." [276.34–277.1]

We may detect a hint of amusement in that most Malorian "as for that, be as be may," and just possibly there is amusement as well as satisfaction in Lancelot's smile a page later (278.3). But these are at most glimmers; in the episode as a whole we are observing heroic knightliness, and we are looking at it from the outside, seeing the *gestes*, not sharing the jests of the hero.[62]

Playful characters are troublesome for Malory; they turn us away from the one thing needful, and they usually require their emotions and motives to be indicated with some explicitness. And Malory is not always able to avoid or rework the frivolities of his sources. It is here, for instance, that Merlin causes him trouble. In *Le Morte Darthur*, as Chambers observes, "Merlin comes and goes, and we are never told who or what Merlin is."[63] The strangeness of this character is I think more the result of Malory's attitude toward play than of his attitude toward *fairye*. Both in the *Morte* and in the French, Merlin keeps turning up in disguise; but in the French it is perfectly clear that Merlin enjoys fooling people, and we are ex-

---

62. Notice, by the way, that the French hero is concerned about his equipment before an encounter (V.309.39–40); the Malorian one praises it afterward.

63. "Sir Thomas Malory," p. 24.

pected to share his enjoyment. In Malory the disguises are often wholly inexplicable—or at least unexplicated.[64] Once he has started upon an episode involving Merlin's japes, Malory will usually risk bewildering his audience rather than make it clear his character's motives are frivolous.

Occasionally in the French romances there is a passage in which the narrator is somewhat playful at the characters' expense. There is a scene in the *Huth Merlin*, for instance, in which Morgan is taking leave of Guinevere. She must go, she says, but will return as soon as she can:

> La roine qui ne l'amoit mie moult, pour chou que elle n'avoit onques veut bien en li, ne li respont mie chou que elle pense, car elle li euust dit: "Dame, alés ent sans ja mais revenir," mais elle li dist: "Dame, n'atenderés vous mie tant que vostre freres soit venus?" "Nenil," fait elle, "car li besoins i est si grans que je ne porroie en nule maniere remanoir." "Ore en alés," fait elle, "a Dieu dont, mais que je vausisse bien s'il vous pleuust, que vous encore remansissiés." "Je nel porroie," fait elle, "faire que je n'i perdisse trop." A tant se part l'une de l'autre.
> [II.218–19]

> [The queen, who did not at all greatly love her, because she had never seen good in her, answers not at all as she thinks, for she would have said, "Madam, go, and never come back," but she said to her, "Madam, will you not remain until your brother comes?" "No," she says, "for so great is the need that I could in no way abide." "Go now," she says, "farewell then, but indeed I would if you pleased that you would abide." "I could not," she says, "or I should lose too much." Therewith the one leaves the other.]

The litotes of "qui ne l'amoit mie moult" is rather arch, and once we know that Guinevere would prefer to say "alés ent sans ja mais revenir," the politeness of "je vausisse bien s'il vous pleuust, que vous encore remansissiés" becomes somewhat comic—vaguely reminiscent of:

64. See, e.g., *Works*, 43.19–44.30.

> My lady Prioresse, by your leve,
> So that I wiste I sholde yow nat greve,
> I wolde demen that ye tellen sholde
> A tale next, if so were that ye wolde.

Malory takes his characters as seriously as they take themselves; he will not amuse us with their small social hypocrisies. He dislikes this kind of passage both because it intereferes with his performance as the respectful, painstaking historian and because it blurs his focus upon the actions rather than the thoughts of his characters. Social hypocrisy is a minor skirmish in a psychomachia, and when he can Malory avoids both psychomachia and that direct narrative of the character's thoughts which usually goes with it in romance. In *Le Morte Darthur* the interview of Guinevere and Morgan is objective, and Malory's queen displays the coldness which is the special mark of her royalty, but no amusing hypocrisy:

> Than she wente unto the quene Gwenyvere and askid hir leve to ryde into hir contrey.
>
> "Ye may abyde," seyde the quene, "tyll youre brother the kynge com home."
>
> "I may nat, madame," seyde Morgan le Fay, "for I have such hasty tydynges."
>
> "Well," seyde the quene, "ye may departe whan ye woll."
>
> [150]

A final observation. The peculiarity of Malory's Merlin, I have said, may have more to do with the author's dislike of frivolity than with his attitude toward *fairye*. This brings me to something I've touched on lightly at several points in this section, but which deserves a somewhat less scattered treatment: the nature of Malory's "position" on such recurrent concerns of Arthurian literature as courtly love, secular and celestial chivalry, the realm of magic and *fairye*, etc.

About such topics there are two kinds of questions to be asked. The first is "what are Malory's ideas on the subject and how do those ideas differ from the ideas of other comparable writers?" This kind of question has been asked many times. The second kind of question is "how much interest does he have in the issue?" Not "what did he think?" but "how much did he care?" With the colossal exception of Professor Vinaver's work, Malorian criticism tends not to ask this kind of question. It is of course a more difficult sort to answer than the other, but it is the sort of question that must be asked about an author who deals with traditional stories and at times is essentially a translator. In stressing the importance of such questions I am perhaps forecasting the nature of my own answer to them, but I want to indicate it more clearly still.

It seems to me that behind the episodes of *Le Morte Darthur* lie not carefully thought out or deeply felt opinions on the nature of true love, or the claims of religion, but indifference. I would certainly agree with R. T. Davies, for instance, in stressing the inconsistencies in both Malory's overt statements and implied attitudes toward courtly love;[65] but I would go further than Davies and suggest that these inconsistencies indicate not that Malory's thinking changes or that he is incapable of abstract thought, but that he is not particularly interested in the subject at all. On the whole Malory seems to be for courtly love when the claims of love work with the claims of knightliness, against courtly love when its claims conflict with the claims of knightliness, and bored with courtly love when its claims have nothing to do with the claims of knightliness. But "claims" is not quite the word. Malory is not the judge, not even the advocate, but the *Dichter* of knightliness, and his re-makings of episodes have more to do with the intensity with which we experience the monocentric within *Le Morte Darthur*, than with Sir Thomas's opinions on religion, sexual morality, or the ontological status of elves. Malory's position on courtly love may well have more to do with the association of courtly love and psychological analysis than with the association of courtly love and adultery. He disapproves of lechery—perhaps. He certainly dislikes clutter.

I began this chapter by discussing one episode in Malory's "Lancelot and Guinevere." In closing it, I would like to touch on another, briefer episode in that tale. Near the beginning of "The

65. "Malory's 'Vertuouse Love,'" *SP* 53 (1956): 459–69, 459.

Fair Maid of Astolat," there is a scene in which Lancelot and
Lavayne, the fair maid's brother, come to Camelot to ride in a tournament. Lancelot wants his identity kept secret at this time, and so
the two knights must find inconspicuous lodgings. The scene is
presented in quick, workmanlike fashion:

> And there was grete pres of kyngis, deukes, erlis, and barownes,
> and many noble knyghtes. But there sir Launcelot was lodged
> pryvaly by the meanys of sir Lavayne with a ryche burgeyse,
> that no man in that towne was ware what they were. And so
> they reposed them there tyll our Lady day of the Assumpcion
> that the grete justes sholde be. [1069]

As we read this, we have no feeling that we ought to be told more.
I spoke earlier in this chapter about the inconsistencies and im-
purities of Malory's style; but in fact by the time we come upon
these sentences, after having read through one thousand pages of
Le Morte Darthur, we have accepted the textures and absorbed the
rhythms of Malorian reality: with Lancelot, we are looking toward
the noble occasion of the jousting, and do not care about that
jousting's non-chivalric context. But Malory's source here is a
slower, more meandering work, and it includes a quite charming
portrait of the burgess with whom the knights lodge:

> Atant lessent le grant chemin et s'en vont droitement et celee-
> ment cele part ou li ostex a la dame estoit. Et quant il furent
> descendu leanz et la dame connut son neveu, si ne veïstes
> onques si grant joie come ele li fist, car ele ne l'avoit puis veü
> qu'il avoit esté chevaliers noviaus; si li dist: "Biaus niés, ou
> avez vos esté des lores que ge ne vos vi mes, et ou avez vos
> lessié vostre frere? Ne vendra il pas a ce tornoiement?—Dame,
> fet il, nenil, car il ne puet, car nos le lessame en meson un pou
> deshetié.—Et qui est, fet ele, cil chevaliers qui est venuz avec
> vos?—Dame, fet il, si m'aïst Dex, ge ne sei qui il est, fors tant
> seulement que preudom me semble; et por la bonté que ge cuit
> en lui, li ferai ge demain compaignie au tornoiement et avrons
> ambedui une meïsmes armes et couvertures d'une maniere."
> La dame vint meintenant a Lancelot et l'apele moult bel et

enneure, et l'enmeinne tantost en une chambre et le fet cou-
chier et reposer en un moult riche lit, car l'en li avoit dit qu'il
avoit toute nuit chevauchié et erré. Toute jor fu Lancelos
leanz et orent grant plenté de touz biens. [*La Mort*, 16]

[Then they leave the highway and go straight and privily
toward where the lady's house was. And when they alighted
there and the lady knew her nephew, you never saw joy so
great as she made him, for she had not seen him since he first
became a knight. So she said, "Fair nephew, where have you
been since last I saw you, and where have you left your brother?
Will he not come to the tournament?" "No, Madam," he says,
"for he cannot, for we left him at home a little unwell." "And
who is this knight," she says," who is come with you?" "Madam," he says, "so God help me, I do not know who he is, only
he seems a worthy man to me; and for the goodness I think is
in him I shall bear him fellowship to the tournament tomor-
row and we shall both have the same arms and caparisons of
one kind." Now the lady came to Lancelot and invites him full
fairly and honorably and led him at once to a chamber and
lette lie down and repose him in a very rich bed, for she had
been told he had ridden and traveled all night. Lancelot was
there all day and they had all good things in great plenty.]

She is more concerned with her family than she is with the Arthurian hero, and inquiries about relatives come before questions
about, even attention to, Lancelot. "Si ne veïstes onques si grant
joie come ele li fist"; the author of the French romance expects us
to enjoy this *gemütlichkeit*, and we do.

What Malory gives up when he omits this kind of passage, what,
finally, he gives up when he leaves out all the dozens of small
details we have watched him exclude, is not just a few pleasant
moments in works which, as wholes, are clearly inferior to his. In
keeping our attention on the one thing needful Malory excludes
from his book something we of the twentieth century want and find
in the greatest works of art—particularly tragic art. This is the sense
of what Coriolanus calls "a world elsewhere"; the kind of awareness conveyed by Homer's narrative style, where, in the words of
a recent critic:

the frequently occurring digression [offers] glimpses briefly
or longer upon moments in time or space which continually
break down the artifice of an arranged view of action; the
world is seen to be as vast, as complex, and as spread out in
time as we know it to be.[66]

Probably the most popular of W. H. Auden's poems is "Musée des
Beaux Arts," which is about this awareness:

About suffering they were never wrong,
The Old Masters: how well they understood
Its human position; how it takes place
While someone else is eating or opening a window or just
    walking dully along;
How, when the aged are reverently, passionately waiting
For the miraculous birth, there always must be
Children who did not specially want it to happen, skating
On a pond at the edge of the wood:
They never forgot
That even the dreadful martyrdom must run its course
Anyhow in a corner, some untidy spot
Where the dogs go on with their doggy life and the torturer's
    horse
Scratches its innocent behind on a tree.

In Brueghel's *Icarus*, for instance: how everything turns away
Quite leisurely from the disaster; the ploughman may
Have heard the splash, the forsaken cry,
But for him it was not an important failure; the sun shone
As it had to on the white legs disappearing into the green
Water; and the expensive delicate ship that must have seen
Something amazing, a boy falling out of the sky,
Had somewhere to get to and sailed calmly on.

It is the world of the quotidian and the coexistent, of dogs that
go on with their doggy life, of the shepherds and dyers who exist
whether Troy stands or falls, of aunts who care about their nephews
whether or not an Arthurian hero is present, the world of nights

66. Charles Rowan Beye, *The Iliad, the Odyssey and the Epic Tradition* (Garden
City, N.Y., 1966), p. 36.

which take time to pass whether or not a hero is ready to act, of
horses that have to be fed, tablecloths to be laid, mountains, valleys,
paths which are there to be crossed whether they are the scenes of
knightly events or not, which is simplified and de-emphasized in
Le Morte Darthur. The Malorian structural originality, so conclu-
sively demonstrated by Vinaver, is essentially of a piece with his
stylistic originality: as Malory rejects the *Arturi regis ambages pul-
cherrimae*, the complex simultaneity of happenings and shifting of
focus from one event to another, so he gives us Icarus without the
coexistent ploughman and ship, Achilles without the rosy-fingered
dawn and the swarming bees. Malory does not like the simulta-
neous or the multicentric, and fixes our eyes on one thing at a time.
Ultimately, Malory's art is lyric rather than epic or dramatic; the
important truth of *Le Morte Darthur* is an attitude, a part of the individual's psychic life, rather than a model of human interaction.
We believe events "out there" are more Homeric and Breughel-
esque than Malorian; the whole world is never watching, and
everything is never at stake.

This singleness of vision which makes *Le Morte Darthur* un-
Homeric (and unShakespearean, unChaucerian, etc.) brings with
it aesthetic risks of a very basic kind as well as aesthetic limitations.
Especially in his early and middle books, Malory can be very
monotonous. Episodes quickly blur into one another in the reader's
memory; one longs for a change in narrative pace, some kind of
local color to keep them distinct. But the particular emotional
experience which Malory's last books offer us depends to a great
extent upon that singleness of vision in the earlier books. We do feel,
when we reach "The Most Piteous Tale of the Morte Arthur
Saunz Guerdon" that Arthur's world is the only world; when the
Round Table fellowship is destroyed, one turns to religion essentially because there is nothing else left. After the last great battle has
been fought, and Arthur has received his death wound,

> . . . sir Lucan departed, for he was grevously wounded in
> many placis; and so as he yode he saw and harkened by the
> moonelyght how that pyllours and robbers were com into the
> fylde to pylle and to robbe many a full noble knyght of brochys

and bees and of many a good rynge and many a ryche juell.
And who that were nat dede all oute, there they slew them for
their harneys and their ryches. [1237–1238][67]

This is a tremendously moving passage in its context, and again it is
moving in large part because in the preceding twelve hundred
pages we have seen so little that is either good or familiar that is not
Arthurian. Chaos is come again; we have so little residual memory
of solicitous aunts or dogs living their doggy lives or even small
details of the landscape that these pillagers in the eerie moonlight
can seem all of the post-Arthurian, non-Arthurian world.

67. This description (as Vinaver points out) is based on the *Stanzaic Morte*. I
should mention that the moonlight is Malory's addition to this passage; the poem
merely refers to the coming of evening at 1.3380—thirty-six lines before the pil-
laging is described. (Note, however, that in the one surviving manuscript copy of
the poem two lines have dropped out of the relevant stanza.)

3

The Last Tales

We read Malory's "Book of Sir Tristram" or his "Tale of King Arthur" to learn (or, it may be, to prove) something about his style, or Arthuriana, or the fifteenth century. But when we come to his two last tales we discover a particular country of the mind. There is a certain part of our emotional lives we understand better for having read these tales; they are irreplaceable, enriching our knowledge of that one area of ourselves in a way no other work does.

These last tales matter for us in a way the earlier ones do not; but the impact of this part of *Le Morte Darthur* depends upon our having experienced what comes before. I say "experienced"; I am not sure that our *ideas* about the tragedy will be much changed if we do not know about the action of the "Tristram" or the "Tale of King Arthur," but the ruin of the Round Table will affect us very differently if we have not gone through the earlier books. In the first thousand pages of *Le Morte Darthur* we have grown used to the singleness of Malory's world. Now we discover a real incoherence there.

This incoherence is mysterious, but somehow it is not alien: we do not feel that the division is imposed from the outside. All is both familiar and strange as we find in this simple world a tragedy strikingly complex in its aspects and causes. " 'Jesu mercy!' seyde the kynge, 'where ar all my noble knyghtes becom? . . .' " (1236.16–17). The reader feels both the inevitability and the bewilderment of this ruin. Clear, familiar, mysterious—described in this way, Malory's last tales sound like a Kafka story. But here terror is not the important thing. Certain nightmare images remain in our minds long after we have closed the book: those robbers in the moonlight, Mordred thrusting himself up to the burr of Arthur's spear. But in this tragedy pity matters more than terror, loss more than destruction.

The Sense of the Past

Malory's historicism is something we feel throughout *Le Morte Darthur;* but it is more important in the last two books than anywhere else. There are some notable changes in the devices of record-keeping here, but at least as significant as what is new is a richer exploitation of techniques used earlier. More than before we are conscious of mediation between ourselves and the events described, and this mediation itself keeps us aware of two things: first, that (as in the earlier tales) the speaker loves the heroes whose deeds he is recording; and second, that a great expanse of time separates those heroes from ourselves. Our awareness of these two things is inseparable from the meaning of the tragedy.

There is in almost every essay on the tragedy of *Le Morte Darthur* a sentence beginning in essentially this way: "Great though their achievements are, Arthur and Lancelot. . . ." A sentence of this kind may include true and even profound perceptions—but yet it must be false to our experience as readers. As long as we hear that narrating voice, we know the greatness of the heroes is not a thing the critic may abandon behind the first suitable comma. Reverence does not preclude assessment, of course, but in these last tales it precedes and conditions it. At times we can hear the emotion in the rhythm of Malory's sentences. There is the indignant repetition of *own* when he describes Mordred's treachery: ". . . and so he thought to beate hys own fadir fro hys owne londys. . ." (1129.20–21); ". . . and there was sir Mordred redy awaytyng uppon hys londynge, to lette hys owne fadir to londe uppon the londe that he was kynge over" (1229.26–28). In moments of ill-fated generosity or bravery, a sentence will be broken by a term of praise in apposition to the subject noun or pronoun—as if the author himself were struck by the full poignance of the thing in the process of describing it:

> So sir Launcelot departed and toke hys swerde undir hys arme, and so he walked in hys mantell, that noble knyght, and put hymselff in grete jouparté. [1165.5–7]
>
> . . . and in the lyfftyng up the kynge sowned, and in the

lyfftynge sir Lucan felle in a sowne, that parte of hys guttis
felle out of hys bodye, and therewith the noble knyght hys
harte braste. [1238.16–19]

But more important for our sense of the speaker's attitude than
such moments of rhetorical or rhythmic emphasis is the kind of
record-keeping discussed in my first chapter. Malory narrates the
tragedy not as a moralist but as a historian, "lowely, and servys-
able" before Arthurian knighthood, and the final books of *Le Morte
Darthur* seem more painstakingly annotated than the preceding
ones. References to sources of information, attempts at geographical
precision, ragged edge and blueprint details, come at moments of
the greatest plangency; and we are especially aware of such details
because they are used at such moments:

> And on the morn all the prystes and clarkes that myght be
> gotyn in the contrey and in the town were there, and sange
> massis of Requiem. And there offrid first sir Launcelot, and he
> offird an hondred pounde, and than the seven kynges offirde,
> and every of them offirde fourty pounde. Also there was a
> thousand knyghtes, and every of them offirde a pounde; and
> the offeryng dured fro the morne to nyght. [1250–1251][1]

> So whan he was howselyd and enelyd and had al that a Crysten
> man ought to have, he prayed the Bysshop that his felowes
> myght bere his body to Joyous Garde. (Somme men say it was
> Anwyk, and somme men say it was Bamborow.) [1257.24–28]

Catalogues are used with increased frequency in these last tales.[2]
As Vinaver points out,[3] when Aggravain and Mordred prepare to
surprise Lancelot in the queen's chamber, the French *Mort* tells us
that Aggravain brought with him *grant compaignie . . . de chevaliers*
and the stanzaic *Morte* mentions that there were twelve of them.

1. This passage is original with Malory. See Vinaver's note.
2. This "increased use of lists" is mentioned by Robert H. Wilson in "Addenda
on Malory's Minor Characters," *JEGP* 55 (1956): 574–75. (Quoted by Vinaver
in *Works*, p. xlvi.) Wilson is interested in this use of lists in another connection and
sees a different, though not contradictory, aim in it.
3. Note to *Works*, 1164.9.

Only Malory lists their names (1164.8–17). There are numerous source references here: almost half of Malory's citations of "the book" and "the French book" occur in this last fifth of *Le Morte Darthur*.[4]

Malory's historicism is chiefly important as a pervasive attitude in these last tales. But here, where he is at his most splendid, his record-keeping also creates beautiful local effects. Perhaps Malory's finest use of the historian's meticulousness is in his discussion of the king's death:

> Thus of Arthur I fynde no more wrytten in bokis that bene auctorysed, nothir more of the verry sertaynté of hys dethe

4. Thirty-four out of seventy. All of Malory's references to "the French book" are cited in Robert H. Wilson, "Malory's French Book Again," *Comparative Literature* 2 (1950): 172–81. One may find their distribution in different parts of *Le Morte Darthur* by retabulating Wilson's citations. These references belong to the rhetoric of history. As F-J. Starke points out (*Populäre englische Chroniken des 15. Jahrhunderts* [Berlin, 1935], p. 110) the phrase "as the book saith" (*wie das Buch sagt*) occurs as frequently in the first part of the *Brut* as it does in Malory. (Starke seems unaware that these references are unevenly distributed in the *Morte*.) We should also notice that Malory chooses this particular *kind* of source reference; for there is another kind, the mention not of the book but of the tale, which he does not like as well. This preference seems to me characteristic of our author. From time to time we do indeed find Malory speaking of the tale; e.g., "NOW TURNYTH THYS TALE UNTO SYR BORS DE GANYS" (949.20): such lines almost always echo references to *li contes* in his sources. But there are strikingly few of these phrases in *Le Morte Darthur* if one considers how frequently the words *ore dist li contes* occur in the French romances. (E.g., *Vulgate Lancelot*, V.87.38, V. 89.13, V. 91.23; *Huth Merlin*, II.75, II.81, II.92.) If there must be a turning, Malory (in this respect like the English metrical romancers) prefers that we rather than the tale do it: "Now turne we to sir Launce-lot" (269.17). (Contrast *Vulgate Lancelot*, V.210.27–30.) Malory's "French book" references, on the other hand, are simply additions: they are not adaptations of references in his sources. Implicit in Malory's cultivation of one kind of source reference and avoidance of another is something like a distinction between history and literature. More precisely, "book" rather than "tale" implies an emphasis on content rather than form. The "tale" is something which leaves off speaking of one matter and turns to speaking of another: it arranges and chooses between facts. The "book" is the repository of facts; it is mentioned in connection with the correctness of what is stated rather than in explanation of narrative technique. Malory speaks to us of the accuracy, not about the manipulation, of our knowledge of the past—and it is here, when he comes to the destruction of Arthur's fellowship, that he makes us most aware of his concern for accuracy.

harde I never rede, but thus was he lad away in a shyp wherein were three quenys; that one was kynge Arthur syster, quene Morgan le Fay, the tother was the quene of North Galis, and the thirde was the quene of the Waste Londis. Also there was dame Nynyve, the chyff lady of the laake, whych had wedded sir Pellyas, the good knyght; and thys lady had done muche for kynge Arthure. (And thys dame Nynyve wolde never suffir sir Pelleas to be in no place where he shulde be in daungere of hys lyff, and so he lyved unto the uttermuste of hys dayes with her in grete reste.)

Now more of the deth of kynge Arthur coude I never fynde, but that thes ladyes brought hym to hys grave, and such one was entyred there whych the ermyte bare wytnes that some-tyme was Bysshop of Caunturbyry. But yet the ermyte knew nat in sertayne that he was veryly the body of kynge Arthur; for thys tale sir Bedwere, a knyght of the Table Rounde, made hit to be wrytten.

Yet som men say in many partys of Inglonde that kynge Arthure ys nat dede, but had by the wyll of oure Lorde Jesu into another place; and men say that he shall com agayne, and he shall wynne the Holy Crosse. Yet I woll nat say that hit shall be so, but rather I wolde sey: here in thys worlde he chaunged hys lyff. And many men say that there ys wrytten uppon the tumbe thys:

HIC IACET ARTHURUS, REX QUONDAM REXQUE FUTURUS. . . .
                                                                    [1242]

Now at this point, as Lumiansky says, Malory is trying to reconcile two versions of the story;[5] but what really matters here is the sense

5. R. M. Lumiansky, "Arthur's Final Companions in Malory's *Morte Darthur*," *Tulane Studies in English* 11 (1961): 9–10. I would like to amplify Professor Lumian-sky's remarks on the ambiguity (or vagueness) or "here in thys worde he chaunged hys lyff." "To change one's life" is reminiscent of the phrase "to change *the* life" (="to die"), which Malory used at *Works*, 906.8. On the other hand, it is notable that a few lines after we are told that Arthur "chaunged hys lyff" Malory ends the section by saying of Guinevere in her life of piety, ". . . all maner of people marvayled how vertuously she was *chaunged*." Is Arthur's change death or

of effort, of a careful weighing of evidence: "bokis *that bene auctory-sed*"; "the *verry* sertaynté"; "*could* I *never* fynde," with its suggestion of years of searching; "knew nat *in sertayne* that he was *veryly* the body"; "*som* men in *many* partys"; "I *wolde* say."[6] The caution of the speaker shows us that for him the death of Arthur is something worthy of careful thought and ought to be written about with the greatest precision. The sincerity of veneration is suggested by the plodding "Note on Sources" where one might expect a threnody.[7]

Vinaver comments, "the speculations about the identity of the man buried in the hermit's chapel (11.11–21) and about the way in which Arthur 'chaunged hys lyff' (11.22–27) are good examples of the author's sceptical turn of mind." But "scepticism" is the wrong word here if it implies support for the "common sense" version of Arthur's death. Malory, first of all, emphasizes the weakness of the case for Arthur's being the body in the tomb as carefully as he stresses his doubts about Arthur's second coming. More important, as readers of, say, Henry James should know, one of the more effective ways to make the supernatural or the extraordinary convincing is to put it in the context of the ordinary. It is the cautious reasonableness of Malory's voice which makes us believe there *may* be something mysterious in Arthur's end. "Scepticism" is wrong also in that it suggests detachment from the events themselves as well as from the versions of those events. What we have here is not so much scepticism as that taking of pains which tells us these events matter.

metamorphosis? Malory appears to suggest both interpretations but give neither. (The phrase "change the [*or* one's] life," meaning "to die," seems to be an uncommon one. In the form "change *the* life" it is not listed by the *ODE* at all; but this does seem to be the form Malory used at 906.8. The *OED* does list *To change* one's *life* meaning "to die" (under "Change *v*, 9b") but marks it "obsc. rare." The only occurrence cited is dated 1546. And this phrase was used in other senses; for instance, under "Change *v*, 6." the *OED* cites "c.1300 *Beket* 258 He gan to changi al his lyf: and his manere also." It would seem, then, that for Malory the phrase in the sense "to die" was uncommon but known, and that the phrase could also be employed in the less baleful way it is still used. Just the right phrase for Arthur's clouded fate.)

6. Caxton has "I *wyl* say."

7. A full threnody here would also lessen the impact of Ector's praise of Lancelot on p. 1259.

The death of Gawain, one of the most moving scenes in *Le Morte Darthur*, ends with this paragraph:

> And so at the owre of noone sir Gawayne yelded up the goste. And than the kynge lat entere hym in a chapell within Dover castell. And there yet all men may se the skulle of hym, and the same wounde is sene that sir Launcelot gaff in batayle. [1232]

The sentence about Gawain's skull is original. It suggests the *gravitas* of the historian, or even the hagiographer (we may recall the passages in saints' lives which tell us where relics are now to be found) but also reminds us that the hero whose dying we have just mourned is in fact long dead. However close we may feel to the fellowship at certain moments in the story, we are far away from them in time: not only Gawain, but the age itself is lost.

There is a similar effect in Lancelot's apologia for sorrow-making:

> "Truly," sayd syr Launcelot, "I trust I do not dysplese God, for He knoweth myn entente: for my sorow was not, nor is not, for ony rejoysyng of synne, but my sorow may never have ende. For whan I remembre of hir beaulté and of hir noblesse, that was bothe wyth hyr kyng and wyth hyr, so whan I sawe his corps and hir corps so lye togyders, truly myn herte wold not serve to susteyne my careful body. Also whan I remembre me how by my defaute and myn orgule and my pryde that they were bothe layed ful lowe, that were pereles that ever was lyvyng of Cristen people, wyt you wel," sayd syr Launcelot, "this remembred, of their kyndenes and myn unkyndenes, sanke so to myn herte that I myght not susteyne myself." So the Frensshe book maketh mencyon. [1256]

We feel close to Lancelot as he speaks these words. But then the reference to the French book reminds us that we are in fact far removed from him, and this sudden reminder increases the poignancy of the moment. Lancelot, whose grief for what is gone we have just been sharing, is himself something in the past, known to us only through books.

These last two passages bring us to that sense of the pastness of the Arthurian age which conditions our experience of the "Lancelot and

Guinevere" and the "Tale of the Death of Arthur" throughout.
Malory's use of tenses, as P. J. C. Field has pointed out, differs
significantly from the usage in his sources and contemporaries. Not
only in these last tales, but throughout *Le Morte Darthur*, the narrative is consistently in the past tense, while those other works make
free use of the historical present. Thus, we are always more aware of
the "pastness" of what is being described in *Le Morte Darthur* than
we are in other romances of the period.[8]

Another device subtly distinguishes the pastness of Malory's
final tales from the pastness of his earlier ones. Throughout the
Morte we come from time to time upon "in those days" or "in king
Arthur's days" explanations.[9] But the use of those expressions in the
"Lancelot and Guinevere" and the "Death of Arthur" contrasts
sharply with their use in the immediately preceding "Quest of the
Holy Grail," and somewhat less sharply with their use in earlier
sections of *Le Morte Darthur*.

In the "Tristram," the fifth and longest of Malory's tales, "at
that time" and "in those days" references tend to be fairly brief and
nonevaluative; that is, they do not as a rule point to either degenera-
tion or progress in contrasting Arthur's days with our own:

> . . . sir Launcelott du Lake that was that tyme named for the
> mervaylyste knyght of the worlde. [377.11–12]

> . . . and they were arayed aftir the gyse that was used that
> tyme in the moste goodlyeste maner. [403.24–26]

> . . . all knyghtes seyde that knew hym that he was one of the
> strengyste knyghtes that was in kynge Arthurs dayes.
> [648.13–15][10]

The texture of the following tale is different. In the "Quest," first

8. *Romance and Chronicle*, p. 54 ff.
9. "Probably the reason Malory did not follow his sources' use of the historic
present is contained in the phrase 'at that time.' In his mind the story of Arthur was
set in a distant past from which it could be contrasted with the degenerate present"
(Ibid., p. 54). But the contrasts between past and present are more complex than
Field indicates. See below.
10. See also, e.g., 371.2–3; 371.10; 376.35–36; 385.7; 493.12–13. 405.2–5 is the
longest of these "Tristram" references.

of all, there are very few "in those days" references, and most of the
ones we do find occur not in narration but in dialogue.[11] Thus they
contrast not our present with the Arthurian past but the Arthurian
period with an earlier one or one Arthurian moment with another.
What is most striking about the "Quest" "in those days" explanations, however, is that on the two occasions when they do occur in
the narration (913.3–9; 1025.28–31)[12] they point out an evil in the
Arthurian period. From a religious perspective (or at least from a
"Quest" perspective) King Arthur's days were the bad old days.
In the final tales there is again a change. Here the references to the
past are more extensive than the ones in the "Tristram" (and of
course than those in the "Quest") and are often idealizing. Now
Arthur's are the golden days, and the gold glitters all the more
brightly because of the contrast with the preceding tale, where the
author was generally silent about the differences between Arthur's
period and ours, and critical of the earlier time on the two occasions
when he did suggest a comparison.

There is something peculiar here, for in one sense the gold is
fool's gold. These late passages on the customs of Arthur's days
move us, but we may wonder if it is intellectually respectable of us
to be moved. The ideas in those passages cannot be considered too
curiously. Early in the seventh tale, for instance, the queen is
brought to the stake, and Malory says

> . . . such custom was used in tho dayes: for favoure, love,
> nother affinité there sholde be none other but ryghtuous juge-
> mente, as well uppon a kynge as uppon a knyght, and as well
> uppon a quene as uppon another poure lady. [1055.11–15]

This works; but certainly not because of its quality as social or legal
thought. The sentence does not even sit well in its context: "another
poure lady" would not have the king asking Bors to be her champion,
and in these very tales Lancelot tells us that he has often rescued the
queen "in wrong and in right." Malory is never very happy with
abstract ideas or analyses of behavioral codes, but I suspect the

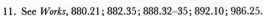

11. See *Works*, 880.21; 882.35; 888.32–35; 892.10; 986.25.
12. The first of these references is in the French also, but the second is not. On
this second passage, see Vinaver's note to *Works*, 1025.18–19.

ideational weakness of such a passage as this is more the result of
inattention than of inadequate philosophical training. Malory
doesn't revere Arthur's civilization because it "stood for" righteous
judgment; it is reverence which is the given. "Rightious judgment"
is an attempt to give a reason for that reverence or, better, to find
an idea around which that reverence may crystallize. The idea need
not be good—only good enough: the tone is what matters. The
quality of justice (1174.19–25); the quality of hermits ("for in thos
dayes hit was nat the gyse as ys nowadayes; for there were none
ermytis in tho dayes but that they had bene men of worship and of
prouesse, and tho ermytes hylde grete householdis and refreysshed
people that were in distresse." [1076.14–17]); the quality of love
(1119.22–1120.13; 1165.10–13); the imaginative truth is the
ideality of Arthur's world, not its particular ideals. Perhaps the key
"in those days" passage (although it refers to part of what I shall call
the time of the "good place" rather than to the whole Arthurian
period) is the one which ends the "Great Tournament" section:

> So than there were made grete festis unto kyngis and deukes,
> and revell, game, and play, and all maner of nobeles was used.
> And he that was curteyse, trew, and faythefull to hys frynde
> was that tyme cherysshed. [1114.29–32]

The time of "*all* maner of nobeles." Our final impression is of
Arthurian Virtue rather than virtues. With the "in those days"
passages Malory creates a sense of nostalgia: earnest and dignified,
but nostalgia nonetheless. Finally the preciousness of the lost era is
not to be explained, and the mode of discourse is really synecdochic,
not analytic.

I have been discussing passages in the last tales which clearly
imply the superiority of Arthur's time to our own. But these tales
also contain nonevaluative "in those days" explanations of the
kind found in the "Tristram":

> And so within fyftene dayes they came to Joyous Garde. And
> there they layed his corps in the body of the quere, and sange
> and redde many saulters and prayers over hym and aboute
> hym. And ever his vysage was layed open and naked, that al

folkes myght beholde hym; for suche was the custom in tho
dayes that al men of worshyp shold so lye wyth open vysage
tyl that they were buryed. [1258][13]

Such references modify the effect of the other, evaluative ones. As
much as the others these keep us aware of the pastness of the past.
But—and this is why they are valuable for Malory—these act to
blur the superiority of the earlier period; to blur, but not to dim it.
En masse, that is, the various "in those days" statements create a
sense of our distance from the events narrated. Insofar as comparative judgments are made, Arthur's days were better than our days.
But it would be difficult to find a common ethical etymon for all
the superiorities of Arthur's days[14]—and some of the differences
(the nonevaluative ones, that is) are not superiorities at all: our
attention is not being directed to a common denominator in all the
lost usages, and we are not given the key to the betterness of a better
society. Nostalgia, then: a general sense of the superiority of
Arthur's age to ours, and of the distance between those ages.[15]

In the last books the characters as well as the author are concerned with history and records, and their concern (seen previously
from time to time in such passages as 864.9–12) echoes and deepens
the sense of pastness in the "Lancelot and Guinevere" and the

13. See also, e.g., 1049.36–1050.3; 1068.34–1069.1; 1121.14–18; 1149.7–32;
1258.27–33.

14. We could and probably should say that "knightliness" is this etymon. But
Malorian knightliness is an omnipresent and undefined essence. We know its mani-
festations, but not the thing in itself.

15. The most famous of Malory's asides draws a great deal of its force from the
way "in those days" passages are used elsewhere in the final tales: "Lo ye all
Englysshemen, se ye nat what a myschyff here was? For he that was the moste
kynge and nobelyst knyght of the worlde, and moste loved the felyshyp of noble
knyghtes, and by hym they all were upholdyn, and yet myght nat thes Englyshe-
men holde them contente with hym. Lo thus was the olde custom and usayges of
thys londe, and men say that we of thys londe have nat yet loste that custom. Alas!
thys ys a greate defaughte of us Englysshemen, for there may no thynge us please
no terme. And so fared the peple at that tyme . . . "(1229.6–15). Implicitly:
love, judgment, hermits, customs of all kinds have changed. But newfangledness—
that is a constant of English character. "What does not change / is the will to
change."

"Morte." Here Lancelot, in a speech original with Malory, says to his men:

> "Than, my fayre felowys," seyde sir Launcelot, "I muste departe oute of thys moste noble realme. And now I shall departe, hit grevyth me sore, for I shall departe with no worship; for a fleymed man departith never oute of a realme with no worship. And that ys to me grete hevynes, for ever I feare aftir my dayes that men shall cronycle uppon me that I was fleamed oute of thys londe. . . ." [1202–1203]

Lancelot has always been concerned with worship and honor, but now he sees them down a long range. Previously he and we had thought about honor within the Arthurian period; now Lancelot wonders what chroniclers will say about him "aftir my dayes," just as the author himself keeps reminding us that what we know about Lancelot, Arthur, and the others we know through a book. When he uses the word "chronicle" in this speech (a word which is fairly uncommon in *Le Morte Darthur*), Lancelot is in fact echoing something he said a page earlier:

> "Moste nobelyst Crysten realme, whom I have loved aboven all othir realmys! And in the I have gotyn a grete parte of my worshyp, and now that I shall departe in thys wyse, truly me repentis that ever I cam in thys realme, that I shulde be thus shamefully banysshyd, undeserved and causeles! But fortune ys so varyaunte, and the wheele so mutable, that there ys no constaunte abydynge. And that may be preved by many olde cronycles, as of Noble Ector of Troy and Alysaunder, the myghty conquerroure, and many mo other: whan they were moste in her royalté, they alyght passyng lowe. And so faryth hit by me," seyde sir Launcelot. . . . [1201]16

The comparison suggests more than just the power of fortune: Lancelot, like Hector and Alexander, is a great figure, but a figure in the past, in history.

16. The references to chronicles and to Hector and Alexander are original. For the motif of a major character concerned, late in the work, with his or her reputation, see, e.g., *Troilus and Criseyde*, V. 1058 ff. and *Othello*, V. ii. 334 ff.

The concern of both the author and his hero for proper records is evident in the "Poisoned Apple" adventure which opens the seventh tale. In the French *Mort* Gaheriz (who, in Malory, is named Patryse) has "Ici gist Gaheriz li Balns de Kareheu, li freres Mador de la Porte, que la reine fist morir par venim" inscribed on his tomb. Now as Vinaver points out,[17] Malory had to change this since, in his version, the tomb is not inscribed until after the combat in which the queen's innocence is proved. What is interesting in this change, however, is first, that Malory does not simply omit the whole subject of the inscription, and second, that we are given a hero concerned with record-keeping. In *Le Morte Darthur* when Mador is defeated and asks for mercy, Lancelot sets a condition:

> "I woll nat graunte the thy lyff," seyde that knyght, "only that thou frely reales the quene for ever, and that no mencion be made uppon sir Patryseys tombe that ever quene Gwenyver consented to that treson." [1057–1058]

The sources do not mention the inscription at this point: it is almost as if in Malory the hero is as much concerned with a proper record as with saving the queen from the fire. Little more than a page later, the "Poisoned Apple" section ends with these paragraphs:

> Than was sir Patryse buryed in the chirche of Westemynster in a towmbe, and thereuppon was wrytten: HERE LYETH SIR PATRYSE OF IRELONDE, SLAYNE BY SIR PYNELL LE SAVEAIGE THAT ENPOYSYNDE APPELIS TO HAVE SLAYNE SIR GAWAYNE, AND BY MYSSEFORTUNE SIR PATRYSE ETE ONE OF THE APPLIS, AND THAN SUDDEYNLY HE BRASTE. Also there was wrytyn uppon the tombe that quene Gwenyvere was appeled of treson of the deth of sir Patryse by sir Madore de la Porte, and there was made the mencion how sir Launcelot fought with hym for quene Gwenyvere and overcom hym in playne batayle. All thys was wretyn uppon the tombe of sir Patryse in excusyng of the quene.
>
> And than sir Madore sewed dayly and longe to have the

17. Note to *Works*, 1059.26–31.

quenys good grace, and so by the meanys of sir Launcelot he caused hym to stonde in the quenys good grace, and all was forgyffyn. [1059–1060]

The author concludes the tale as the knight concluded the combat— with his attention turned to the record.

These final tales contain two letters, Elaine's final letter of complaint and the letter from Gawain to Lancelot, and it is instructive to compare them. Gawain is a figure in history. His letter (which is not in Malory's sources) is a wonderfully moving thing, but clearly a document. We notice not only the form of salutation, but the insistence upon date, place and time at the beginning and at the end:

> "Unto the, sir Launcelot, floure of all noble knyghtes that ever I harde of or saw be my dayes, I, sir Gawayne, kynge Lottis sonne of Orkeney, and systirs sonne unto the noble kynge Arthur, sende the gretynge, lattynge the to have knowlecche that the tenth day of May I was smytten uppon the olde wounde that thou gaff me afore the cite of Benwyke, and thorow that wounde I am com to my dethe-day . . .

> ". . . And so the tenth day of May last paste my lorde kynge Arthur and we all londed uppon them at Dover, and there he put that false traytoure, sir Mordred, to flyght. And so hit there mysfortuned me to be smytten uppon the strooke that ye gaff me of olde.

> "And the date of thys lettir was wrytten but two owrys and an halff afore my dethe, wrytten with myne owne honde and subscrybed with parte of my harte blood. And therefore I requyre the, moste famous knyght of the worlde, that thou wolte se my tumbe." [1231–1232]

The sentence before the text of this letter is "And than he toke hys penne and wrote thus, *as the Freynshe booke makith mencion*. . . ." The reference to the French book is original with Malory, and serves to emphasize the historicity and *gravitas* of the account, just as Gawain's own references to the tenth day of May do.

Elaine, when compared to Gawain, is still a figure in romance. Her letter gives us emotion, but few *data*:

> "Moste noble knyght, my lorde sir Launcelot, now hath dethe made us two at debate for youre love. And I was youre lover, that men called the Fayre Maydyn of Astolate. Therefore unto all ladyes I make my mone, yet for my soule ye pray and bury me at the leste, and offir ye my masse-peny: thys ys my laste requeste. And a clene maydyn I dyed, I take God to wytnesse. And pray for my soule, sir Launcelot, as thou arte pereles."
> [1096]

This letter does of course "document" Elaine's virginity and the cause of her death, but there is no statement of time and place, no identification by family, no epistolary salutation. This does not have the texture of a document, as Gawain's letter does. It is the most central characters in the last books who share the author's concern with record-keeping.

The Good Place: The Function of Malory's Seventh Tale

Intensified, the prosaic record-keeping of late medieval narrative becomes a distinctive poetry in the last tales. We believe what this voice tells us and we accept the attitudes it suggests. But of course the power of the "Lancelot and Guinevere" and "Tale of the Death of Arthur" does not come only from the narrator's tone. Structure is of great importance here, especially the relation of the seventh tale to the final one. It is this seventh tale more than anything else which makes the ruin of Arthur's kingdom at once inevitable and unexpected.

The "Lancelot and Guinevere" and the "Death of Arthur" go together; we sense that these two narratives form a unit not simply by virtue of their quality, but in their content; and yet it is at first difficult to say why that seventh tale is so important a part of the tragedy. In terms of plot, we learn little here which we must know when we come to the "Tale of the Death of Arthur." The adultery is resumed; the love of Lancelot and Guinevere is spoken of in court, and Aggravain and Mordred watch the lovers closely, waiting

for a chance to put them to a "rebuke and a shame"(1046.15–
17;1153.32–34). Lavayne and Urry are introduced and come to be
closely associated with Lancelot. There is not much else in the
"Lancelot and Guinevere" which we must know to follow the story
of the "Morte." That eighth tale, in fact, probably contains fewer
specific references to events in the "Lancelot and Guinevere" than
to occurrences in such earlier tales as "Sir Launcelot du Lake,"
"Sir Gareth of Orkney," "Sir Tristram," and the "Tale of the
Sankgreal."[18] In the seventh tale we are concerned with Elaine,
Meliagaunt, Pynnel, and (as a victim) Patryse, none of whom is
referred to in the "Morte Arthur."

The "Lancelot and Guinevere" focuses on no important Arthurian deaths. In this it contrasts strongly not only with the eighth tale,
but with the fifth, in which there are many adventures and the death
of Sir Lamerak, and the sixth, the last part of which is devoted to
the adventures and death of Galahad. Reading the seventh tale
we are certainly aware of the deaths of noble knights,[19] but such
deaths are in the past, in the background: portents, but portents
glimpsed only for a moment. The principal deaths in the episodes
themselves are those of Patryse, whom we never see except at the
very moment when he dies, Meliagaunt, an unattractive villain, and
Elaine. Elaine is one of Malory's most appealing characters, but she
is outside the Arthurian circle, and hers is a bittersweet, graceful
death which does not disturb our sense of order in the world. By the
end of the "Lancelot and Guinevere," Lancelot has those two
pleasant new followers, Urry and Lavayne; but on the whole the
seventh tale gives us very little sense of change in the fellowship's
composition.

What then is the function of the "Lancelot and Guinevere?"
Edmund Reiss subtitles his account of this section "The Pause that

18. See, respectively: 1162.14–17 and 1198.27–34; the many references to
Gareth's knighting; 1170.26–29; 1153.11–14.

19. In a wonderfully effective rearrangement of material, Malory tells for the
first time of the slaying "with treason" (and the charge of treason will echo all
through the destruction in the following tale) of Tristram in the "Healing of Urry"
section of the "Lancelot and Guinevere"; that is, in the section which tells us of
the final triumph of the Arthurian company. See 1149.28–35. There are earlier
references to the deaths of noble knights at 1049.1–3, 1121.21–27, and 1149.7–11.

Regresses,"[20] and sees a central irony in the post-Grail-Quest chivalry of this book: "For man to return to worldly aims after glimpsing higher purposes and values is for man to be either frustrated or deceived into thinking that he is still leading a good and worthwhile life. . . . Although chivalry is stale, it is all they know. The Christian *novus homo* is no more, and the worldly knights are now only spiritual old men."[21] Now certainly the seventh tale shows us failures of the Arthurian company, but to find only "staleness" in this chivalry is to shut one's ears to tone. The respect for the Arthurian age discussed above is hard to understand in terms of spiritual old men: when we find a section ending "So than there were made grete festis unto kyngis and deukes, and revell, game, and play, and all maner of nobeles was used. And he that was curteyse, trew, and faythefull to hys frynde was that tyme cherysshed" (1114.29–32) we feel the pity of it, feel that this is soon to end, may feel, even, that to be courteous, true, and faithful to one's friend is not enough. But we feel it is not enough and wish that it could be, not "it is not enough—how futile it all is."

A pattern in Malory's vocabulary is significant here. If we examine the way the word "noble" is used in the four last tales, we discover a variation rather like the variation in Malory's use of "in those days" explanations. With both the "in those days" passages and the word "noble" there is what seems a normative Malorian use in the fifth tale, a very light use in the sixth, and then a heavy use in the seventh and eighth. Both patterns create the same effect. The element relatively forgotten in the "Grail" section—the section in which we are not comparing the Arthurian and the modern, but the temporal and the eternal—appears with renewed force in the last tales, and reminds us that, whatever the failings of the Arthurian heroes and period from a religious perspective, they are superb from an earthly (which is, in Malory, a normal) perspective. The sixth tale teaches us that gold is not platinum; in the seventh we learn again how beautiful gold is.

Some word counts. "Noble," as we might expect, is one of Malory's

20. *Sir Thomas Malory*, p. 158.
21. Ibid., pp. 158, 159.

favorite terms.[22] In the section of the "Tristram" beginning on p. 727 of the *Works* and ending on p. 846 (106 pages of Malorian text) there are fifty occurrences of words of the *noble* group ("noble," "nobler," "noblest," "nobly," "noblesse," etc.) and thus an average of .47 occurrences per page of text.[23] Now at the end of the "Tristram" we're told "HERE FOLOWYTH THE NOBLE TALE OF THE SANKEGREALL" (845.32–33), but in the "Quest" itself words of the *noble* group are used only three times: "And there mette hym twenty noble squyers" (861.4–5); "the quene dud on a noble jesseraunce uppon hym" (864.21–22); "the noble knyght sir Launcelot" (1018.15–16).[24] There do not seem to be new adjectives of praise which replace *noble* in this tale; rather the high-frequency adjectives which appear alongside "noble" in the other tales (especially "good," "better," "best"; "gentle," "worthy," etc. to a lesser extent) simply fill the gap left in Malory's vocabulary of approbation. In the seventh tale, "The Book of Sir Lancelot and Queen Guinevere," words of the *noble* group occur appreciably more often than in the 106 pages of the "Tristram": sixty-two uses in ninety-four pages of text, and thus an average of .66 occurrences per page.[25]

22. Field says that "noble knyghtes" is "the most important thematic phrase of the *Morte Darthur*" (*Romance and Chronicle,* p. 75), and suggests that this phrase is used heavily "throughout all the books" but especially in the last tale (Ibid., p. 82). But see my comments on the "Quest" below.

23. The occurrences are: 733.5; 736.5; 736.21; 736.22; 737.4; 739.30; 740.1; 742.15; 744.10; 745.31; 748.15; 755.14; 761.11; 761.18; 762.1; 762.23; 764.3; 764.15; 769.23; 769.32; 776.19; 776.27; 777.4; 778.12; 778.15; 779.14; 780.23; 780.24; 781.7; 785.11; 793.12; 796.1; 796.2; 808.12; 809.26; 810.6; 814.32; 815.3; 815.4; 815.10; 815.24; 819.10; 829.5; 839.31; 840.4; 840.7; 843.2; 843.11; 843.28; 845.32.

24. It is curious that only one of these occurrences involves a noble knight; "knight" is probably the noun which more frequently follows "noble" in the other tales.

25. These occurrences are: 1047.17; 1049.25; 1053.33; 1054.1–2; 1054.13; 1055.2; 1056.36; 1065.18; 1067.21; 1068.29; 1069.2; 1069.21; 1071.27; 1074.22; 1074.25; 1076.2; 1077.1; 1077.10; 1078.19; 1079.10; 1079.23; 1079.37; 1083.25; 1085.31; 1088.29; 1088.34; 1093.12; 1094.1; 1096.28; 1098.12; 1103.32; 1107.15; 1109.7; 1111.12; 1111.18; 1114.13; 1114.30; 1121.23; 1121.33; 1122.11; 1112.20; 1123.10; 1123.14–15; 1124.31; 1125.5; 1125.19; 1127.18; 1134.13; 1138.21–22; 1146.6; 1146.17; 1146.31; 1147.14; 1149.2–3; 1149.8; 1149.19; 1149.28; 1150.15; 1150.23; 1151.20; 1153.28; 1153.30.

This average in turn is almost doubled in the next book, "The Tale of the Death of Arthur." There are 102 uses of words of the *noble* group in these eighty-one pages of text: an average of 1.26 occurrences per page.[26]

Clearly "noble" is a word Malory associates with earthly, Arthurian chivalry but not with the religious chivalry of the Grail quest; stylistically, the avoidance of this word in the sixth tale contributes to the reader's impression that here he is moving in a different world. That difference, however, is indeed a *difference* in texture. We do not feel there is an inferiority in things described as "noble": in *Le Morte Darthur* this is surely a term of unequivocal praise. By reserving such a term of approbation for the earthly chivalric, and then using it very heavily in his two last tales, Malory subtly molds our attitudes toward the Round Table world. Whatever we saw in the "Quest," Arthurian chivalry is not just a second-rate version of celestial chivalry: there is a term of high praise which belongs to earthly chivalry alone. The knightliness of Lancelot and Gareth is not just a degree, but a particular kind of goodness. And we are doubly impressed with how important that kind of goodness is because Malory now makes us see everywhere the thing we had forgotten in the preceding tale.

The noble world of the "Lancelot and Guinevere" is not a perfect world. The materials of the final explosion are here, and we understand their explosiveness. In the second paragraph Malory tells us "sir Launcelot began to resorte unto quene Gwenivere agayne . . ." (1045.10–11) and there is talk of this love in the court. The poisoning

26. These occurrences are: 1161.22; 1162.18; 1162.32; 1165.6; 1165.31; 1166. 13; 1171.6; 1174.15; 1174.16; 1175.31; 1176.16; 1176.18; 1177.29; 1177.33; 1178.15; 1178.16; 1183.4; 1183.8; 1183.11; 1185.17; 1187.6; 1187.27; 1187.31; 1187.35; 1191.30; 1192.18; 1194.13; 1194.14; 1197.15; 1198.22; 1198.24; 1199.19; 1199.24; 1200.8; 1201.9; 1201.16; 1202.11–12. 1202.26–27; 1203.1; 1203.9; 1203. 32; 1203.34; 1204.2; 1204.22; 1204.24; 1205.1; 1205.22; 1211.1–2; 1212.10; 1212.12; 1212.15; 1214.2; 1214.5; 1214.10; 1214.13; 1215.8; 1215.30; 1216.13; 1219.25; 1220.23; 1228.29; 1229.7; 1229.8; 1229.16; 1229.30; 1230.4; 1230.25; 1230.28 (twice); 1231.8; 1231.10; 1231.22; 1231.26; 1231.27; 1233.8; 1234.17; 1234.22; 1236.2 (twice); 1236.7; 1236.16; 1237.23; 1238.1; 1238.19; 1238.23; 1239.7; 1239.21; 1239.30; 1241.30; 1243.2; 1249.18; 1249.23; 1249.27; 1251.9; 1252.9; 1252.11; 1254.38. 1255.12; 1255.20; 1256.30; 1259.28; 1260.17.

in the first episode is connected with Gawain's killing of Sir Lamorak (1049.1–5) and in the final episode we are reminded that Lamorak was *with treason* slain "by sir Gawayne and hys brethirn"
(1149.34–35). Yet the tale as a whole presents a kind of "Indian
summer" of the Round Table, whose culmination is the wonderfully
poignant "Healing of Sir Urry." Here Keats is a better teacher
than Augustine; there is a pause, as Reiss tells us, but it is the pause
that "spares the next swath and all its twined flowers." We do not
lose sight of the weaknesses of Arthurian civilization, but we are
most aware of what is good in that civilization and we are savoring
it for the last time.[27]

The "Lancelot and Guinevere" is a reprieve. The human failings
which contribute to the fall of the Round Table are already present. If the Grail quest announces the insufficiency of earthly
knighthood, the announcement has already been heard. There are
adequate causes for tragedy and yet there is no tragedy here. Whatever their failings, the Arthurian heroes show themselves "curteyse,
trew and faythefull," and none of them dies. Problems arise, but
are solved; disruptions of order can be avoided or contained. The
contrast between this reprieve and the disaster which befalls this
world in the next tale makes the final tragedy all the more desolat-
ing and bewildering.

Early in the "Lancelot and Guinevere," just after the lovers
have quarreled, Lancelot says to Bors, "Brother . . . wyte you
well I am full loth to departe out of thys reallme, but the quene
hath defended me so hyghly that mesemyth she woll never be my
good lady as she hath bene" (1047.25–28). This speech is original
with Malory, and interesting in a number of ways. It is the first of
the great number of phrases, situations, and motifs which occur in
the seventh tale and then echo, either loudly or faintly, in the
eighth. Lancelot is loth "to departe out of thys reallme," and there
will be another time when he "muste departe oute of thys moste
noble realme" (1202.36–1203.1). But more significant than this

27. Professor Reiss conveys very well the autumnal, retrospective quality in the
"Healing of Sir Urry" list of knights and achievements, though I think he stresses
the pre-winter aspect of the autumnal somewhat too heavily. See *Sir Thomas Malory*,
p. 170 f.

slight echo of phrase and situation is the sentiment expressed. Lancelot is wrong, and this is a notable state of affairs, since in *Le Morte Darthur* heroes and author do tend to see things from a single, correct point of view. The paradigm laconic warrior, Lancelot, is guilty of what we now call overreacting. The situation is not as dismal as he thinks. Bors judges what has happened more accurately:

> "Sey ye never so," seyde sir Bors, "for many tymes or this she hath bene wroth with you, and aftir that she was the first that repented hit."
>
> "Ye sey well," seyde sir Launcelot, "for now woll I do by your counceyle and take myne horse and myne harneyse and ryde to the ermyte sir Brastias. . . ." [1047]

At the end of the episode the queen looks at Lancelot and weeps, thinking of the great kindness he had done her when she had shown him great unkindness (1058.36–1059.2). Lancelot's gloom, his deflected judgment in a work where the judgment of heroes is usually undeflected, has two functions. First, with a kind of dramatic irony at once faint and complex, it foreshadows the "departure" in the following book, a departure which will really call for such pessimism. Second, it functions within the seventh tale as a kind of crying "wolf," a false alarm. We start by giving a certain credence to Lancelot's first, emphatic judgment; and even if Bors can calm him down, when Lancelot sees the damage of the quarrel as irreversible, we more than half expect that it will be irreversible. But of course it is not: Lancelot is wrong, and what this means is that anyone, anything, that points to irreversible damage, is wrong. There are no permanent consequences in this tale: the center does hold, even if Lancelot himself thinks that it will not. The feeling of the "Lancelot and Guinevere" is a combination of the sense of the charmed, unexplained, "in-spite-of" security of the Arthurian world suggested to us by Lancelot's false reaction in this first episode, and the sense of the preciousness of that security, that wholeness, conveyed by the final "Healing of Sir Urry."

The "Lancelot and Guinevere" is permeated by nostalgia, and a sense of the pastness of the Arthurian age. In itself, the mood of this

penultimate tale might be expected to lend a certain bittersweet
quality to the tragedy of the final "Morte Arthur Saunz Guerdon,"
and indeed it does. But Malory does not achieve his effects by a
simple juxtaposition of the two tales; as I have indicated, he links the
"Lancelot and Guinevere" and the "Morte" with a large number of
situational and verbal echoes which *en masse* create for the reader a
haunting remembrance of the seventh tale in the eighth; a remembrance, in Dante's phrase, of a time of happiness in a time of misery.

The numerousness of these echoes is important, but even more
important is their variety. They differ widely in audibility. As the
reader moves through the eighth tale certain incidents and turns of
phrase will clearly recall parts of the "Lancelot and Guinevere";
at other moments in the eighth tale that reader will have only the
faintest sense of *déjà vu* (or *déjà entendu*). The echoes also vary greatly
in their thematic import. The incidents linked to one another are
sometimes very much alike in what they show us about the Arthurian world, sometimes strikingly in contrast, sometimes only
partially in contrast. The lack of a thematic common denominator
in the linkages is, in a sense, like the absence of an important common denominator in the "in those days" passages. The excellence of
the Round Table civilization is not to be defined, and the meaning
of the change from the charmed circle of the seventh tale to the
tragic world of the eighth is not to be specified. Ultimately we cannot translate the echo patterns into a single ethical meaning; but
certainly we can say that the felt multiplicity of those patterns, and
their varied audibility contribute to our sense of a mysterious complexity half-observed within the singleness of Malory's world.

The two May passages constitute the most obvious of the links
between books seven and eight. In the "Lancelot and Guinevere"
Malory writes:

> And thus hit passed on frome Candylmas untyll after Ester,
> that the moneth of May was com, whan every lusty harte
> begynnyth to blossom and to burgyne. For, lyke as trees and
> erbys burgenyth and florysshyth in May, in lyke wyse every
> lusty harte that ys ony maner of lover spryngith, burgenyth,
> buddyth, and florysshyth in lusty dedis. For hit gyvyth unto all

lovers corrayge, that lusty moneth of May, in somthynge to constrayne hym to som maner of thynge more in that moneth than in ony other monethe, for dyverce causys: for than all erbys and treys renewyth a man and woman, and in lyke wyse lovers callyth to their mynde olde jantylnes and olde servyse, and many kynde dedes that was forgotyn by neclygence.

For, lyke as wynter rasure dothe allway arace and deface grene summer, so faryth hit by unstable love in man and woman, for in many persones there ys no stabylité: for we may se all day, for a lytyll blaste of wyntres rasure, anone we shall deface and lay aparte trew love, for lytyll or nowght, that coste muche thynge. Thys ys no wysedome nother no stabylité, but hit ys fyeblenes of nature and grete disworshyp, whosomever usyth thys. . . . Wherefore I lykken love nowadayes unto sommer and wynter: for, lyke as the tone ys colde and the othir ys hote, so faryth love nowadayes. And therefore all ye that be lovers, calle unto youre remembraunce the monethe of May, lyke as ded quene Gwenyver, for whom I make here a lytyll mencion, that whyle she lyved she was a trew lover, and therefor she had a good ende.

So hit befelle in the moneth of May, quene Gwenyver called unto her ten knyghtes of the Table Rounde. . . . [1119–1120]

In itself, this is a very interesting, if somewhat perplexing discussion.[28] Arthur's Age, in this the longest of Malory's "in those days" passages, is a golden past. But the nostalgia here is as much a matter of attitude as of specific differences between then and now. What May does is significant: it "constrains" lovers not to passion or directly to noble behavior but to remembrance, and to remem-

28. This famous passage has been much examined by critics interested in Malory's idea of love and in the question of Lancelot's lack of steadfastness. See especially R. T. Davies, "Malory's 'Vertuous Love,'" *SP* 53 (1956): 461 f. and Reiss, *Sir Thomas Malory,* p. 168. f. Roger Sherman Loomis cuts through the difficulties of the passage by suggesting that Malory was drunk when he wrote it. (*The Development of Arthurian Romance* [New York, 1963], p. 175.) This is certainly not impossible. In any case, here as elsewhere Malory conveys the tone of earnestness that goes with true love far more clearly than he does its doctrine. The tone was, I believe, more real to him than the doctrine.

brance not of beauty or of passion but of "olde jantylnes and olde
servyse, and many kynde dedes that was forgotyn by neclygence."
In this nostalgic world, love itself is a form of nostalgia: there is a
harmony between the author and the reader thinking of Arthur's
distant time and the lover sighing over "many kynde dedes that was
forgotyn by neclygence." Guinevere was a true lover "and therefor
she had a good ende": this is not a jarring phrase, but it does remind ✓
us that this queen is a figure in the past, and that her end has already
come—very much a "Lancelot and Guinevere" phrase.

Now in the eighth tale Malory echoes this passage in at least two
ways. There Lancelot speaks to Arthur of the remembrance of old
service and kind deeds:

> ". . . And at suche tymes, my lorde Arthur," seyde sir Lance-
> lot, "ye loved me and thanked me whan I saved your quene
> frome the fyre, and than ye promysed me for ever to be my good
> lorde. And now methynkith ye rewarde me evyll for my good
> servyse. . . . " [1188]

> ". . . And therefore, my lorde, I pray you remembir what I
> have done in many placis, and now am I evyll rewarded."
>
> So whan kynge Arthur was on horsebak he loked on sir
> Launcelot; that the teerys braste oute of hys yen, thynkyng of
> the grete curtesy that was in sir Launcelot more than in ony
> other man. [1192]

> ". . . And therefore, my lorde Arthur, remembir you of olde
> kyndenes, and howsomever I fare, Jesu be youre gyde in all
> placis." [1218.15–17]

But here the king, who does remember old kindness and was never
negligent, can do nothing. Something has happened: the emotions
and patterns of behavior we saw in the seventh tale have not
changed, but they are no longer enough.

The second echo of the "Lancelot and Guinevere" passage is of
course the description of May which opens the eighth tale. It stuns
us:

> In May, whan every harte floryshyth and burgenyth (for, as

the season ys lusty to beholde and comfortable, so man and
woman rejoysyth and gladith of somer commynge with his
freyshe floures, for wynter wyth hys rowghe wyndis and blastis
causyth lusty men and women to cowre and to syt by fyres),
so thys season hit befelle in the moneth of May a grete angur
and unhappe that stynted nat tylle the floure of chyvalry of
alle the worlde was destroyed and slayne. [1161.1–8]

This second passage strongly recalls the first because it too is a
description of May opening a section of the work, because Malory
so rarely pays attention to season or flora, and because of the heavy
use of doublets and marked similarity in wording. The shock comes
from the similarity. Nowhere else in *Le Morte Darthur* is the fuzziness
of the fifteenth-century *so* exploited as tellingly. We are in the midst
of another praise of May, again (and "again" in that the traditional
nature of the panegyric brings non-Malorian echoes to the reader
as well as echoes of the seventh tale)[29] man is like the budding
plants; but instead of moving to the expected discussion of love, we
move to the destruction of the Round Table by way of that vague
so. It is done superbly: Malory's voice does not change in the
slightest. The doublets he has been using quite properly in an "ele-
vated," traditional panegyric of May and love ("floryshyth and
burgenyth," "man and woman rejoysyth and gladith," "rowghe
wyndis and blastis") he continues to use ("a grete angur and
unhappe," "destroyed and slayne"). The traditional man-flower
comparison of the May panegyric is combined with the equally
traditional *flower* of chivalry; but now men are *not* like other
plants, chivalry's *not* like other flowers: this May is not their time
of flourishing, but the beginning of their destruction.[30] Our reaction is a "double-take"; we were not prepared for such an idea at

29. Note that for Wolfram von Eschenbach, writing early in the thirteenth
century, the May setting of Arthurian adventures was already something of a
cliché: "Arthur is the man of May, and whatever has been told about him took
place at Pentecost or in the flowering time of May." (*Parzival*, trans. Helen M.
Mustard and Charles E. Passage [New York, 1961], p. 153.)

30. Notice also that it is "on the tenth day of May" that Gawain is fatally struck
upon his old wound (1231.11–13).

the end of this passage, and for a moment we do not quite realize what it is Malory has said.

We are no longer in "the good place." With this use of the May motif to announce destruction rather than flourishing, Malory shows us what his basic strategy will be in echoing the seventh tale in the eighth. Things, actions, phrases we associated with an area of the imagination in which he that was "curteyse, trew and faythefull to hys frynde" was cherished—in which death was mostly off-stage, adding poignancy to, but not destroying, the Arthurian world; in which Lancelot could prevent his adultery from having political consequences—now reappear in tragic contexts. These echoes do not teach us why the change took place; they sadden and bewilder us with the fact of the change.

"For hit ys an olde-seyde sawe, 'there ys harde batayle thereas kynne and frendys doth batayle ayther ayenst other,' for there may be no mercy, but mortall warre." This olde-said saw applies very well to the events of the eighth tale, but actually occurs in the seventh (1084.4–7); it is quoted by Lancelot when Sir Bors rebukes himself for having wounded him in combat. In the seventh tale we are mostly aware of the woundings of Lancelot as the occasions for Elaine's nursing, but Lancelot's injury at Bors's hands is also a foreshadowing of Lancelot's killing of Gareth. When Gawain in this earlier book discovers Lancelot is the knight Bors has wounded, he says, "Truly . . . the man in the worlde that loved beste hym hurte hym" (1079.27–28). Arthur exclaims in the final book ". . . Merci Jesu . . . why slew he sir Gaherys and sir Gareth? For I dare sey, as for sir Gareth, he loved sir Launcelot of all men erthly" (1183.19–21). Lancelot himself says, "as for sir Gareth, I loved no kynnesman I had more than I loved hym . . ." (1199.13–14) and in a notably intricate variation on the ground pattern, "I wolde with as good a wyll have slayne my nevew, sir Bors de Ganys, at that tyme" (1189.18–19).

That killing of Gareth is the central event of the Round Table tragedy, and we are being prepared for it in the "Lancelot and Guinevere." Malory emphasizes Gareth's loyalty to Lancelot at a number of points in the seventh tale, and he also plays carefully with foreshadowings and inversions of the situation in which Gareth dies. In "The Great Tournament," which is essentially of Malory's invention, Gareth, disguised, fights superbly on Lancelot's side "and yet . . . sir Launcelot knew nat sir Gareth; for and sir Trystram de Lyones other sir Lamorak de Galys had ben on lyve, sir Launcelot wolde have demed he had bene one of them twayne" (1112.3–13). Here it is literally inconsequential that Lancelot cannot recognize Gareth, and that the unknown knight reminds him of heroes who have been killed, just as it does not matter in the seventh tale that Bors wounds Lancelot.[31]

The story of Elaine, the maid of Astolat, contains a number of motifs which reappear in the "Morte." The "barget" that carries Elaine's body (1095 ff.) reappears as a death motif in the "greate boote" containing the fatally wounded Gawain (1230.3 ff.) and the "lytyll barge" in which the three ladies come for Arthur (1240. 12 ff.).[32] When dying both Elaine and Gawain compose letters to Lancelot. In Malory (but not in his sources) we have this description of Elaine's body:

> . . . and there he saw the fayryst woman ly in a ryche bed, coverde unto her myddyll with many rych clothys, and all was of cloth of golde. *And she lay as she had smyled.* [1096.14–16]

And recalling it, this description of Lancelot's:

> So whan syr Bors and his felowes came to his bedde they founde hym starke dede; *and he laye as he had smyled,* and the swettest savour aboute hym that ever they felte. [1258.15–17][33]

Lancelot rebukes the hermit who tells him his excessive "sorowmaking" for Guinevere and Arthur displeases God (1256.20–39). There is a scene like this in the seventh tale also. Elaine grows steadily weaker and realizes she is dying: she confesses and takes

31. In the seventh tale Guinevere also sounds this theme of non-recognition when she admonishes Lancelot not to ride disguised into any jousts or tourneys without warning his kinsmen, and making sure they will know him (*Works*, 1103. 16–22).

32. This pattern is in Malory's sources also.

33. See also *Romance and Chronicle*, p. 82.

the sacrament, but continues to "complain upon" Sir Lancelot. Her confessor bids her leave such thoughts, and Elaine replies with a speech as moving as Lancelot's praise of Arthur and Guinevere—that wonderful lament in which dying for love seems not only an honorable, but a sensible, down-to-earth, self-respecting course of action (1093.2–1094.3). Shortly before we are told of their deaths, both Elaine and Lancelot, chided by religious figures for excessively lamenting worldly things, defend their actions eloquently.

But perhaps the most poignant echoes of Elaine's death are heard in that central killing of Gareth. Both characters are entirely devoted to Lancelot, and Lancelot is in one sense responsible and in another sense not responsible for the death of each. After Elaine's letter has been read to him, he declares "I was never causar of her deth be my wyllynge . . ." (1097.8–9); later he will say "I slewe never sir Gareth nother hys brother be my wyllynge" (1199.26–27). In the *locus amoenus* the brother of the dead innocent absolves Lancelot from any blame;[34] in the eighth tale the brother will seek vengeance unremittingly.

The "Knight of the Cart" story is of course not original with Malory but it is he who makes it one of the Arthurian last things; thus the connections between this adventure and the following tragedy are particularly interesting. In the earlier section Lancelot is in the inner court of Meliagaunt's castle crying, "Thou traytour knyght, com forthe!" (1128.21);[35] in the eighth tale Gawain, riding before the chief gate of Benwick, cries "Where arte thou, sir Launcelot? Com forth, thou false traytoure knyght and recrayed . . ." (1219.1–2). To be sure Lancelot in the "Death of Arthur" episode is not hiding from Gawain out of fear, but there are parallels in the two situations. Both Meliagaunt in the earlier scene and Lancelot in the later one are trying to avoid a challenge, each is under attack in his own castle, and neither would be in this situation had he not loved Guinevere. Now the similarities certainly do not mean that

34. See Lavayne's speech to his father, 1091.11–15. Lavayne's silence when Lancelot says "and that woll I reporte me unto . . . sir Lavayne" clearly indicates assent.

35. See also 1127.24.

Mel stealing Guin like L's stealing

Lancelot is really "just as bad as" Meliagaunt. Such reductive irony, "deere ynogh a jane," is not Malorian. Meliagaunt is perhaps the most contemptible of Lancelot's major adversaries—a more cowardly opponent than, say, Tarquin in the third tale; the true shame is that there is *any* similarity between Lancelot and Meliagaunt.[36]

Again in the "Knight of the Cart," as in the death of Elaine, there are elements which foreshadow the killing of Gareth. Gareth and Gaherys are "unarmed and unawares" (1177.34) when they are killed, and Gawain rebukes Lancelot for this: "And two of hem thou slew traytorly and piteously, for they bare none harneys ayenste the, nother none wold do" (1199.8–10). It is of course *because* Lancelot could not recognize them without their harness that he does not spare them; nonetheless, as we read this we may recall the earlier episode where Meliagaunt attacks unarmed knights escorting Guinevere as Lancelot does in the "Morte" (1122). The Queen's Knights, who are Guinevere's escort in the "Knight of the Cart," are "the moste party . . . yonge men that wolde have worshyp" (1121.16–17); Gawain tells Arthur in the following tale that Gaherys and Gareth, unlike himself, will not refuse to be at Guinevere's execution because "they ar yonge and full unable to say you nay" (1176.27–28).

Wilfred L. Guerin has pointed out the relation between another "Knight of the Cart" incident and a scene in the last book.[37] When, in the earlier adventure, Lancelot tells Lavayne that he must go to speak with Guinevere, Lavayne replies, "Sir . . . let me go with you, and hyt please you, *for I drede me sore of the treson of sir Mellyagaunte*" (1131.1–3). Later, in the first section of the "Morte," it is Bors Lancelot tells he is going to speak with the queen. Bors attempts to dissuade him:

> "Sir, for I drede me ever of sir Aggravayne that waytith uppon you dayly to do you shame and us all. And never gaff my harte

36. Notice also that the Lancelot who in the final conflict of the "Knight of the Cart" entices Meliagaunt into continuing a battle, in the last tale tries to entice Gawain into ending one. Repetition of *proffer* (and *offer*) helps connect these two scenes (1139.8, .15, .17, .19; 1199.29, 1200.13–14).

37. " 'The Tale of the Death of Arthur'; Catastrophe and Resolution," *Malory's Originality*, p. 258.

ayenste no goynge that ever ye wente to the quene so much as
now, for I mystruste that the kynge ys oute thys nyght frome
the quene bycause peradventure he hath layne som wacche for
you and the quene. *Therefore I drede me sore of som treson.*" [1164]

Lancelot takes the advice of his follower in neither episode, and in
both cases there is indeed a trap. But in the "good place" of the
seventh tale that trap has no ultimate consequence: it is simply the
occasion for a knightly adventure. The trap in the eighth book leads
to the destruction of the Round Table.

Another echo of the "Knight of the Cart" is quite poignant.
Meliagaunt throws himself on Guinevere's mercy, begging her "to
rule my lorde sir Launcelot" (1128.12); she replies, "Ye sey well
. . . *and bettir ys pees than evermore warre*, and the less noyse the more
ys my worshyp" (.16–.17). Lancelot's followers, in the last tale,
want to fight with Arthur's army rather than "coure in castels"
(1212.14). Lancelot disagrees: "Howbehit we woll as at this tyme
kepe oure stronge wallis. And I shall sende a messyngere unto my
lorde Arthur a tretyse for to take, *for better ys pees than allwayes warre*"
(1212.25–26). Lancelot, who has never cowered in his life now tries
(and tries, of course, unsuccessfully) to avoid a fight, and the adage
he quotes in that attempt recalls a moment when Guinevere could
patronize a man terrified at the prospect of fighting with this same
Lancelot.[38]

The climax of the "Knight of the Cart" is Lancelot's rescue of
Guinevere, and this rescue motif is in itself the largest of the patterns
joining the last two books. In the eighth tale Lancelot pleads that
he is now being blamed for rescuing the queen, where he has always been praised for doing so in the past (1188.19–27). The reader

38. Another minor verbal echo from the "Knight of the Cart" in the eighth tale
is Lancelot's "And now I had levir than to be lorde of all Crystendom that I had
sure armour uppon me. . . . "(1166.33–34), which recalls his "I had lever . . .
than all France that I had bene there well armed" (1125.6–7). Notice too "harte
full colde" (1129.17) and "full colde at the harte-roote" (1162.9). "As reason is,"
Malory makes use of rings as links. The queen sends a ring to Lancelot in the
"Knight of the Cart" (1123.34 ff.) and the lovers exchange rings in the last book
(1169.1–2). The two ring passages seem to be original. (See Vinaver's notes to
Works, 1123.25, etc. and 1168.26–1169.3.)

shares some of the hero's bewilderment at the change: both the
"Poisoned Apple" and the "Knight of the Cart," two of the five
episodes in the earlier tale, have as their climax just such a rescue;
now, in the eighth tale, Lancelot again does what in a sense he has
always done (in Gawain's fine Malorian phrase "he hath done but
knyghtly" [1184.22–23]) but here Gareth and Gaherys are killed.[39]

Not only the rescue of Guinevere, but the accusation against her
in the "Poisoned Apple" section echoes in the last tale. Bors, in the
earlier section, attempts to defend the queen's reputation and his
decision to act as her champion:

> Many answerd hym agayne: "As for oure moste noble kynge
> Arthure, we love hym and honoure hym as well as ye do, but
> as for quene Gwenyvere, we love hir nat, because she ys *a
> destroyer of good knyghtes.*"
>
> "Fayre lordis," seyde sir Bors, "mesemyth ye sey nat as
> ye sholde sey, for never yet in my dayes knew I never ne harde
> sey that ever she was *a destroyer of good knyghtes,* but at all tymes,
> as far as ever I coude know, she was a maynteyner of good
> knyghtes. . . ."[40] [1054]

We may half-remember this charge and defense when the queen,
in her last interview with Lancelot, speaks Malory's most haunting
line: ". . . thorow the and me ys the floure of kyngis and knyghtes
destroyed" (1252.24–25). Guinevere defends herself in the earlier
section by saying " 'Alas . . . I made thys dyner *for a good entente
and never for none evyll,* so Allmyghty Jesu helpe me in my ryght, as I
was never purposed to do such evyll dedes, and that I reporte me

39. Edmund Reiss discusses the progression of the three rescues in his *Sir Thomas
Malory,* pp. 160–62. Notice also that Malory underlines the repetition by making
death by fire the threatened punishment in all three episodes. He follows his
sources when he makes burning the punishment in the last of these stories. But the
fire in the "Poisoned Apple" section is not found in the French *Mort*; Malory is
here enlarging on a reference in the stanzaic poem. (On the relation of *Le Morte
Darthur* to its sources here, see E. Talbot Donaldson, "Malory and the Stanzaic Le
Morte Darthur," *SP* 47 [1950]: 460–72, 465 n.) The "Knight of the Cart" fire is
not found in any of the French versions, and seems to be borrowed, as Vinaver
suggests (note to *Works,* 1137.6–7) from the earlier one in this seventh tale.

40. The "destroyer of good knights" sentences are original with Malory.

unto God' " (1050.28–31). We may recall both the phrasing and
the situation here when Gawain urges the king not to be too hasty
in judging Guinevere, who has been surprised with Lancelot:

> ". . . And peradventure she sente for hym *for goodnes and for
> none evyll*, to rewarde hym for his good dedys that he had done
> to her in tymes past. And peradventure my lady the quene
> sente for hym to that *entente*, that sir Launcelot sholde a com
> prevaly to her, wenyng that hyt had be beste in eschewyng and
> dredyng of slaundir; *for oftyntymys we do many thynges that we wene
> for the beste be, and yet peradventure hit turnyth to the warste*. . . .
> [1175]

As Edmund Reiss has pointed out,[41] the fact that Lancelot "for no
stated reason" fights against Arthur's knights in "The Great Tournament" section of "The Book of Lancelot and Guinevere" fore-
casts "Lancelot's actual fight against the king in the next tale." The
same is of course true of Lancelot's decision in the "Fair Maid of
Astolat" section: ". . . at that justys I woll be ayenste the kynge
and ayenst all hys felyship" (1066.11–12). The strategem which
gave Lancelot opponents worthy of him, and which we as readers
enjoyed because it let us see him performing at his best, becomes
the tragic division of the last book. As we read of the endless weeping
in the "Morte," we may recall that when Arthur first saw Lancelot
come to Astolat to fight against his companions, the king smiled
(1067.2).[42]

Malory uses one minor character not only to connect but almost
to epitomize certain things in these last tales. This is Nynyve, the
Lady of the Lake. According to the "Index of Proper Names" in
the *Works*, there are ten references to Nynyve in the "Tale of King
Arthur" and one in the "Tristram." She is not referred to at all
between pages 490–492 and page 1059,[43] but then is mentioned four
times in the last tales. The first of these late references (none of which
appears in Malory's sources) comes at the end of the "Poisoned

41. *Sir Thomas Malory*, p. 166.
42. The smiling and of course the choice of side in the "Fair Maid of Astolat"
are found in Malory's sources as well as in *Le Morte Darthur*.
43. But there is one reference to a different lady of the lake on p. 796.

Apple" episode—the adventure which opens the "Tale of Lancelot
and Guinevere." Nynyve appears as a *dea ex machina* to elucidate the
mystery which has not yet been explained:

> And so hit befelle that the Damesell of the Lake that hyght
> Nynyve, whych wedded the good knyght sir Pelleas, and so
> she cam to the courte, for ever she ded grete goodnes unto
> kynge Arthure and to all hys knyghtes thorow her sorsery and
> enchauntementes. And so whan she herde how the quene was
> greved for the dethe of sir Patryse, than she tolde hit opynly
> that she was never gylty, and there she disclosed by whom hit
> was done, and named hym sir Pynel, and for what cause he
> ded hit. [1059]

The second reference (this not directly to Nynyve herself, but to
"the chief lady of the lady of the lake") is in the "Healing of Sir
Urry" list of knights, and is an explanatory digression on the hither-
to unknown Sir Severause le Brewse:

> For, as the booke seyth, the chyff lady of the Lady off the Lake
> fested sir Launcelot and sir Severause le Brewse, and whan she
> had fested them both at sundry tymes, she prayde hem to gyff
> her a done, and anone they graunted her. And than she prayde
> sir Severause that he wolde promyse her never to do batayle
> ayenste sir Launcelot, and in the same wyse she prayde sir
> Launcelot never to do batayle ayenste sir Severause, and so
> aythir promysed her. (For the Freynshe booke sayth that sir
> Severause had never corayge nor grete luste to do batayle
> ayenste no man but if hit were ayenste gyauntis and ayenste
> dragons and wylde bestis.) [1148]

The third comes two pages later, further on in the list of knights:

> . . . sir Pelleas that loved the lady Ettarde (and he had dyed
> for her sake, had nat bene one of the ladyes of the lake whos
> name was dame Nynyve; and she wedde sir Pelleas, and she
> saved hym ever aftir, that he was never slayne by her dayes;
> and he was a full noble knyght). . . . [1150]

And the last of these references is to Nynyve as one of the ladies in the ship which carries off the wounded Arthur:

> . . . Also there was dame Nynyve, the chyff lady of the laake, whych had wedded sir Pellyas, the good knyght; and thys lady had done muche for kynge Arthure. (And thys dame Nynyve wolde never suffir sir Pelleas to be in no place where he shulde be in daungere of hys lyff, and so he lyved unto the uttermuste of hys dayes with her in grete reste.) [1242]

As Professor Guerin has said, in *Le Morte Darthur* the happy marital relationship of Pelleas and Nynyve contrasts sharply with the relationships between men and women in Arthur's world;[44] but I think the happy love of Nynyve and Pelleas is only part of what interests Malory here. In her late appearances Nynyve always suggests a kind of "islands of the blessed" existence. She and the "chief lady of the lady of the lake" represent a realm where there is no tragedy: Nynyve saves Pelleas from death, and as long as she lives he will never be slain. The eighth book is about war between kin and friends, but in the last episode of the preceding tale we hear of Lancelot, the center of the fighting in the coming tragedy, promising the chief lady of the Lady of the Lake never to do battle against Sir Severause; and Severause, of whom we hear nowhere else, is a knight who wishes to fight giants and dragons, but not men. Soon Lancelot will be responsible for the deaths of some of those he loved best in the world; here, when he is near the Lady of the Lake, we see him for an instant pledging peace.

In the seventh tale there are the elements of tragedy, but no tragic results; this is a narrative whose last episode is about healing and whose first episode ends with the words "and all was forgyffyn." Nynyve and her lady epitomize all that is present in this tale but will vanish in the final one. Harmony, a peaceful love, a kind of immortality: not only do these things exist in the barely-glimpsed realm of the lake, but the realm in which they exist touches the Arthurian one. Nynyve cares about Arthur and his knights, and she

44. " 'The Tale of the Death of Arthur,' " p. 255.

enriches the harmonies of the seventh tale: she removes Guinevere's last difficulty in the first episode, and thanks to her the queen is excused; she is invoked, her knightly lover is present, at the making whole of Sir Urry in the last episode—and in that same last episode we learn that her chief lady has arranged harmony between two men, one of whom doesn't want to fight with any man.

What then is the function of Malory's last reference to Nynyve? Even as Arthur lies wounded she reminds us of the harmony that has been lost; reminds us of it both because we remember the earlier scenes at which she was present and because of the mention of Pelleas: the knight whom she keeps out of danger, and who avoids the fate of Arthur. In the last book Nynyve is a reminder of a time of happiness in a time of misery.

Again and again phrases and situations from the "Lancelot and Guinevere" echo in the last tale. We are always being reminded of a better time when things like these were done and said, but the result was different. As we read the eighth tale our memories of the seventh tale not only make the later events seem sadder by contrast to the events they recall, but also bewilder us: why do the characters, the plans, the loyalties that availed then not avail now? We never learn why the "great anger and unhap" comes at this particular point; why suddenly the suspension ends, and all the weaknesses of Arthurian civilization combine with one another (and with what are apparently chance occurrences) to produce disaster rather than surmountable difficulties. It is a change whose imaginative truth we recognize, but not a change we understand.

THE CAUSES

At the last meeting of Guinevere and Lancelot the queen says to her ladies:

> "Thorow thys same man and me hath all thys warre be wrought, and the deth of the moste nobelest knyghtes of the worlde; for thorow oure love that we have loved togydir is my moste noble lorde slayne. Therefore, sir Launcelot, wyte thou well I am sette in such a plyght to gete my soule hele. And yet I truste, thorow Goddis grace and thorow Hys Passion of Hys

woundis wyde, that aftir my deth I may have a syght of the blyssed face of Cryste Jesu, and on Doomesday to sytte on Hys ryght syde; for as synfull as ever I was, now ar seyntes in hevyn. And therefore, sir Launcelot, I requyre the and besech the hartily, for all the love that ever was betwyxt us, that thou never se me no more in the visayge. And I commaunde the, on Goddis behalff, that thou forsake my company. And to thy kyngedom loke thou turne agayne, and kepe well thy realme frome warre and wrake, for as well as I have loved the heretofore, myne harte woll nat serve now to se the; for thorow the and me ys the floure of kyngis and knyghtes destroyed. And therefore go thou to thy realme, and there take ye a wyff, and lyff with hir wyth joy and blys. And I pray the hartely to pray for me to the Everlastynge Lorde that I may amende my mysselyvyng." [1252]

"For thorow oure love that we have loved togydir is my moste noble lorde slayne. . . . For thorow the and me ys the floure of kyngis and knyghtes destroyed." Here is our rational explanation of the fall: the conflict of love and loyalty. Yet if Malory wants us to see this conflict as *the* cause rather than *a* cause, he has left us with a great many false clues, not all of which can be traced back to the tangle of stories he inherited from his predecessors, and none of which we can dismiss out of hand *merely* because it is inherited and seems to conflict with other explanations.

One more echo. As Vinaver points out, the speech I have just quoted is based on lines in the stanzaic *Morte*,[45] but, like other phrases here, the words "for all the love that ever was betwyxt us" are not in the corresponding section of the poem.[46] This is a phrase Malory had used some twenty pages earlier in the letter the dying Gawain writes to Lancelot: "Also, sir Launcelot, for all the love that ever was betwyxte us, make no taryyng, but com over the see in all the goodly haste that ye may . . ." (1231.24–26).[47] Here the echo

45. See Vinaver's note to *Works*, 1252.8–1253.27.

46. The closest thing to it is "For my loue now I thee pray" (3663). But the Malorian phrase does seem to be a remembrance of lines elsewhere in the poem. See 55, 72, 742, 1661, 1701, 1818, 2024, 2937.

47. The text of Gawain's letter is original with Malory.

draws attention to the parallel situations: both the queen and Gawain are bidding farewell to Lancelot and looking back on the ruin of the Round Table. And there is a similarity in reaction as well as in situation, for Gawain takes the blame for what has happened upon himself, saying to Arthur, just before he composes the letter: "And thorow me and my pryde ye have all thys shame and disease, for had that noble knyght, sir Launcelot, ben with you, as he was and wolde have ben, thys unhappy warre had never ben begunne . . ." (1230.24–27). So Guinevere, before she speaks to Lancelot, says to her ladies "Thorow thys same man and me hath all thys warre be wrought. . . ."

Guinevere's statement does not supercede Gawain's; in that earlier speech, which is one of the finest things in Malory, Gawain may be nobly myopic in looking only at his own failings, but he is certainly not mistaken. The parallelism of the two scenes creates symmetry of blame. Both Gawain and the queen see themselves as responsible. Both are right, but obviously neither is entirely right, since each leaves out the explanation given by the other. And of course Guinevere herself is not the last character to explain the tragedy. Lancelot, in a speech quoted earlier in this chapter, will say "by my defaute and myn orgule and my pryde . . . [Arthur and Guinevere] were bothe layed ful lowe . . ." (1256.33–34). Lancelot's explanation does not replace Guienvere's; hers does not replace Gawain's. The disasters are brought about through Gawain and his pride and they are brought about through Lancelot's "orgule and . . . pryde." In these last books of *Le Morte Darthur* causation is multiple and complex. Had Lancelot and Guinevere not loved, or not resumed their love, Arthur's civilization would not have fallen, and it is Guinevere's nobility and intelligence, not any kind of masochism, which allows her to see this. Yet it is also true that if Gawain had acted differently, if the adder had not been there, if Arthur, after the last battle, had left Mordred alone, the flower of kings and knights would not have been destroyed. Gawain, Lancelot, and Guinevere each take absolute responsibility for the disaster because each could have prevented it, not because each entirely caused it.

What does cause the tragedy? Is there a *tertium quid* to which we

can give a name? Here we must look carefully at the various causes
that are named, and at the way we, as readers, experience those
causes.

The May passage which opens Malory's last book is again a useful
starting point for discussion. As I have pointed out, that first paragraph plays upon our memories of the May encomium in the
seventh tale and upon the general expectations the topic raises by
suddenly telling us about destruction when we expected to hear
about love and flourishing. The rhetoric with which this paragraph
opens does not prepare us for that theme of destruction; but in one
sense the preceding tale clearly did. Aggravain was waiting at the
beginning and the end; the adultery continued; there were references to "off-stage" destruction (e.g. the death of Tristram). But
nothing made us expect destruction *right now*: the killings of good
knights *were* offstage; we grew used to happy or bittersweet endings
onstage. *O Deth, thou comest whan I had the leest in mynde*! Everyman
knows all men are mortal, and the reader of "The Tale of Lancelot and Guinevere" understands what the dangers to knights and
civilization are, but neither expects suddenly to face that annihila-
tion he knows is coming. In "The Tale of the Death of Arthur" we
first experience the destruction of the Round Table as something
sudden and overwhelming, rather than as the long-expected
consequence of certain failings of character.

If the first paragraph tells us only that in this particular May a
"grete angur and unhappe" "befelle" and did not end until the
flower of chivalry was destroyed—if, in other words, it suggests no
human agency or cause for the destruction—the second paragraph
does assign blame:

> And all was longe uppon two unhappy knyghtis whych were
> named sir Aggravayne and sir Mordred, that were brethirn
> unto sir Gawayne. For thys sir Aggravayne and sir Mordred
> had ever a prevy hate unto the quene, dame Gwenyver, and to
> sir Launcelot; and dayly and nyghtly they ever wacched
> uppon sir Launcelot. [1161.9–14]

"And all was longe uppon . . . sir Aggravayne and sir Mordred."
This line will cause us a great deal of trouble if we are determined to

find one basic cause and meaning for the fall of the Round Table. And the line cannot be dismissed;[48] it is clear Malory does want this strong initial emphasis upon the responsibility of Aggravain and Morded, for he stresses that responsibility not only in the second paragraph of the eighth tale, but in the *Explicit* of the seventh: "And bycause I have loste the very mater of Shevalere de Charyot I departe from the tale of sir Launcelot; and here I go unto the morte Arthur, and that caused sir Aggravayne."

This early emphasis upon Mordred—and especially upon Aggravain—is extremely important, and I shall have more to say of it below. But notice that even in these opening paragraphs of the "Morte" Malory gives us a second explanation of the tragedy—or at least a second attitude toward it—intertwined with the first. This second attitude is implicit in those words "hit befelle . . . a grete angur and unhappe . . . that stynted nat . . ." which present the destruction as an occurrence of unknown or at least impersonal causation rather than as a human action. It is also implicit in the word "unhappe" in the first paragraph and "unhappy" in the second. Malory is pointing to luck, fate, fortune, chance, rather than moral responsibility.

In her study, "Malory's Book of Balin," Laura Hibbard discusses

48. C. S. Lewis sees the fall of the Round Table as essentially the fulfillment of the Grail section prophecies. "They are, no doubt, worked out through a tangle of human motives . . . . Of course. The fulfilment of the prophecies about Oedipus came about through seemingly free agents obeying human motives. That is how prophecies are fulfilled in good stories . . ." ("The English Prose *Morte*," 20). But there is a difficulty here. The great *Oedipus* is, as it happens, a play rather than a story; we listen to characters, but not an authorial voice. There *could*, no doubt, be a good narrative version of *Oedipus*. But not one where the author begins by telling us the destruction of the Theban royal house was all caused by an unhappy king named Laius. In a story of prophecies being fulfilled, or a story of divided loyalties destroying a civilization, or a story with any other "real" cause underlying apparent causes, the author can and often should remain silent. This is itself mimesis; in life it is difficult to see the real cause beneath the apparent ones: let the reader have the same difficulty in art. But let the reader have the same difficulty for similar reasons. Lewis's analogy won't hold up because he looks only at the kinds of misleading evidence, not at the way the evidence is used. A reliable narrator who begins by giving us an erroneous interpretation is an imitation of paranoia, not of life.

the effective repetition of "unhappy" in the "Balin" and also in Lancelot's lament (i.e., 1249.12–29).[49] "Unhappy" and related words are in fact used at key moments throughout the eighth tale, and there is a cluster of them on the opening page: besides "angur and *unhappe*" and "two *unhappy* knightes," there are Gawain's words to Mordred, "ever unto all *unhappynes*, sir, ye woll graunte" and "so hyt myssefortuned sir Gawayne and all hys brethirne were in kynge Arthurs chambir," the words which introduce the first scene. (This last is a striking usage, since malice aforethought—or at least malice foreseeable—could easily account for what happens without any reference to *misfortune*).

The killing of Gareth is seen in terms of *misfortune*. "And so in thys russhynge and hurlynge, as sir Launcelot thrange here and there, hit *mysfortuned* hym to sle sir Gaherys and sir Gareth, the noble knight . . ." (1177.31–33). Some knights describe the killing to Arthur: "And as they were unarmed, he smote them and wyst nat whom he smote, and so *unhappely* they were slayne" (1183.24–26). Lancelot explains " . . . And alas, that ever I was so *unhappy* . . . that I had nat seyne sir Gareth and sir Gaherys!" (1189.20–21) and ten pages later, "And as Jesu be my helpe, and be my knyghthode, I slewe never sir Gareth nother hys brother be my wyllynge, but alas that ever they were unarmed that *unhappy* day!" (1199.25–28). Later, when Arthur's forces must oppose Lancelot's, the king laments, "Now alas . . . that *ever thys unhappy warre began*!" (1218.18–19), and later Gawain echoes this phrase even as he accepts the blame for what has happened: "And thorow me and my pryde ye have all thys shame and disease, for had that noble knyght, sir Launcelot, ben with you, as he was and wolde have ben, *thys unhappy warre had never ben begunne* . . ." (1230.24–27). Gawain informs Lancelot he received his death wound when "hit *mysfortuned* me to be smytten uppon the strooke that ye gaff me of olde . . ." (1232.4–5). After the adder's appearance has destroyed the truce between Mordred's forces and his own, Arthur cries, "Alas, this *unhappy* day!" (1235.28); still later, Lucan advises the king to leave Mordred alone" . . . for he ys *unhappy*. And yf ye passe this

49. "Malory's Book of Balin," *Medieval Studies in Memory of Gertrude Schoepperle Loomis*, ed. Roger Sherman Loomis (New York, 1927), 175–195, pp. 184–185.

unhappy day ye shall be ryght well revenged . . ." (1236.28–30). Finally, in the lament Hibbard mentions in her article, Lancelot says:

> ". . . And in an *unhappy* owre was I born that ever I shulde have that *myssehappe* to sle firste sir Gawayne, sir Gaherys, the good knyght, and myne owne frynde sir Gareth that was a full noble knyght. Now, alas, I may say I am *unhappy* that ever I shulde do thus. And yet, alas, myght I never have *hap* to sle that traytoure, sir Mordred!" [1249]

Words of the *unhappy-misfortune* group are not outstandingly numerous in the last tale (I have cited all occurrences except one at 1219. 10) but we hear them at critical moments. "Hap" and "fortune" are part of the texture of the work.

Part of the texture, but only part. As I have said, those opening paragraphs intertwine suggestions of fatality with the responsibility of Aggravain and Mordred, and it is time to look more closely at these characters and the use Malory makes of them.

The two are not equally prominent. Both Mordred and Aggravain are responsible for the attempt to trap Lancelot in the Queen's chamber but Aggravain is the more important conspirator. In that *Explicit* to the seventh tale, it is only Aggravain Malory mentions as causer of the ruin, and even earlier, at the beginning of the tale, he singled out "sir Aggravayne, sir Gawaynes brothir" (1045.20–21) among those who spoke of the love of Guinevere and Lancelot. Aggravain is the first to talk against the lovers in the opening scene of the "Morte" (1161.19–23), and Bors singles him out as the man to be wary of (1164.23). Aggravain and Mordred speak together in the entrapment itself, but it is only the former Lancelot addresses by name in this scene.[50] When the king assigns responsibility, Mordred is an appendage to his brother just as he was in the plot itself:[51]

---

50. Aggravain is also the more important of the two plotters in the corresponding sections of the *Stanzaic Morte* (ll. 1167–1863) and the French *Mort* (88 ff.).

51. Notice not only that Mordred is mentioned while Aggravain is addressed, but that Arthur omits *sir* when addressing Aggravain. As I have said before, this is rare in Malory, and suggests both that this is a moment of intense emotion and that Aggravain is more vividly present to Arthur's mind than is Mordred.

". . . wyte you well, my harte was never so hevy as hyt ys
now. And much more I am soryar for my good knyghtes losse
than for the losse of my fayre quene; for quenys I myght have
inow, but such a felyship of good knyghtes shall never be togydirs in no company. And now I dare sey," seyde knyge Arthur,
"there was never Crystyn kynge that ever hylde such a felyshyp
togydyrs. And alas, that ever sir Launcelot and I shulde be at
debate! A, Aggravayne, Aggravayne!" seyde the kynge,
"Jesu forgyff hit thy soule, for thyne evyll wyll that thou haddist
and sir Mordred, thy brothir, unto sir Launcelot hath caused
all this sorow." [1183–1184]

This speech is Malory's invention,[52] and is especially interesting
because of the point in the story where it occurs. When Arthur
learned of the attempt to trap the lovers he first marvelled at
Lancelot's prowess (a splendidly Malorian reaction) and then showed
more grief than anger (1174.12 ff.). What anger he did display
at that time was toward Lancelot and the queen; Arthur thought of
Aggravain as "a full good knyght" (1175.29). It is only now, when
he finds out Lancelot has killed Gaherys and Gareth that the king
speaks against Aggravain who of course died before the episode in
which Gaherys and Gareth were killed. Why does Malory have
Arthur denounce Aggravain at this point in the story?

The important thing here is the audience's reaction to Aggravain.
He is the first major character to die because of the mischief he
worked. Hoist on his own petard, of course; but there is more to it
than this. At the opening of the tale, recall, references to the responsibility of Aggravain and Mordred are combined with suggestions of fatality. Now one of the meanings of "unhappy," the key
word in those suggestions, is "causing misfortune or trouble (to
oneself or others); objectionable or miserable on that account"
(*OED*, s.v.l). "To oneself or others": Aggravain brings calamity to
both, and his early death separates the idea of causation from the
idea of control. There would have been no final disaster were it not
for Aggravain's evil; but he has a perfect alibi for every disaster in
the chain after the first one.

52. See Vinaver's note.

To hate a particular villain is one way to rationalize tragedy, and in the speech quoted above the king is trying to do just this. The disaster he is lamenting, the killing of Gareth, is the pivotal event in the fall of Arthur's civilization, and it is important that this is the event *no one* wanted to happen. It is a completely senseless event, but Arthur tries to make sense out of it by finding someone to blame, and vicariously the reader joins in the king's effort. But why does Malory have Arthur settle on Aggravain rather than, say, Lancelot or himself? Precisely because the reader *must* find this explanation emotionally unsatisfying. Aggravain, who will be mentioned only once more by Malory in a comparatively unimportant context (1197.26–27), who was never a particularly interesting villain, and who, being dead himself and only an indirect causer of Gareth's death, cannot be hated very passionately by the reader. To blame this man for the death of Gareth is logically different from saying Gareth died by "unhap" and misfortune; but emotionally there is not much to choose between the explanations.

Aggravain is unsatisfying as a villain. We cannot hate him with much conviction, and when we say he caused the ruin of the Round Table we understand that ruin only in the way we understand Ivan Ilych's death when we say it was caused by a domestic accident. On the other hand there is too great an emphasis upon Aggravain in the first part of this eighth tale for us to ignore him or look through him to more profound failures in more interesting characters. Malory usually means what he says: ". . . and here I go unto the morte Arthur, and that caused sir Aggravayne." This is not the only cause, but it is a cause, ineradicable and nonconvertible. The ruin is the fault of Aggravain, and of Gawain, and of Guinevere, and of Lancelot; it is also an unhap, a misfortuning. Malorian tragedy is multicentric: we understand all the parts, but not the whole.

Before saying more about the major events of the tragedy, I want to look at the background of those events. The handling of minor characters is significant. In the final tales of *Le Morte Darthur* there is no one supernumerary of greater complexity than the supernumeraries of the earlier tales, but now the minor characters are less homogeneous *en masse*. Largely because of an increased use of ragged edge and blueprint details, our eye is attracted from time to

time by some motion at the rear of the stage. There is now a complication of background action to complement and add to the
multiplicity of tragic causation.

Sometimes this new complication is a matter of one phrase. When,
in the "Poisoned Apple" episode, Bors says he will be the queen's
champion and argues for her innocence, Malory, but not his source,
adds that "somme were well pleased and some were nat" (1054).
More interesting is the last tale's eighteen line catalogue of the
knights who follow Lancelot (1170), which includes: ". . . Sir
Neroveus, sir Plenoryus (for thes two were knyghtes that sir Launcelot wan uppon a brydge, and therefore they wolde never be ayenst
hym) . . . sir Bellangere le Bewse that was sir Alysaundir le Or-
phelyne sone; bycause hys modir was Alys la Beale Pelleryn, and
she was kyn unto sir Launcelot, he hylde wyth hym. . . . Than
there felle to them, what of Northe Walys and of Cornwayle, for
sir Lamorakes sake and for sir Trystrames sake, to the numbir of
seven score knyghtes." Any one of the explanatory phrases might
add a particular thematic emphasis if it were the only such phrase
in the list. But the three explanations in one catalogue impress us
with the variety of honorable motives among these knights. Earlier
in the same part of the "Morte," and again in an original catalogue,[53] Malory names the knights who go to trap Lancelot and the
queen. After listing them, he says "So thes twelve knyghtes were
with sir Mordred and sir Aggravayne, and all they were of Scotlonde, other ellis of sir Gawaynes kynne, other well-wyllers to hys
brothir" (1164). The range of motives may be modest, but Malory
now wants us to know that it was a number of different things which
brought those knights together.

When the king prepares to lay siege to Joyous Garde, we are told
that "anone sir Launcelot harde thereof and purveyde hym of
many good knyghtes; for with hym helde many knyghtes, som for
hys owne sake and some for the quenys sake" (1186.32–33). The
alternative motive—for the queen's sake—is a notable addition
in light of Malory's handling of the "Poisoned Apple" episode,

53. See Vinaver's note. The French *Mort* says only that Aggravain was accom-
panied by "grant compaignie" of knights; the *Stanzaic Morte* gives their number
but does not name them.

for instance; there, typically, the queen's plight arouses far less
sympathy among the English knights than among their French
models. For a moment, and, it would appear, simply for the sake of
background complexity, Guinevere is allowed to have some drawing
power independent of her role as Arthur's wife and Lancelot's
lady. Some knights are sorry and some are glad when Arthur and
Lancelot are at debate (1178.17–19); many people support Mordred's revolt because they think life with Mordred is joy and bliss
and with Arthur war and strife (1228.34–1229.5); others draw to
the king, and say Mordred wars upon Arthur wrongly (1232.29–31);
those who love Lancelot support Mordred, and also many people
from London, Kent, Sussex, Surrey, Essex, Suffolk and Norfolk
(1233.5–10).[54] In the final parts of Arthur's reign, as in the earlier
parts, battles are settled by heroes rather than masses of anonymous
troops; Gawain dies of a blow from an unknown hand, but that
blow is struck "upon the wound *Lancelot* had dealt him." But the
setting is now more complex, and we have a sense of many motivations converging in the great ruin.

That sense of background movement strengthens our impression
of tragic multicentricity; the impression itself is created by the
changing emphases in the foreground. We are concerned with
Aggravain early in the eighth tale; but the final catastrophe, the
king's fight with Mordred, centers around a new group of dangers
and possibilities. Before this battle Gawain appears to Arthur in a
vision, and says to his uncle:

> ". . . Thus much hath gyvyn me leve God for to warne you
> of youre dethe: for and ye fyght as to-morne with sir Mordred,
> as ye bothe have assygned, doute ye nat ye shall be slayne, and
> the moste party of youre people on bothe partyes. And for the
> grete grace and goodnes that Allmyghty Jesu hath unto you,
> and for pyté of you and many mo other good men there shall
> be slayne, God hath sente me to you of Hys speciall grace to
> gyff you warnyng that in no wyse ye do batayle as to-morne,

54. Malory intends the reader to see a contemporary parallel to the composition of Mordred's army. See George R. Stewart, "English Geography in Malory's
'Morte D'Arthur,' " *MLR* 30 (1935), 204–09, esp. 208–09.

but that ye take a tretyse for a moneth-day. And proffir you
largely, so that to-morne ye put in a delay. For within a moneth
shall com sir Launcelot with all hys noble knyghtes, and
rescow you worshypfully, and sle sir Mordred and all that
ever wyll holde wyth hym." [1234.6–19]

Arthur takes this advice, and a treaty is arranged. A knight raises
his sword to kill an adder; the peace is broken; the two armies
fight, and no one is left alive but Arthur, Lucan, Bedwere, and
Mordred. The king sees Mordred and wants to continue the fight
but Lucan tries to dissuade him:

"Sir, latte hym be," seyde sir Lucan, "for he ys unhappy. And
yf ye passe this unhappy day ye shall be ryght well revenged.
And, good lord, remembre ye of your nyghtes dreme and what
the spyryte of sir Gawayne tolde you tonyght, and yet God of
Hys grete goodnes hath preserved you hyddirto. And for
Goddes sake, my lorde, leve of thys, for, blyssed be God, ye
have won the fylde: for yet we ben here three on lyve, and with
sir Mordred ys nat one on lyve. And therefore if ye leve of now,
thys wycked day of Desteny ys paste." [1236–1237]

But Arthur will not let Mordred escape him now and is mortally
wounded as he kills his son.

Although the events just described are not invented by Malory,
this whole episode is vital to our understanding of the eighth tale.
This is not mechanical translation. Lucan's speech, as Vinaver
points out, is Malory's addition to the narrative: obviously he is
interested in the prophecy motif, not just tolerant of it. But we see
most clearly how Malory makes the old episode his own by comparing the verse original of Gawain's advice to the king with the
Malorian version. This is Gawain's entire speech, starting with his
answer to Arthur's question about his companions, as it appears in
the stanzaic *Morte:*

> "Sertis, syr," he sayd A-gayne,
> "They byde in blysse ther I motte be.
>
> lordys they were And ladyes hende,
> Thys worldys lyffe that hanne for-lorne;

Whyle I was man on lyffe to lende,
A-gaynste her fone I faught hem forne;
now fynde I them my moste Frende:
They blysse the tyme that I was borne;
They Asked leve with me to wende
To mete with yow vpon thys morne.

A monthe day of trewse moste ye take
And than to batayle be ye bayne;
yow comethe to helpe lancelot du lake,
With many A man mykell of mayne:
To-morne the batayle ye moste for-sake
Or ellys, certis, ye shall be slayne."

[3206–3221][55]

In *Le Morte Darthur* Lancelot's rescue is described in more detail
("For within a moneth shall com sir Launcelot with all hys noble
knyghtes, and rescow you worshypfully, and sle sir Mordred and
all that ever wyll holde wyth hym"), and so is more substantial,
more fully there as a vision of the future. The divine source of
Gawain's message is also more explicitly and solemnly given (". . .
for the grete grace and goodnes that Allmyghty Jesu hath unto
you . . . God hath sente me to you of Hys speciall grace to gyff
you warnyng. . ."). The possibility of a happy ending is stronger
in Malory than it was in the poem: we can see what Lancelot will
do if the truce is obtained; Gawain is sent by God (there is no reason
to doubt the spirit's word) and while we don't know very much
about Malory's God, one would assume He does not send useless
recommendations.

This is not a tragedy in which a single flaw of character (or even
a single conjunction of flaws of characters) or one fateful event is
the root of destruction. Gawain has been killed already, but the
thing is not yet determined; a happy, "Lancelot and Guinevere"
ending is still possible. Lucan's speech suggests this possibility
even later: "And therefore, if ye leve of now, thys wycked day of
Desteny ys paste." When only four men are left alive the king re-

55. See also *La Mort*, 176.1–46. But here Malory seems to be working from the
poem.

jects Lucan's advice, crying "Now tyde me dethe, tyde me lyff . . .
now I se hym yondir alone, he shall never ascape myne hondes!
For at a bettir avayle shall I never have hym" (1237.5–7). It is
certainly possible (though I think mistaken) to detect a moral
flaw in Arthur here: excessive wrath, lack of regard for prophecies,
or something of the kind. But the essential point is that even if
Arthur dies in one sense because he is, e.g., wrathful, he dies in
another sense because an adder came out of a little heath bush and
stung a knight in the foot.[56] The early part of the eighth tale draws
our attention to Aggravain, a comparatively minor character, as
the cause of the coming disasters; the last episodes in Arthur's
career draw our attention to the chance appearance of a snake,
the king's hatred for Mordred, and Bedwere's love of a rich sword[57]

56. The adder story is found in the stanzaic poem, but probably was not in
Malory's French source. (See Vinaver's note to *Works*, 1235.20–29.) Here Malory
is choosing to follow one version of the story and rejecting another; this is not
mechanical translation. One might say that what matters is not the adder itself but
the mutual distrust which lets so small a thing start a battle. But this does not seem
to me an attractive reading. Why *shouldn't* the armies distrust one another? Why
shouldn't Arthur be suspicious of Mordred? More important, if we rationalize the
adder as representing "any little thing," we must conclude that the truce was
bound to fail. But if this is so, Gawain's message was useless and Malory's solemn
references to Christ and God in Gawain's speech were, to say the least, in rather
bad taste. To rationalize this scene is to emasculate it. If an adder hadn't happened
to be there, Arthur would have been rescued by Lancelot in a month's time.

57. That scene between Bedwere and Arthur before the barge comes to take
the king away is a significant one. When Lucan dies, Arthur says ". . . and I
myght lyve myseff, the dethe of sir Lucan wolde greve me evermore. But my tyme
passyth on faste . . ." (1238.30–31). Here Malory's king, like the Arthurs of the
other versions, is clearly dying. Notice, however, that after the second time Bedwere
tries to hide Excaliber Arthur says to him "But now go agayn lyghtly; for thy longe
taryynge puttith me in grete jouperté of my lyff, for I have takyn colde . . ." (1239.
31–33). This reference to Arthur's condition, which is not found in the source
versions, leads us to think the king's wound is not *necessarily* a mortal one—but the
delay Bedwere causes is aggravating the situation dangerously. Two pages later
Morgan la Fee says to the king, "A, my dere brothir! Why have ye taryed so
longe frome me? Alas, thys wounde on youre hede hath caught overmuch coulde!"
(1240.23–25). This is once again based on the poem, 11.3506–3509. As Lumiansky
shows in his "Arthur's Final Companions" and as I have said above, Malory
throughout this episode is careful to keep alive a reasonable doubt about what
happens to Arthur. What is to the point here, however, is that even in the king's

as causes of Arthur's death. Many things could have prevented the ruin, but no one thing made it inevitable: the fate of the Round Table is fixed only at the very last minute. There are morals aplenty to be found in this last book; but if we are to respond to that book's artistry rather than improve upon it we must take the whole range of those morals. Malory didn't want a Q.E.D. on his work.

Except for incest (an exception the Man of Law would no doubt have approved) Malory seems to include all the likely explanations for ruin in this last tale. At the beginning of Arthur's dream (the dream which ends after Gawain's appearance and counsels) there is the Wheel of Fortune motif:

> So uppon Trynyté Sunday at nyght kynge Arthure dremed a wondirfull dreme, and in hys dreme hym semed that he saw uppon a chafflet a chayre, and the chayre was faste to a whele, and thereuppon sate kynge Arthure in the rychest clothe of golde that myghte be made. And the kynge thought there was undir hym, farre from hym, an hydeous depe blak watir, and therein was all maner of serpentis and wormes and wylde bestis fowle and orryble. And suddeynly the kynge thought that the whyle turned up-so-downe, and he felle amonge the serpentis, and every beste toke hym by a lymme. [1233]

The Fortune-theme is not as central to Malory's eighth tale as it is to the *Mort Artu*. Yet it is not accurate to say, as Professor Vinaver does, that Malory shifts attention from this theme if by this one means he tries to avoid that theme as much as possible. Malory does indeed omit the explanation of the wheel symbol given in the French, but not many of his early readers would have failed to recognize the wheel for what it is; then too, Malory is never very fond of expounding symbolism. But more important here is one of Lancelot's speeches earlier in this same book:

> "Moste nobelyst Crysten realme, whom I have loved aboven all othir realmys! And in the I have gotyn a grete parte of my

---

very last scene his fate *may* be unfixed, the delay caused by Bedwere's greed *may* determine whether Arthur recovers or dies of the wound Mordred gave him. Not even that blow, rich in suggestions of myth and nightmare, makes the end inevitable.

worshyp, and now that I shall departe in thys wyse, truly me repentis that ever I cam in thys realme, that I shulde be thus shamefully banysshed, undeserved and causeles! But fortune ys so varyaunte, and the wheele so mutable, that there ys no constaunte abydynge. And that may be preved by many olde cronycles, as of noble Ector of Troy and Alysaunder, the myghty conquerroure, and many mo other: whan they were moste in her royalté, they alyght passyng lowe. . . ." [1201][58]

Along with much else, Malory adds the mention of Fortune to what he finds in the French version.[59] This does not mean he is emphasizing Fortune-tragedy *rather than* what Vinaver calls human tragedy; clearly Vinaver is right to emphasize the omission of Sagremor's speech on Fortune in the Malorian last battle.[60] But if Malory is concentrating on "human tragedy," he is not aiming at a *purely* ✓ human tragedy; his preference in causation is "more A than B," not "A rather than B."

Late in this eighth tale, when Arthur's forces are divided against Lancelot's, Mordred engages our attention. He too complicates things, and demands that we widen our understanding of the tragedy. If Aggravain was oddly mediocre for his role as the central

58. The opening of this, Lancelot's farewell to England, "Moste nobelyst Crysten realme," echoes his farewell to Guinevere when they are surprised together in her chamber. That earlier speech began "Moste nobelest Crysten quene. . . " (1116.13) and there too the phrase (indeed the entire speech) was original with Malory. (See Vinaver's note to *Works*, 1166.11–1167.6). The symmetry of phrasing reminds us of the symmetry of Lancelot's affections: the realm, in which he has won much of his worship, and the queen—but that symmetry of phrasing also reminds us that these affections now make conflicting claims upon the hero.

59. See Vinaver's note to *Works*, 1201.9–15 and *La Mort*, 123.

60. Though one might say that Malory's most striking omission in describing the last battle is the last battle itself. *La Mort le Roi Artu* describes the fighting in some detail and at length (180 ff.); even in the stanzaic poem it occupies thirty-five lines (3348 ff.). In *Le Morte Darthur*, after 1200 pages, after the catalogues and blueprint details and record-keeping, that last battle, in which the Round Table is destroyed and one hundred thousand men die, occupies only about fifteen lines (1235.30 ff.). " 'Jesu mercy!' seyde the kynge, 'where ar all my noble knyghtes becom? . . . ' " (1236.16–17). We share the king's bewilderment: the slaughter is almost total, and it all takes just a few sentences. This is what a battle is like when it is part of a "great anger and unhap," a nameless but felt design.

villain of the beginning, Mordred seems too dynamic to be the central villain of this last part. The forces of good are divided; if the meaning of events lies in those tragic flaws of the good characters which allow this division to occur, Mordred should be a mediocrity, dangerous only because his betters are divided against themselves. But Mordred is not Everychurl. He is *extraordinarily* evil. Malory is plainly shocked by Mordred's behavior, and particularly by the violation of family loyalty: ". . . and there [Mordred] seyde playnly that he wholde wedde her (*which was hys unclys wyff and hys fadirs wyff*) . . ." (1227.8–10). As I pointed out earlier, we hear this indignation particularly in Malory's repetition of *owne:* ". . . and so he thought to beate hys owne fadir fro hys own londys . . ." (1229.20–21); ". . . and there was sir Mordred redy awaytyng uppon hys londynge, to lette hys owne fadir to londe uppon the londe that he was kynge over" (1229.26–28).[61] Shocking as his behavior is, however, he is a fine knight in battle: "But ever kynge Arthure rode thorowoute the batayle of sir Mordred many tymys and ded full nobely, as a noble kynge shulde do, and at all tymes he faynted never. And sir Mordred ded hys devoure that day and put hymselffe in grete perell" (1236.1–5). The nightmare wounding of Arthur (Mordred's thrusting of himself up to the burr of the king's spear—a detail Malory found in neither the French nor the English version of the story)[62] also shows Mordred as a figure of

61. See also 1249.6–7 and the Bishop of Canterbury's speeeh, 1227.31–1228.7.

62. C. O. Parsons believes Malory borrowed this detail from *The Original Chronicle of Andrew Wyntoun*; see Vinaver's note to *Works*, 1237.16–18. The important thing, however, is that Malory *wants* this kind of detail enough to move away from his immediate Arthurian sources. Notice, by the way, that in departing from those usual sources here Malory leaves out a detail Dante found memorable. Arthur wounds Mordred; the French *Mort* adds "l'estoire dit que après l'estordre del glaive passa par mi la plaie uns rais de soleill si apertement que Girflet le vit, dont cil del païs distrent que ce avoit esté sygnes de corrouz de Nostre Seigneur" (190.56–60). ["The story says that after the glaive's stroke a sunbeam passed through the wound so clearly that Girflet saw it, of which those of the country said this had been a sign of Our Lord's anger."] In the *Inferno* Mordred is he "a cui fu rotto il petto e l'ombra / con esso un colpo per la man d'Artù"—"whose breast and shadow were pierced with a single blow from Arthur's hand" (XXXII.61–62; Sinclair translation). Dante wants the emphatic blow against evil, the "corrouz de Nostre Seigneur"; Malory prefers a detail suggesting that, in the time of ruin, the very weapon and

immense energy and resolve. Mordred does not simply fill a power vacuum; in evil and intensity, if not in intelligence, he is a Malorian Richard III. When good men quarrel among themselves they can expect to find evil men trying to exploit their division; but Mordred is too extraordinary a character to represent what's *bound* to happen in any situation. Like the adder, he suggests meanings, but remains irreducibly himself.[63]

The "human tragedy" of *Le Morte Darthur,* the interaction of the king, the queen, Lancelot, and Gawain, is what matters and what moves us most. But the "most important" part must be seen in the context of the rest: though the speeches of regret or self-recrimination by Lancelot, Guinevere, and Gawain are the most poignant thematic statements in the work, the other explanations of the fall are there because Malory wants them to be there. Things *misfortune,* characters and days are *unhappy;* Fortune's wheel turns. *Alas! Who may truste thys world?* says Lancelot at 1254.12: the sublunary is unstable; yet God sends Gawain to Arthur with a prophecy and a quite secular plan, which miscarries because an adder suddenly appears and stings a knight's foot. The king might still survive, but

---

blow that should assure Arthur's victory can be the means to his destruction. (Dante's debt to the *Mort* here is pointed out in Antonio Viscardi's "Arthurian Influences on Italian Literature from 1200 to 1500," *ALMA,* p. 423.)

63. Reiss views Mordred quite differently: "Just as Galahad was in a sense contained within Lancelot, so Mordred symbolizes a side of the king's character. Now that the realm is collapsing, Mordred is able to exist. A shadowy figure throughout the earlier tales, Mordred now comes into his own and exists as a challenge to Arthur. When chaos is unleashed, he appears as its symbolic representative as well as its unleasher" (*Sir Thomas Malory,* p. 183). Now Mordred does not "feel" like this kind of emanation; certainly he is more fully "there" than Galahad is. But I should also say that Reiss's reading, like all readings which emphasize Arthur's faults and culpability, comes up against the difficulty of Arthur's lack of tragic knowledge. At or near the end of their lives, Gawain, Lancelot, and Guinevere have speeches in which they take responsibility for what has happened—total responsibility, as it seems. Given this context, surely it is monstrous that Arthur, the most noble Christian king, should be killed by what is symbolically part of his own nature and do no more than *regret* being against Lancelot (1238.10–14) or say (hauntingly, but cryptically) to Bedwere, "Comforte thyselff . . . and do as well as thou mayste, for in me ys no truste for to truste in" (1240.31–35). The king's speeches of loss and sorrow in the last book are too poignant for us to accept this as Arthur's recognition that he is deeply to blame for the tragedy.

cannot bear to let Mordred escape him. And what of Bedwere and
the sword? Is it this knight's desire for a sword which "causes" the
king's death? Out of the corners of our eyes we see supernumeraries
taking sides and changing sides for a number of different reasons;
Aggravain, a comparatively minor character, seems the central
villain in the early part of the tale, Mordred is the central villain
at the end. In the "Tale of the Death of Arthur" as in the "Nun's
Priest's Tale" there are too many meanings for us to take the fruit
and leave the chaff.

In one sense a variety of explanations affects us much as the
absence of explanation does: the reader takes away from Malory's
last tale a sense of the sorrow at the loss which is far deeper and
clearer than his sense of the reason for that loss, or its lesson. It is
part of our emotional being rather than our understanding of
politics or ethics or religion which says "yes, of course" to the "Tale
of the Death of Arthur." *Le Morte Darthur* is in various ways unlike
the tragedies which now mean most to us. But in Malory's last
books, as in many of the great tragic works, we glimpse unnamed
patternings, mysterious interlacings, under the surface of the world
we know.

SHAME AND NOISE

When news of the quarrel between Lancelot and the king spreads
through Europe, the Pope orders Arthur to "take his quene agayne
and accorde with sir Launcelot" (1194.18–19). The lovers return;
and when Lancelot appears with Guinevere before the assembled
company, he delivers a long and for most modern readers a very
troublesome speech: dignified, respectful of both his king and
himself, beautifully modulated, and morally outrageous:

> So whan sir Launcelot saw the kynge and sir Gawayne, than
> he lad the quene by the arme, and than he kneled downe and
> the quene bothe. Wyte you well, than was there many a bolde
> knyght wyth kynge Arthur that wepte as tendirly as they had
> seyne all their kynne dede afore them!
> So the kynge sate stylle and seyde no worde. And whan sir
> Launcelot saw hys countenaunce he arose up and pulled up the
> quene with hym, and thus he seyde full knyghtly:

"My moste redouted kynge, ye shall undirstonde, by the Popis commaundemente and youres I have brought to you my lady the quene, as ryght requyryth. And if there be ony knyght, of what degré that ever he be off, except your person, that woll sey or dare say but that she ys trew and clene to you, I here myselff, sir Launcelot du Lake, woll make hit good uppon hys body that she ys a trew lady unto you.

"But, sir, lyars ye have lystened, and that hath caused grete debate betwyxte you and me. For tyme hath bene, my lorde Arthur, that ye were gretly pleased with me when I ded batayle for my lady, youre quene; and full well ye know, my moste noble kynge, that she hathe be put to grete wronge or thys tyme. And sytthyn hyt pleased you at many tymys that I shulde feyght for her, therefore mesemyth, my good lorde, I had more cause to rescow her from the fyer whan she sholde have ben brente for my sake.

"For they that tolde you tho talys were lyars, and so hit felle uppon them: for by lyklyhode, had nat the myght of God bene with me, I myght never have endured with fourtene knyghtes, and they armed and afore purposed, and I unarmed and nat purposed; for I was sente unto my lady, youre quyne, I wote nat for what cause, but I was nat so sone within the chambir dore but anone sir Aggravayne and sir Mordred called me traytoure and false recrayed knyght."

"Be my fayth, they called the ryght!" seyde sir Gawayne.

"My lorde, sir Gawayne," seyde sir Launcelot, "in their quarell they preved nat hemselff the beste, nother in the ryght." [1196–1197]

One's first impulse is to take this as Malory's condemnation of Lancelot through his own words: here is the noblest knight of the world reduced to lying, sophistry, blasphemy. Now there are other speeches like this in "The Death of Arthur,"[64] and one can read the human tragedy of the last tales as suitable to such a condemnation: this is what comes of forgetting the promise and perfection of the Grail quest, of being caught up again in this world unstable. Or

64. See, e.g., 1195.28–1196.4; 1201.9–21 (esp. 11–14); 1202.4–8; 1202.17–21.

rather, one can *try* to understand the tales in this way—for the thing does remain troublesome. That speech sounds so much like injured innocence, for one thing, but notice also that authorial "full knyghtly": the reader seems forced to take that description as ironic; yet such bitter irony (whether at the expense of knighthood or the expense of Lancelot) is just not Malorian. A more basic difficulty is the reader's attitude toward Lancelot himself. We may want a guilty Lancelot, but we also want a tragic hero with whom we can sympathize, and once we start thinking of this kind of speech as hypocritical, we soon lose all sympathy whatever. Lancelot is not at all uncomfortable about his lying and disingenuousness: he seems brazenly to accuse Arthur of inconsistency in praising him for rescuing Guinevere in the past yet being displeased with this last rescue—the different circumstances are apparently unimportant. God was with him; otherwise he could not have killed the knights in the queen's chamber. He seems ready to go on killing knight after knight to cover up a lie, and as far as one can tell it never matters to him in the least that it *is* a lie. If this is the best knight in the world, there is not much to regret in the destruction of the Round Table.

Putting aside the question of whether Lancelot's speech is defensible or not, we can say that it is classifiable. It makes sense—even, I think, the note of reproachfulness—if we see Lancelot as acting within a shame system rather than a guilt system. That is, what matters for Lancelot here is not the fact of his guilt or innocence of the adultery and his personal awareness of that fact, but the public recognition of the charge, the public machinery for making the charge good, and the way the public accusation and public "making good" affect his reputation and the queen's. For Lancelot the important values are not guilt and innocence but shame and honor. The usefulness of the shame-guilt distinction for an understanding of how Lancelot and other characters behave in *Le Morte Darthur* was first pointed out by D. S. Brewer in his edition of Malory's final tales,[65] and his insight is of fundamental importance.

65. *The Morte Darthur: Parts Seven and Eight,* "Introduction," part vi, pp. 23–35. See also the discussion of shame, appearance and reality in S. J. Miko's extremely interesting "Malory and the Chivalric Order," *Medium Aevum* 25 (1966): 211–230. My idea of the nature of shame in *Le Morte Darthur* is closer to Brewer's than to

It seems to me, in fact, that the distinction is even more basic than Professor Brewer considers it to be. It is Malory himself, not just his characters, for whom honor and shame are more real than innocence and guilt. *Le Morte Darthur* is *of* rather than *about* a shame ethos. When Malory describes Lancelot's speech as "full knightly" he is not being ironic.

For the author as for the character the *fact* of the lie does not really exist; or we might say it exists only in the ghostly way the mountain and valley of Perceval's island exist: it has no imaginative weight. The narrative style of *Le Morte Darthur*, as I have been describing it in this book, obviously works well with an emphasis on public recognition rather than private knowledge. Guilt may matter in Lancelot's world; in the imagined world of Sir Lancelot, where one's official, social identity is one's real identity, shame is more significant. Malory's style presents values and states as objectively demonstrable and palpable, existing on the same plane of reality as physical objects. It is what might be called the stylistic converse of this demonstrability of states and values that the state which is not demonstrated does not fully exist: shame matters, not guilt. The important thing is not one's own knowledge of what one has done (the inner life is not very significant in Malory), but public recognition of one's actions. Lancelot really is indignant. His observable behavior is what it always was, and he has passed the tests: what right do people have to make trouble? "Liars," for him, means almost "those who say what they cannot make good" rather than "those who say what is false." Strange as it may seem, he believes what he says here about the might of God. In the entrapment itself he exclaims, just before opening the door to fight his accusers, ". . . God deffende me frome such a shame! But, Jesu Cryste, be Thou my shylde and myne armoure" (1167.4–7).[66] He does not think at all about the morality of his presence in the queen's chamber; what matters is the attempt of Aggravain and the others to

---

Miko's, but I am more nearly in agreement with Miko than with Brewer on the relation of the author's attitudes to the characters's.

66. This passage is original with Malory, though I suspect there is a memory of Ephesians VI in it. Lancelot and the Red Crosse knight are protected by the same armor.

cause trouble about that presence: God would side with Lancelot rather than Aggravain, the stirrer up of strife.

When we think of Malory as a writer to whose imagination shame and honor were more vivid than guilt and innocence a good many things in *Le Morte Darthur* make more sense than they did before: things ranging from Malory's attitude toward the adultery of Lancelot and Guinevere to the paragraph to paragraph emphases of the narration. Inconsistencies remain, of course; here as elsewhere Malory's imagination recasts but does not reblend. Yet the reader will find that a shame-reading solves more puzzles than it creates. In this section I want to look at some of the ways in which Malory's shame-orientation manifests itself; but I should take a moment first to say a few things about the context of this shame/guilt contrast and its appropriateness for the study of a late medieval writer.

In literary criticism the shame/guilt distinction occurs most commonly when Homeric and post-Homeric values are being compared.[67] We have learned to see Homer as the poet of a shame-culture, and Aeschylus, his contemporaries, and successors as the poets (perhaps even the creators) of a guilt-culture, Generally speaking, there is a value judgment explicit or implicit in these contrasts: shame cultures are "primitive," guilt-cultures "more sophisticated";[68] the discovery of guilt, responsiveness to internal sanctions, is an advance in civilization. Is it not improbable then that Malory, living in a society well acquainted with the values of innocence and guilt, would respond more deeply to the primitive values of honor and shame? Not as improbable as it may seem, I think.

First, the shame-culture/guilt-culture distinction is not really like a quill/fountain pen distinction. It is obvious enough from a glance at any day's newspaper that "shame" and "honor" never become obsolete concepts. Classicists such as Snell and Dodds tell us not that shame and honor do not matter in post-Homeric writings but

67. See the first two chapters of E. R. Dodds, *The Greeks and the Irrational* (Berkeley and Los Angeles, 1951) and the first chapter of Bruno Snell, *Scenes from Greek Drama* (Berkeley and Los Angeles, 1964).

68. Snell, *Scenes from Greek Drama*, p. 11.

that new and sometimes competing values have been introduced. For any anthropologist, I believe, a guilt-culture is one in which internal sanctions matter more than external sanctions, rather than one in which shame and honor are entirely replaced by guilt and innocence.[69] Second, it is unnecessary to assume that because Christian thought stressed guilt and innocence all of medieval Christendom was a single guilt-culture. Honor can be more important than innocence even for those who have been "exposed" to the more advanced value and might know better; it is quite possible for ideas of guilt and innocence to exist, but not lodge as deeply or as widely in a society's imagination as its ideas of shame and honor. Even now a good many parts of Christendom are better described as shame-cultures than as guilt-cultures. Our fifteenth-century Englishman may seem rather out of place among samurai, Homeric, and Navaho warriors; but a twentieth-century village in Andalusia might also be called a shame-culture,[70] and in this setting Malory looks somewhat more at home. Perhaps the most important point to be made here, however, is that the terms "shame" and "guilt" are meaningful for psychological as well as anthropological description and classification.[71] All men—like all or most cultures—have both a

69. I think most contemporary anthropologists would also maintain that there are guilt elements in all shame-cultures. See, e.g., Philip K. Bock, *Modern Cultural Anthropology: An Introduction* (New York, 1969), p. 69.

70. For a study of honor in such a village, see Julian Pitt-Rivers, "Honour and Social Status," in *Honour and Shame: The Values of Mediterranean Society*, ed. J. G. Peristiany (London, 1966), pp. 19–77. Professor Brewer uses this volume, and particularly the Pitt-Rivers essay, as points of reference for his discussion of honor in Malory. The title of this book is of course quite relevant to what I am saying here. I might also point out, while on the subject of shame-orientation in a Christian society, that Eugene Vance has described *The Song of Roland* as the expression of a shame-culture. (*Reading the Song of Roland*, p. 36.) Despite the Christian context of the *Roland*, "respect for public opinion" is "the strongest moral force its characters know." In the terms I used before, there has been exposure to "higher" values, but those higher values have not really taken. We might also recall that the last word in *Beowulf* is *lofgeornost*, "most eager for praise."

71. Gerhart Piers, in Part I of the influential *Shame and Guilt: A Psychoanalytic and a Cultural Study* by Gerhart Piers and Milton B. Singer (New York, 1971 [originally published 1953])offers a post-Freudian description: "Whereas guilt is generated whenever a boundary (set by the superego) is touched or transgressed, shame oc-

sense of shame and a sense of guilt, and the relative strengths of the two will vary from individual to individual. Now assuming that (however much the psychologist may want to refine the anthropologist's understanding of the origins, dynamics and interrelationships of shame and guilt) both psychologist and anthropologist are referring to the same or closely related things when they use these terms, we may stress the variety of attitudes possible not only from culture to culture but also within a given culture. Saying that shame was more real, that it loomed larger in Malory's imagination than guilt, and that Malory was likely far less sensitive to guilt and innocence than, say, Chaucer, does not mean we see *Le Morte Darthur* as an inexplicable throwback to the Homeric age.[72]

Malory's sense of shame is not atavistic, but it is nonetheless remarkable. A stanza from Chaucer's *Troilus* placed next to a passage from *Le Morte Darthur* points up not only the Malorian concentration on shame but also the single minded gravity of that concentration:

> Pandare answerde, "Frend, thow maist, for me,
> Don as the list; but hadde ich it so hoote,
> And thyn estat, she sholde go with me,
> Though al this town cride on this thyng by note.
> I nolde sette at al that noys a grote!
> For whan men han wel cryd, than wol they rowne;
> Ek wonder last but nyne nyght nevere in towne. . . ."
>
> [4:582–88]

"My lorde, myne uncle, what woll ye do? Woll ye now turne agayne, now ye ar paste thys farre uppon youre journey? All the worlde woll speke of you vylany and shame."

"Now," seyde kynge Arthur, "wyte you well, sir Gawayne,

---

curs when a goal (presented by the ego ideal) is not being reached. It thus indicates a real 'shortcoming.' Guilt anxiety accompanies transgression; shame, failure" (p. 24). I am certainly not competent to evaluate this description (or Singer's critique of earlier anthropological work) but it does seem to me that for both Malory and his hero failure is indeed more real than transgression.

72. It would be useful to consider the relation between Malory's shame-orientation and his taste for English heroic poems.

I woll do as ye advyse me; and yet mesemyth," seyde kynge
Arthur, "hys fayre proffers were nat good to be reffused. . . ."

[1213]

Pandarus's advice may not be very good but, good or bad, it is
possible, discussable advice in *Troilus and Criseyde*. In the last book of
the *Morte Darthur* where the hero does in fact perform an action
somewhat like the one Pandarus proposes, the attitude Pandarus
advises is almost unimaginable. "Noise"—a word used frequently
in the early scenes of Malory's last tale[73]—*does* matter. Gawain's
argument is unanswerable; at least no one in Malory would think of
answering it with Pandarus's argument. As Lancelot says on
another occasion, "as for worldis shame, now Jesu deffende me!"
(1136.15)

In Sir Lancelot's world, there are no imagined holidays from
honor. But if one gives up such holidays in going from Chaucer to
Malory one also leaves guilt behind; or at least one leaves the word
behind. Thanks to the Chaucer *Concordance* it is easy to compare the
occurrences of *guilt* and *shame* in Chaucer and Malory, and the
results of such a comparison are striking. *Guilt, guilty, guiltless*, etc.
seem to be extremely rare in *Le Morte Darthur*. I have looked through
330 pages of Malory's text for occurrences of *shame* and related words
(*shamed, shamefully*, etc.) and of *guilt* and related words. In those
pages there are just three uses of *guilty* (1054.16; 1059,17; 1174.22)
to 135 occurrences of *shame* words.[74] The *Concordance* indicates that

73. E.g., 1163.2; 1163.17; 163.21; 1165.31; 1166.9; 1167.11; 1167.33; 1168.4.
74. These occurrences are:

In the "Gawain, Ywain, and Marhalt" section of "The Tale of King Arthur"
(pp. 157–80): 160.9; 164.9; 167.12; 170.30; 172.2; 172.20.

In the first twenty-one pages of "The Noble Tale of Sir Launcelot du Lake" (pp.
253–73): 258.18; 265.26; 269.23.

In the first forty-five pages of "The Tale of Sir Gareth of Orkney" (pp. 293–337):
299.4; 299.13; 301.24; 303.17; 303.35; 305.20; 305.37; 305.38; 306.3; 306.6;
307.24; 307.26; 308.23; 310.20; 311.4; 312.24; 312.31; 315.10; 315.15; 319.24;
319.26; 320.1; 320.9; 320.16; 320.21; 321.4; 322.13; 322.14; 322.18; 324.28;
324.29; 324.33; 325.24; 334.6; 334.7; 334.13; 336.23; 337.22.

In the "Round Table" section of "The Book of Sir Tristram de Lyones" (pp.
545–72): 546.35; 547.24; 549.15; 554.5; 557.34; 561.2; 563.31; 565.8.

In the "Sir Launcelot," "Sir Gawain," and "Sir Bors" sections of "The Tale of

Chaucer uses the word *guilt* thirty-nine times and *shame* 160 times: a ratio of about 1 : 4; if one counts occurrences not only of *shame* and *guilt* but of related words (*shame, shamed, shamefastness, shameful, shames, shameth, fore-shamed, ashamed; guilt, guiltless, guilts, guilty, giltif, a-gilt, a-gilte, a-giltest*) one finds 110 occurrences of *guilt* words, 200 of the *shame* group: a ratio of about 1 : 2.

Obviously one cannot quite assert that Chaucer and Malory distinguished between the words *shame* and *guilt* in exactly the way either Ruth Benedict or Piers and Singer do. In fact, a careful investigation of Chaucer's use of the two words would be a very valuable, though formidable project. It would also be good to have an analysis of semantically related terms (e.g., the positives to these negatives, such as *honor, worship, innocence, virtue, cleanness*; the words *abasshed, sinful, corrupt, disworship, culpable*). But at the moment I see no reason not to assume that both Chaucer and Malory distinguish between *guilt* and *shame* roughly as we do now, and that Malory's infrequent use of the word *guilt* can be traced to his lack of interest in the thing.

With word-counts one is talking about broad stylistic patterns; let me turn to some slight but illuminating changes in wording Malory makes in adapting an important scene from *La Queste del Saint Graal*: the interview in which Lancelot confesses to a hermit that he has "loved a quene unmesurably and oute of mesure longe" (897.16).

Just before the interview, Malory's Lancelot speaks bitterly of the

the Sankgreal" (pp. 925–75): 932.17; 948.34; 961.11; 961.16; 962.15; 970.1; 970.2; 972.11.

In the "Lancelot and Guinevere" (pp. 1045–1154): 1046.26; 1049.13; 1049.21; 1049.26; 1050.3; 1050.15; 1052.13; 1052.20; 1053.32; 1053.34; 1054.12; 1054.14; 1056.9; 1057.2; 1058.25; 1058.29; 1083.21; 1083.26; 1113.15; 1113.16; 1114.14; 1114.24; 1122.9; 1122.12; 1122.13; 1122.26; 1122.29; 1124.30; 1126.3; 1127.19; 1129.3; 1129.10; 1129.13; 1132.20; 1133.1; 1133.17; 1136.13; 1136.15; 1137.11; 1138.10; 1139.4; 1151.30.

In "The Morte Arthur Saunz Guerdon" (pp. 1161–1260): 1161.19; 1161.21; 1161.23; 1166.2; 1166.8; 1167.5; 1171.29; 1171.33; 1172.1; 1172.3; 1172.17; 1172.26; 1173.16; 1175.24; 1176.21; 1189.11; 1192.19; 1195.25; 1195.30; 1201.13; 1203.7; 1203.29; 1211.19; 1213.17; 1215.19; 1217.12; 1221.7; 1228.1; 1239.20; 1249.14.

failure in the quest his sinfulness has brought him. This speech is explicitly concerned with shame and honor in a way its source is not:

> Et lors comence un duel grant et merveilleux, et se clame chaitif dolent et dit: "Ha! Diex, or i pert mes pechiez et ma mauvese vie. Or voi je bien que ma chetivetez m'a confondu plus que nule autre chose. Car quant je me deusse amendeʀ, lors me destruit li anemis, qui m'a si tolue la veue que je ne pui veoir chose qui de par Dieu soit. Et ce n'est mie de merveillese je ne puis veoir cler: car des lors que je fui primes chevaliers ne fu il hore que je ne fusse coverz de teniebres de pechié mortel, car tout adés ai habité en luxure et en la vilté de cest monde plus que nus autres." [*La Queste*, 61–62]

[And then he begins a great and marvellous lament, and calls himself a miserable wretch and says: "Ah, God, now my sin and my wicked life appear! Now well I see that more than any other thing my wretchedness has undone me. For when I ought to have amended myself, then the fiend destroyed me, who so blinded me that I could see nothing that was of God. And it is no marvel that I cannot see clearly: for since I was first a knight, there has been no hour in which I was not covered by the shadows of deadly sin, for more than anyone else I have dwelled altogether in lust and in this world's vileness."]

And than he called hymselff a verry wrecch and moste unhappy of all knyghtes, and there he seyde,
"My synne and my wyckednes *hath brought me unto grete dishonoure!* For whan I sought worldly adventures for worldely desyres I ever encheved them and had the bettir in every place, and never was I discomfite in no quarell, were hit ryght were hit wronge. And now I take uppon me the adventures to seke of holy thynges, now I se and undirstonde that myne olde synne hyndryth *and shamyth me*, that I had no power to stirre nother speke whan the holy bloode appered before me." [895–896]

In itself, this increased emphasis on shame might be taken merely as Malory's characterization of Lancelot: a tone of worldliness even in his remarks about holy things. But Malory's hermit, as much the voice of God as his original, is also concerned with shame and worship. In the French the hermit is astonished to learn that the man seeking his help is Lancelot, "li hons ou monde de qui len disoit plus de bien" (63.10–11). Malory translates "de qui len disoit plus de bien" into "worldly worship," and that worship becomes not the reason for the holy man's astonishment, but the first of the things for which Lancelot should thank God:

> "Sir," seyde the ermyte, "ye ought to thanke God more than ony knyght lyvynge, for He hath caused you to have more worldly worship than ony knyght than ys now lyvynge. And for youre presumpcion to take uppon you in dedely synne for to be in Hys presence, where Hys fleyssh and Hys blood was, which caused you ye myght nat se hyt with youre worldely yen, for He woll nat appere where such synners bene but if hit be unto their grete hurte other unto their shame. And there is no knyght now lyvynge that ought to yelde God so grete thanke os ye, for He hath yeven you beauté, bownté, semelynes, and grete strengthe over all other knyghtes. And therefore ye ar the more beholdyn unto God than ony other man to love Hym and drede Hym, for youre strengthe and your manhode woll litill avayle you and God be agaynste you." [896–897]

The parable of the talents, which occurs at this point in the French, is omitted;[75] God's gifts to Lancelot now call for gratitude rather than investment, and indeed it is difficult to think of worship, now the most prominent of God's gifts, as a talent to be used.

Later in their conversation Lancelot tells the *Queste* hermit that he will live chastely, but cannot give up the life of chivalric adventure. The hermit rejoices to hear him say so, and tells him, "if you would leave the sin of the queen, I tell you truly that Our Lord would love you again and send you succour and look upon you with pity and give you power to achieve many things your sin

75. Though note that Malory's explication of what the voice said to Lancelot comes at 897.3 ff.

now keeps you from" (71.5–9). Malory changes the power to accomplish things to the reward for accomplishment—worship:

> "Sir, loke that your harte and your mowth accorde," seyde the good man, "and I shall ensure you ye shall have the more worship than ever ye had." [897.29–31]

The shift in emphasis is subtle but it is there; and there not just in the attitude of Malory's hero, but of Malory's work as a whole.

Another thing worth considering here is what might be called the argument from loose ends: a consideration, like the one in my discussion of the Perceval on the Island episode, of what kind of thing Malory is careless about when he is careless. The loose end I want to consider here is one pointed out by R. M. Lumiansky in his study of the seventh tale: the blood stains in the queen's bed.

This loose end—which as we will see in a moment, Professor Lumiansky regards as part of an ingenious bow—is found in the story of Meliagaunt, the most contemptible of Malory's villains. On coming into the queen's chamber, Meliagaunt discovers that her bed has been bloodied. He then accuses Guinevere of treason in the form of adultery with one of the wounded knights who lay in her chamber during the night. Technically, the queen is not guilty of the charge. But only technically: it was Lancelot, not one of those wounded knights who shared her bed, and the blood came from a deep cut in Lancelot's hand. After reprimanding him for opening the queen's bed without permission, Lancelot agrees to act as Guinevere's champion against Meliagaunt, and eventually fights and kills him. This section, "The Knight of the Cart," then closes with the words "And than the kynge and the quene made more of sir Launcelot, and more was he cherysshed than ever he was aforehande" (1140.11–13).

The problem is that bloodied bed. Don't the characters wonder whose blood it is and how it got there? Professor Lumiansky assumes that they *must* wonder about it, even though there is no evidence that they do:

> When told of Meleagant's charging the Queen with infidelity and of Lancelot's challenging Meleagant, Arthur says, "I am

aferde sir Mellyagaunce hath charged hymselff with a grete charge." Here Arthur is completely noncommittal about what presumably is uppermost in his mind—the bloodstained bed as evidence of the Queen's infidelity—and simply adds that Lancelot will almost certainly appear to defend the Queen.[76]

[At the end of "The Knight of the Cart"] Arthur has good reason to suspect the adultery, for though the Queen has been saved and the disturbance caused by Meleagant has been successfully quieted, the King has had absolutely no explanation for the bloodstained bed. Since he established that no one of the wounded knights was guilty, circumstances point straight toward Lancelot as the culprit.[77]

But we are left wondering why at the end of this episode Arthur is making *more* of Sir Lancelot than ever before, and why Malory is so silent about what is uppermost in the king's mind.

It seems to me that Malory's silence about the blood and stress on Arthur's gratitude make sense if we understand Malory, Arthur, and Lancelot to be concerned with the queen's shame rather than her guilt: we focus not on whether adultery was committed, but on whether the charge of treason can be made good. I do not think the non-resolution of the blood question is a literary strategy: it is simply a loose end—a kind of loose end that Chretien did not leave[78] and that neither Professor Lumiansky nor I would be likely

76. R. M. Lumiansky, " 'The Tale of Lancelot and Guenevere': Suspense," *Malory's Originality*, p. 227. f.

77. Ibid., p. 228.

78. See *Le Chevalier de la Charrete*, 11.4775–4784. I should point out that Malory himself ties up a comparable loose end with an original passage at the end of the "Poisoned Apple" section. See Vinaver's note to *Works*, 1059.11–19. The interpretation of Malory's interests which Professor Vinaver suggests in this note is quite unlike the one I am presenting in this section. I would guess that Malory included this explanation primarily because, as Vinaver also mentions, it introduced the Lady of the Lake into the narrative—and as I said earlier in this chapter, the motif of the Lady of the Lake as a bringer of peace is an important one in the last tales. In other words, I suspect the change was more the result of an opportunity seen than of a dissatisfaction felt. We should also notice that although the French *Mort* never makes the truth of the murder openly known, the stanzaic poem does (11. 1648 ff.); Malory does not discover a loose end—rather he changes one kind of bow for another.

to leave if we were writing this story. The question "what did
Arthur think about the bloody bed?" has much the same answer as
the question "what happens to the fool in *King Lear*?" : nothing;
the question may matter to us, but it did not matter to the author.[79]

   Malory's shame-orientation is important for our understanding
of the love of Lancelot and Guinevere and the kind of responsibility
those lovers have for the ruin in the eighth book. If we assume the
author must want us not to look at questions of shame but to look
through them to the real issues of guilt, we will see "and that caused
sir Agravain" as Malory being banal in interpreting his own work,
and most of the other causes I have discussed will seem fake columns
in the tragic edifice. If we see the tragedy primarily in terms of a
shame-ethos, Aggravain does really cause it: we view Lancelot and

79. See also Miko's discussion of this loose end, "Malory and the Chivalric
Order," p. 215. Let me suggest two other points in the story of Meliagaunt's accusation where a shame interpretation is useful. Lancelot's first reaction to the story
of Meliagaunt's discovery and accusation is fury at Meliagaunt's breach of eti-
quette in touching the queen's bed (1133.10–17); Meliagaunt has done "unwor-
shypfully and shamefully." The accuser then answers "Sir, I wote nat what ye
meane . . . but well I am sure there hath one of the hurte knyghtes layne with her
thys nyght" (1133.18–20). Now here, as with Lancelot's speech when he returns
Guinevere to Arthur, we see Malory's hero as either a peculiarly brazen hypocrite,
very stupid, or shame-oriented. Surely the third possibility is the most attractive.
If Meliagaunt does not understand what Lancelot means it is because he is a churl
as well as a coward.
   The wounded knights are "sore ashamed" when they see the blood discovered
by Meliagaunt (1133.1–2). What is likely to be our first assumption here—that
they are "ashamed" because they think the queen had committed adultery—may
well be right. But perhaps not. These knights are all willing to champion the
queen's cause after seeing the evidence as well as before seeing it, and Malory
doesn't suggest either that they have to struggle with their consciences or that they
continue to be willing to champion the queen *in spite of* the evidence they have seen.
When Malory says these knights are "ashamed," his emphasis, I suspect, is on
their embarrassment that the hated Meliagaunt has the queen "at suche avaunt-
age," rather than on the guilt that evidence points toward; their reaction may be
like that of a defense attorney when the prosecution introduces unexpected new
evidence. Perhaps the most curious manifestation of the shame ethos here is the
obliviousness of both Malory and his characters to the nature of the ancient motif at
the center of this episode. No one seems very interested in the fact that the queen is
innocent only through a technicality, that it is merely the letter of the law which
puts her "in the right." Lancelot could not be more single-willed defending Una's
chastity than he is defending Guinevere's innocence.

Guinevere as victims rather than culprits, their love as the occasion
and not the root of the anger and unhap. For Malory, I believe,
Lancelot's tragedy is not so much the tragedy of having caused as
of having failed to prevent disaster.

The love of Lancelot and Guinevere calls for a good deal of discussion, and I will be taking it up in the next section. Here I want
to conclude by looking at a structural pattern whose full importance
we don't feel until we realize the centrality of shame in *Le Morte
Darthur*. The pattern is the recurrent motif of noise.

Just before Lancelot dies, he summons his last companions, the
hermit and his remaining fellows, and speaking "wyth drery steven"
asks to be given the last rites. They tell him this is not necessary; he
will be "wel mended" in the morning. Lancelot replies, "My fayr
lordes . . . wyt you wel my careful body wyll into th'erthe. I have
warnyng more than now I wyl say. Therefore gyve me my ryghtes"
(1257). That "I have warnyng more than now I wyl say" is not in
the sources, and it is somehow very moving; if Lancelot dies as a
Christian man, he also dies as a Malorian knight, anxious to do
rather than talk about. "But he seyth but lytil, but he doth much
more," Arthur's praise of Torre in the first book (131.28–29) might
apply to any of the Round Table knights; most recently to the dying
Lucan (1238.5–26), and here to the greatest of those heroes even
when all that is left to do is to prepare for his own death and burial.
This laconism is the mark of Arthurian knighthood, and the thing
which destroys that knighthood is its opposite: an insistent noise,
a saying which cannot be ignored.

We are told, at the beginning of the seventh tale, that when
Lancelot and Guinevere resumed their love "many in the courte
spake of hit, and in especiall sir Aggravayne, sir Gawaynes brothir,
for he was ever opynne-mowthed" (1045.19–21).[80] Thus, although
Aggravain can in fact use the laconic style on occasion (" 'Lat us
deale!' seyde sir Aggravayne and sir Mordred" [1164.5]), Malory
makes us associate his destructive quality with an unchivalric gar-

80. In his note to this passage Vinaver suggests that "open-mouthed" came from
a misreading of the French. This seems to me possible, but the epithet is powerful
and right, however it got there.

rulousness. We find this same emphasis on unbearable noise and open speech in the first of the calamities of the eight tale:

> Sy hyt myssefortuned sir Gawayne and all hys brethirne were in kynge Arthurs chambir, and than sir Aggravayne *seyde thus opynly, and nat in no counceyle, that manye knyghtes myghte here.* . . .[81] [1161.15–18]

> But thus as they were togydir there cam sir Aggravayne and sir Mordred wyth twelve knyghtes with them of the Rounde Table, and they seyde *with grete cryyng and scaryng voyce,*
> "Thou traytoure, sir Launcelot, now ar thou takyn!"
> *And thus they cryed with a lowde voyce, that all the courte myght hyre hit.* [1165]

> But ever sir Aggravayne and sir Mordred cryed, "Traytour knyght, come oute of the quenys chambir! For wyte thou well thou arte besette so that thou shalt nat ascape."
> "A, Jesu mercy!" seyde sir Launcelot, "*thys shamefull cry and*

---

81. This passage, and especially the words "opynly, and nat in no counceyle," are particularly striking if we know the French *Mort*. There, on an earlier occasion, Aggravain had spoken to Arthur of the adultery in this way: "Sire, ge vos diroie une chose *a conseill,* se ge ne cuidoie que il vos en pesast. Et sachiez que ge le di por la vostre honte vengier.—Ma honte? fet li rois, va donc la chose si haut que ma honte i est?—Sire, fet Agravains, oïl, et ge vos dirai comment. *Lors le tret a une part et li dist a conseill . . .*" (*La Mort,* 6.7–13). ["Sire, I would tell you a thing *in counsel,* if I did not think it would grieve you. And know that I tell you it to avenge your shame." "My shame?" said the king. "Is it then so high a thing that my shame lies there?" "Sire, yes," said Agravain. "And I shall tell you how." *Then he drew him to one side and said to him in counsel. . . .*] In the French scene which corresponds to Malory's, Aggravain and his brothers are "parloient de cest chose *moult a estroit"* (85.40–41). The king draws near, Gawain tells Aggravain to keep quiet, and Aggravain says he will not. The king overhears this, and wants to know what Aggravain was speaking about so loudly. Arthur insists on knowing: Aggravain will not tell him, nor will the others; Arthur only extracts the information from Aggravain by taking up a sword and threatening to cut off his head if he doesn't speak. The French Aggravain, obviously, is far less open-mouthed than the Malorian one. The Aggravain of the *Stanzaic Morte* occupies a more-or-less intermediate position between the discreet French accuser and the reckless Malorian one. See 11.1672 ff.

noyse I may nat suffir, for better were deth at onys than thus to endure *thys payne*." [1166]

Pathetically, and hopelessly, Arthur tries to keep Gawain from hearing of his brothers' deaths (1183.15–18).[82] But of course Gawain does learn what has happened, and when he comes to take his revenge he uses speech as if it were a battering ram.

> . . . And so sir Gawayne made many men to blow uppon sir Launcelot, and so all at onys they called hym "false recrayed knyght."
>
> But whan sir Bors de Ganys, sir Ector de Marys and sir Lyonell harde thys outecry they called unto them sir Palomydes and sir Lavayne an sir Urré wyth many mo knyghtes of their bloode, and all they wente unto sir Launcelot and seyde thus:
>
> "My lorde, wyte you well we have grete scorne of the grete rebukis that we have harde sir Gawayne sey unto you; wherefore we pray you and charge you as ye woll have oure servyse, kepe us no lenger wythin thys wallis, for we lat you wete playnly we woll ryde into the fylde and do batayle wyth hem. . . ." [1190][83]

> Than hit befelle uppon a day that sir Gawayne came afore the gatis armed at all pecis, on a noble horse, with a greate speare in hys honde, and than *he cryed with a lowde voyce* and seyde,
>
> "Where arte thou now, thou false traytoure, sir Launcelot? Why holdyst thou thyselff within holys and wallys lyke a cowarde? Loke oute, thou false traytoure knyght, and here I shall revenge uppon thy body the dethe of my three brethirne!"
>
> And all thys langayge harde sir Launcelot every deale. Than hys kynne and hys knyghtes drew aboute hym, and all they seyde at onys unto sir Launcelot,

82. He does so in the *Stanzaic Morte* also, but not in the French. See Vinaver's note to *Works*, 1183.15–16.

83. Here again, and in the next passage quoted, Malory is following the English poem. See Vinaver's note to *Works*, 1187.15–1190.20.

"Sir, now muste you deffende you lyke a knyght, othir ellis
ye be shamed for ever, for now ye be called uppon treson, hit ys
tyme for you to styrre! For ye have slepte over longe, and
suffirde overmuche."

"So God me helpe," seyde sir Launcelot, "I am ryght hevy
at sir Gawaynes wordys, for now he chargith me with a grete
charge. And therefore I wote as well as ye I muste nedys deffende me, or ellis to be recreaunte." [1215][84]

In this eighth book Gawain pounds at Lancelot with words not
only before he can reach him with other weapons but when he is
past doing so:

. . . sir Gawayne sanke downe and sowned. And anone as he
ded awake he waved and foyned at sir Launcelot as he lay,
and seyde,

"Traytoure knyght, wyte thou well I am nat yet slayne.
Therefore com thou nere me and performe thys batayle to the
utteraunce!"

"I woll no more do than I have done," seyde sir Launcelot.
"For whan I se you on foote I woll do batayle uppon you all
the whyle I se you stande uppon youre feete; but to smyte a
wounded man that may nat stonde, God defende me from
such a shame!"

And than he turned hym and wente hys way towarde the
cité, and sir Gawayne evermore callyng hym "traytoure
knyght" and seyde,

"Traytoure knyght! Wyte thou well, sir Launcelot, whan I
am hole I shall do batayle with you agayne, for I shall never
leve the tylle the tone of us be slayne!" [1220–1221][85]

Except for Mordred's wounding of Arthur, the thunder of the
captains and the shouting are far more vivid than either the smells
or the sights of battle in this last tale. That high volume of sound—
sound which not only marks but brings about the ruin of Arthur's

84. See also 1218.27–1219.19.

85. In the *Stanzaic Morte*, which Malory is still following here, Gawain defies
Lancelot but does not continue to hurl charges at him (2914–2921).

kingdom—probably has a good deal to do with the mysterious poignancy of one bit of detail late in the work. After Lancelot's final interview with Guinevere all day and night he rides weeping through a forest; then he comes to the place where he will remain for the rest of his life: "And atte last he was warre of an ermytage and a chappel stode betwyxte two cliffes, and than he herde a lytel belle rynge to masse. And thyder he rode and alyght, and teyed his hors to the gate, and herd masse" (1254.2–6). Less than a page later, Bors too comes upon this chapel: "And so syr Bors herde a lytel belle knylle that range to masse . . ." (1254.28–29). Malory is working from the stanzaic poem here,[86] but one of his additions to the story is that *little* describing the bell. Not an astonishing epithet, but exactly right: after all the noise and shouting, the audibility of a *little* bell suggests the quiet of the life Lancelot and his fellows now take up.

Two of the most striking features of Malorian heroic speech, I have said, are knightly laconism and a liking for performative utterances. Both of these things are particularly significant as parts of the ideal destroyed in the last book. Destruction comes as noise, as shameful shouting and accusation. This shouting is in one sense the opposite of the knighthood it destroys; the heroic knight is the laconic knight, and if there were no noise there would be no ruin. On the other hand, speech is action: formally in the heroic performative utterance, effectively in the noise which destroys Arthur's world. "He seyth but lytil, but he doth much more"; the Malorian attitude is usually that garrulousness, jangling, babbling are bad because they are empty substitutes for action. But there is another and an opposite reason for knightly laconism: in a world of shame and worship, a public word has great power.[87]

"ALL THE LOVE THAT EVER WAS BETWIXT US": LANCELOT AND GUINEVERE, LANCELOT AND GAWAIN

Of the many things which contribute to the ruin of the Round Table, two especially interest and trouble us: the love of Lancelot

86. See Vinaver's notes to 1253.32–33 and the following pages.
87. See also Brewer's remarks, *The Morte Darthur: Parts Seven and Eight*, pp. 29–30.

and Guinevere and the relation of Lancelot to Gawain and Gareth; the human tragedies. We are troubled because Malory's presentation will not quite make sense; we are interested because these are obviously the most complex areas of responsibility and Malory associates them with one another. That phrase "all the love that ever was betwixt us" links Gawain's last communication to Lancelot with Guinevere's; both Lancelot and Gawain blame their pride for what has happened; these three noble characters are the only ones who take the blame for the disaster upon themselves.

There are difficulties here. Some of them grow out of our misconceptions, but others are Malory's own. He knows a number of ideas about love and loyalty: he knows the story of Arthur's fall; most deeply of all, he knows the sobriety and dignity of his own Lancelot —and he seems to feel all of these things must cohere, when they just do not. Sensing the problems in Malory's presentation, the critic may try to fly above them, and look for a broad ideational design. I prefer to move under them, and will spend most of my time seeking the real (if not the total) Malory at ground level. I want to look closely at the narrative presence of the two relationships, at how the reader actually experiences them. This, I think, ✓ is the level at which the important coherencies of Malory's presentation will be found.

Arthur's civilization falls because of adultery. But as Malory presents it, that adultery is not so much the disease organism as the point of infection. The relationship of Arthur, Guinevere, and Lancelot contains no poison; none of the three characters considers the infidelity in itself an important evil—nor, I think, does, Malory; at least not with any conviction. The love of Lancelot and Guinevere is, to change the image, an unprotected flank.[88]

The reader of the *Morte* will certainly be puzzled by Malory's treatment of the adultery. There are internal contradictions here traceable to differing attitudes in Malory's sources and for that

88. In *Le Morte Darthur* even more than in the source versions Lancelot is concerned about not having armor when he is trapped in the queen's chamber. This atypical focusing upon equipment is altogether appropriate: at this moment not only Lancelot but the whole civilization is unprotected against attack.

matter to differing attitudes in his society. He has not thought the whole thing out. Nonetheless, Malory's attitude is *fairly* consistent, and our basic difficulty is with the strangeness of that attitude. Malorian *gravitas* is quite foreign to most works condoning adultery; on the other hand, those books which do earnestly tell us the world is well lost for adulterous love present that love as a loyalty or a desire differing immensely from other loyalties and desires in kind or in degree. *Le Morte Darthur* fits into neither of these groups.

Here as elsewhere it is good to begin by comparing *Le Morte Darthur* with its French sources. It is also rather amusing to do so, for unexpectedly we discover that in one respect the treatment of adultery in Malory's last three books is closer to what we find in the French *Graal* than to *La Mort le Roi Artu*. For Malory, the cuckolding of Arthur is in itself not very important. His "Quest" condemns the love of Lancelot and Guinevere simply as lechery (859–99); nothing is said about adultery as an especially evil form of lechery, or about any betrayal of the king. In itself, this silence is quite consistent with the *Queste del Saint Graal*; but there the author seems to find the whole genus lechery so loathesome that the particular species is hardly worth discussing. Now in Malory's last tales there is much the same silence about the betrayed husband that we find in his "Quest." The lovers accept responsibility for the ruin that has come; they (especially Lancelot) achieve what tragic wisdom there is to be achieved; but it does not occur to either of them that the adultery in itself was an injury to the king. Malory himself does not think of Arthur as wronged; and here the English version is quite unlike the French in content as well as in spirit.

The king of *Le Morte Darthur* is not Lancelot's rival. Arthur is distinctly more interested in the preservation of the fellowship than he is in Guinevere. When Mordred tells him about Lancelot's escape from the queen's chamber, he is "sore amoved" that Guinevere must now be put to death but it is the breaking of the Round Table he mentions first (1174.12–18). Later, and more strikingly, he says, ". . . much more I am soryar for my good knyghtes losse than for the losse of my fayre quene; for quenys I mught have inow, but such a felyship of good knyghtes shall never be togydirs in no company" (1184.1–5). But the French king loves Guinevere passionately.

Rather than have her die a shameful and villainous death he would lose his whole kingdom. "For," he says, "I have never loved anything in the world as much as I have loved you and love you still" (79.40–41). When the pope commands him to take Guinevere back he is angry; he knows she has wronged him; "nonetheless, he loved the queen with so great a love . . . that he was easily won over [*vaincus*]" (117.16–20).

Earlier in the work, when he once suspects infidelity he must find out *la pure verité;* he will never be at ease until he does (53.57–59). (Indeed, much of the narrative suspense of *La Mort le Roi Artu* rises from the way either luck or prudence lulls the king's suspicions.) But Malory's king feels no need to find out *la pure verité;* he is able to live with "a deeming":

> For, as the Freynshe booke seyth, the kynge was full lothe that such a noyse shulde be uppon sir Launcelot and his quene; for the kynge had a demyng of hit, but he wold nat here thereoff, for sir Lancelot had done so much for hym and for the quene so many tymes that wyte you well the kynge loved hym passyngly well. [1163]

On the strength of this passage Malory's Arthur is sometimes thought of as a *roi fainéant*, a contemptible wittol, which he certainly is not. Nothing else we know about the character will support such a reading; but it is more to the point here that Malory changes not only the king's attitude toward adultery but, by omission, that of the society as a whole—or at least the attitude of its men of good will. In the French we have a perfectly familiar set of values. No man can endure this betrayal; as Morgan says, "il n'est pas rois ne hom qui tel honte suefre que l'en li face" (53.67–68). It is apparently the act itself which injures the cuckold, rather than public accusations. Thus, for instance, when the queen learns, *before* there has been any public charge of treason, that Lancelot wore a maiden's sleeve in a tournament, she says she has been tricked by the man for whose love she has dishonored the most valiant man in the world [*pour l'amour de lui avoie honni le plus preudome del monde!*] (33.23–27).[89]

89. See also, e.g., Bors's words at 90.90–92; the clash between Gawain and Arthur (and between two views of adultery) at 87.55–61; and the remarks of

In Malory, the admirable characters have no sense that the love of Lancelot and Guinevere is an injury to the king; the adultery is something to be used by men of evil will, an excuse for action more than a reason for it. We are told at the beginning of the seventh tale that many at court spoke of the love of Lancelot and Guinevere; but Aggravain and Mordred, the ones who want to do something about it, are watching the lovers because of "a prevy hate unto the quene, dame Gwenyver, and to sir Launcelot" (1161.12–13), and Malory's king understands this "real" motive perfectly well (1184.8–11). The nearest thing to a condemnation of the adultery by a sympathetic character is Bors's "Insomuch as ye were takyn with her, *whether ye ded ryght othir wronge,* hit ys now youre parte to holde wyth the quene, that she be nat slayne and put to a myschevous deth" (1171.30–32). And this parenthetical, oblique condemnation is oblique not because indirection gives it a greater sting, but because the issue raised does not matter deeply to Malory. The love of Lancelot and Guinevere is not as much like theft or fraud as like reckless driving which eventually ends in an accident. Disaster comes not from the thing itself, but from a particular combination of that thing and external circumstances: neither the reckless driver nor the Malorian adulterer experiences guilt or shame if there is no "accident." On the other hand, after a disaster both adulterer and driver feel deeply tainted, not because either entirely caused the unhap or accident ("to cause an accident" is a slightly odd phrase) but because either could have entirely prevented it:[90]

> "Thorow thys same man and me hath all thys warre be wrought, and the deth of the moste nobelest knyghtes of the worlde; for thorow oure love that we have loved togydir is my moste noble lorde slayne. Therefore, sir Launcelot, wyte thou well I am sette in suche a plyght to gete my soule hele. . . . for as well as I have loved the heretofore, myne harte woll nat serve now to se the; for thorow the and me ys the floure of kingis and knyghtes destroyed. . . ." [1252]

Guinevere and Lancelot on Arthur's willingness to take the queen back, 118.12–14 and 28–31.

90. This, as I've said, is the kind of responsibility we find throughout Malory's last book.

Adultery is not the same kind of sin in Malory as in the French *Mort;* in *Le Morte Darthur* the lovers are not felt to be guilty of betrayal but to be risking shame and disaster. What matters most in Malory, however, is not what we think about the issue of adultery, but how we see the adulterers in the narrative. And the essential thing is this. Lancelot the Lustful is a forpinéd ghost, the wispiest of doppelgängers; the plot condemns him to haunt the narrative, and Malory's sense of his warrior condemns him to insubstantiality. The Lancelot we see is Lancelot the noble knight.

In his fine speech of self-reproach, Lancelot explains his grieving to the hermit. That sorrow-making is not "for ony rejoysyng of synne":

> ". . . for whan I remember of hir beaulté and of hir noblesse, that was bothe wyth hyr kyng and wyth hyr, so whan I sawe his corps and hir corps so lye togyders, truly myn herte wold not serve to susteyne my careful body. Also whan I remembre me how by my defaute and myn orgule and my pryde that they were bothe layed ful lowe, that were pereles that ever was lyvyng of Cristen people, wyt you wel," sayd sir Launcelot, "this remembred, of their kyndenes and myn unkyndenes, sanke so to myn herte that I myght not susteyne myself."
>
> [1256]

Notice the movement of Lancelot's thought: from the queen herself to the queen and king together. It is often and truly said that Lancelot's is a tragedy of divided loyalties. However, those loyalties are divided not because there are two souls dwelling in Lancelot's breast, but because there are two horns to his dilemma. Basically he has one bicornuate loyalty, and it is that fundamental single loyalty Lancelot returns to in this speech. I think it is a sense of that same radical unity which makes Lancelot charge Arthur with inconsistency in the speech quoted at the beginning of the previous section. This singleness of loyalty is a vivid truth to Lancelot in the last tales, perhaps most notably in his story (which does not occur at this point in Malory's sources) of how he was knighted by Arthur and "done worship" by Guinevere on the same day; because of this he "ought of ryght ever to be in youre quarell and in my ladyes the quenys quarell" (1058.21–23).[91] Arthur too sees Lancelot's devotion (or acts of service) to himself and Guinevere as one thing. The king, as I have pointed out, did not want to hear of the adultery even though he had a deeming of it: "for sir Launcelot had done so much for hym and for the quene so many tymes that wyte you well the kynge loved hym passyngly well" (1163.23–25). A peculiar, Bloomsbury idea: the king is grateful to Lancelot for things Lancelot has done for the queen, so he would rather not look too closely at the possibility of Lancelot's adultery with the queen. But of course what the sentence really tells us is that for Arthur as for Lancelot, the division into what is for the king's sake and what is for the queen's is superficial. Gawain also speaks of the king and queen together when he begins to describe the debts of gratitude owed to Lancelot: "Also, brothir, sir Aggravayne . . . ye muste remembir how oftyntymes sir Launcelot hath rescowed the kynge and the quene. . . . " (1162.6–8), and Malory himself presents them as a pair rejoicing in Lancelot's return at the opening of the seventh tale, and thanking him at the conclusion of the "Knight of the Cart" episode.

It is significant that in the final tales both Lancelot himself and other characters speak of this knight's loyalty to king and queen—his loyalty as it existed before the entrapment—as a single thing. Yet the passages I have just cited would not count for much—might, in a different kind of writer, even be taken as ironic—if the passion of Lancelot and the queen (and particularly Lancelot's passion *for* the queen) were real to us; but it is not. Consider just what one does see of the lovers as lovers. In the early tales that love is a thing referred to, but rarely observed. There, as Professor Reiss says, Guinevere is "merely the consort of Arthur and the queen who appears briefly at several points."[92] It is in the seventh tale (and

91. See also 1166.13 ff. Notice the words "in ryght and in wronge" here. This formula occurs a number of times in this last book. Malory *may* want us to respond by thinking "yes, that's the trouble," but I'm not sure that he does. In at least some English romances the character who says he will fight for someone "in right and in wrong" seems to be pledging a noble loyalty rather than revealing moral insensitivity. See Tristram's pledge (*Works*, 391.23–33) and *Sir Degrevant*, 553ff.: ". . . I shall faythfully fyghte / Bathe in wrang and in righte, / With sqwyere and als with knyghte . . . ."

92. *Sir Thomas Malory*, p. 160.

the entrapment scene in the eighth) that we do most of our observing
of the lovers together and in any case it is the picture of love as it
existed between Lancelot's return from the quest and the killing of
Aggravain we remember most clearly as we read of the calamities.
What is it we see?

In his commentary on the "Tale of Lancelot and Guinevere"
Professor Reiss says: "Now the love between Lancelot and Guinevere is explicitly revealed in all its physical desire. It is no longer
manifested as loyalty or courtesy; now it is desire, even lust; and as
such it will be the efficient cause of the final conflict and the destruction of the Round Table."[93] The seventh tale begins well if
we are looking for such an explicit revelation: ". . . and so they
loved togydirs more hotter than they dud toforehonde, and had
many such prevy draughtis togydir that many in the courte spake of
hit . . ." (1045.17–20). The language is strong, and of course the
line is particularly important because it comes on the very first page
of the tale. But once Malory has introduced the idea of lust he returns to it only occasionally. In fact, as I will show later, he begins
to modify our impression the moment he creates it. This opening is
ominous: the knight and queen love "more hotter" than before and
many speak of it; but it is worth remembering that in the French
Lancelot is not only more reckless than before at this point (4.5–18)
but grows still more reckless and more passionate as the story goes
on.[94] Once Malory has set up the situation in which Aggravain is
lying in wait and many in the court are talking about the love of the
knight and queen, the erotic passion of the lovers, and particularly
Lancelot's passion, is for the most part off stage, a *datum*. It is the
thing which explains, e.g., why this knight is trying to please this
lady, rather than an emotion we observe directly. Although Lancelot is sometimes exasperated, the passion most strongly present in
him is the passion to serve well, as a loyal knight should serve.

As a narrative presence, his love is most often a chivalric obligation. When the queen has been captured by Meliagaunt, she gives
her ring to a child of her chamber, saying "Now go thou . . . and
beare thys rynge unto sir Launcelot du Laake, and pray hym as he
lovythe me that he woll se me and rescow me, if ever he woll have

93. Ibid., p. 159.
94. See, for instance, 85.33–39.

joy of me . . . " (1123.34–1124.2). Lancelot responds to the message as a loyal and worshipful knight:

> "Alas!" seyde sir Launcelot, "now am I shamed for ever, onles that I may rescow that noble lady frome dishonour!" Than egirly he asked hys armys. [1124.30–32]

Change the word *lady* to *king*, and perhaps substitute *shame* or *a rebuke* for *dishonour*, and Lancelot might use the same speech on hearing that Arthur had been captured. The knight is concerned with the honor of his lord or mistress, but he is concerned with his own honor as well. The proper adjective for Guinevere is *noble*, just as it would have been for Arthur.

The central exchange between Lancelot and Guinevere is in the entrapment scene and here too the emphasis is on nobility of conduct. Notice first what Malory has his hero say to Bors as he sets out for the queen's chamber. In the stanzaic *Morte* Lancelot had answered the advice to stay by saying he would go to his lady "Som new tythandes for to lythe" and would not stay long (1784–1791); the French hero was "moult liez" when he saw the messenger bringing Guinevere's summons; when Bors tried to dissuade him, he just insisted that he would indeed go (89.24–34). Malory's hero, like the poem's, will go and "make no taryynge";[95] when Bors continues to object, he adds, "Fayre neveawe . . . I mervayle me much why ye say thus, sytthyn the quene hath sente for me. And wyte you well, *I woll nat be so much a cowarde*, but she shall undirstonde I woll se her good grace" (1164.34–1165.2). The emphasis is not upon Lancelot's desire to go to the queen's chamber, but upon his duty to go and his dread of seeming a coward—unknightly, rather than unloving—if he does not. It is Lancelot's heroism which Malory points to in the lines following this conversation: not any betrayal of Arthur, not even the contingent risks to fellowship, kin, and indeed the queen herself, but the immediate physical danger to himself: "So sir Launcelot departed and toke hys swerde undir hys arme, and so he walked in hys mantell, that noble knyght, and put hymselff in grete jouparté." (1165.5–7).[96] Lancelot's fault here is more like Byrhtnoth's *ofermod* than lechery.

---

95. Malory's phrasing is echoed in Gawain's letter to Lancelot, 1231.25.
96. This seems to be based on lines 1792–1799 of the *Stanzaic Morte*. But the

The next change is more striking. Both the source versions tell us that when Lancelot arrives the lovers go to bed. But Malory writes, "the quene and sir Launcelot were togydirs. And whether they were abed other at other maner of disportes, me lyste nat thereof make no mencion, for love that tyme was nat as love ys nowadayes" (1165.-11–13). This is not "desire, even lust" but the ideal love of king Arthur's time. For Malory and his heroes, feminine courtliness is merely quirkiness; and when he comes upon stories where Guinevere makes it difficult for Lancelot to win worship, Malory tends to be either far less interested in or far less sympathetic to the queen than are the French romancers. But here, where love is really a form ✓ of heroism, his queen is splendid:

> "And therefore, myne owne lady, recomforte youreselff, whatsomever com of me, that ye go with sir Bors, my nevew, and sir Urré and they all woll do you all the plesure that they may, and ye shall lyve lyke a quene uppon my londis."
>
> "Nay, sir Launcelot, nay!" seyde the quene. "Wyte thou well that I woll nat lyve longe aftir thy dayes. But and ye be slayne I woll take my dethe as mekely as ever ded marter take hys dethe for Jesu Crystes sake."
>
> "Well, madame," seyde sir Launcelot, "syth hit ys so that the day ys com that oure love muste departe, wyte you well I shall selle my lyff as dere as I may. And a thousandfolde," seyde sir Launcelot, "I am more hevyar for you than for myselff! And now I had levir than to be lorde of all Crystendom that I had sure armour uppon me, that men myght speke of my dedys or ever I were slayne."
>
> "Truly," seyde the quene, "and hit myght please God, I wolde that they wolde take me and sle me and suffir you to ascape." [1166–1167][97]

I have spoken of Lancelot and *ofermod*. This part of *Le Morte Darthur* does remind me of the *Battle of Maldon;* most strikingly when, a few

---

heroism there is of a much more swaggering kind: "There was no man vndyr the mone / he wende with harme durste hym haffe soughte." The poem emphasizes the confidence, but not the risk.

97. This exchange is original with Malory. See Vinaver's note to *Works,* 1166.11–1167.6.

pages after this, Lancelot's followers vow to stand by him: "Sir,"
seyde sir Bors, "all ys wellcom that God sendyth us, and as we have
takyn much weale with you and much worshyp, we woll take the
woo with you as we have takyn the weale" (1169.24–26). The
splendor of the heroic world, the nobility of the last-ditch effort, is
available to Malory's imagination in a way sensibility is not, and
here the queen can share in that splendor. We are watching
Lancelot and Guinevere as they are caught in a snare, but we are
not thinking of it as the snare of lust.

Both artistically and personally, Guinevere is at her greatest in
that entrapment scene. Malory can make her majestic there—and
by *can* I mean both has the kind of imagination required to do so
and can afford to do so. This second consideration was I think an
important one for Malory as he wrote the seventh tale. Much of
what we see of the queen there makes better sense if she is thought
of not as a psychologically consistent portrait but as a foil for
Lancelot.

It is difficult to serve Guinevere. The seventh tale begins with
Malory's statement that after the Grail quest Lancelot began to
resort to the queen again and many spoke of it.[98] But as the reader
moves to the first episode proper, he finds the lovers engaged in a long
quarrel (1045.30–1047.11),[99] and both the issues and the atmosphere

98. Lancelot himself reminds Guinevere, both here, near the beginning of the
seventh tale (1045.30–1046.27) and again near the conclusion of the eighth
(1253.7–19) that he might have succeeded in the Grail quest were it not for their
love. But we must not be too quick to understand the force of these references.
In these speeches the prominent values are shame and honor. Though Lancelot
says the high service of the Grail may not be lightly forgotten, for him and for
Malory the thing lost is essentially eminence, worship, rather than sanctity—less
a Beatrice or an Una than a Christianized Briseis. "I saw in that my queste as
much as ever saw ony synfull man lyvyng, and so was hit tolde me. . . . I had sene
as grete mysteryes as ever saw my sonne sir Galahad, Percivale, other sir Bors
. . . . [I]f I had done so . . . I had passed all the knyghtes that ever were in the
Sankgreall excepte syr Galahad, my sone." Lancelot does not feel tainted or stained
by lust; in neither passage is he exactly regretting his failure in itself; rather, he is
indignant that his sacrifice of worship is not being properly valued.

99. There is no source for this dialogue in the *Mort Artu* and the corresponding
passage in the English poem (11.65–80) is far shorter. Malory gives his readers a
bitterer first interview between Lancelot and Guinevere than his sources do.

of that quarrel modify the impression created by the datum. It was explained that the two loved "more hotter than they dud tofore-honde," and many in the court spoke of this; but the quarrel begins when Guinevere says to Lancelot "I se and fele dayly that youre love begynnyth to slake" (1045.32–33). He explains his conduct: his labor in the high service of the Grail "may nat be yet lyghtly for-gotyn" (1046.12–13); he is also trying to avoid the "shame and sclaundir" which their bold conduct might produce (1046.25–27). *contradicts* What we see of Lancelot as lover is quite unlike what we were told of him; he "forgate the promyse and the perfeccion that he made in the queste," but a page later he says his high service may not yet be lightly forgotten. The lovers's conduct becomes a topic of conversa-tion, but immediately both the author and the character tell us Lancelot is keeping away from the queen in order to stop that talk-ing. Guinevere is not an appealing character here, but her very unpleasantness makes Lancelot more admirable. The hero's reck-less, overwhelming passion is a premise of the story which we accept but which neither we nor Malory believe. Lancelot is prudent, loyal, and long-suffering. We believe he serves the queen because he is a noble and faithful knight, not because her presence brings him great pleasure.[100]

As the seventh tale opens, then, the lovers are sharply contrasted and the Lancelot we see and hear is long-suffering rather than lustful. We are vividly aware of that endurance at the end of the next episode (" 'Thys ys nat the firste tyme,' seyde sir Launcelot, 'that ye have ben displese with me causeles. But, madame, ever I muste suffir you, but what sorow that I endure, ye take no forse' " [1098.5–8]), and of course the story of the Fair Maid of Astolat shows us both the queen's jealousy and her regal inconsistency. But once the initial contrast between the lovers has been vividly and

100. The opening quarrel scene is the only one in the "Poisoned Apple" section where the lovers are alone together; in the later part of the episode, it is the unity of his obligation to king and queen which Lancelot stresses (1058.21–25). The queen then weeps for sorrow "that he had done to her so grete kyndenes where she shewed hym unkyndenese" (1058.36–1059.2); her emotion is very like what Arthur will feel as he thinks of Lancelot in the next tale (1192.20–33), and her wording is recalled when Lancelot contemplates the dead king and queen together, and remembers "their kyndenes and myn unkyndenes" (1256.36–37).

firmly made, Malory has little need for the nearly hysterical Guinevere of the opening.

One notices that the beginning of the second section of "Lancelot
and Guinevere" presents a more reasonable queen than did the
opening of the first section. In this scene, as in the earlier one, the
lovers are quarreling (1065.31–1066.18). Lancelot, as Lumiansky
says, "is here sharply ironic with the Queen; and she is unpleasantly
formal with him."[101] And this quarrel too is about discretion. But
there is a difference: now both lovers are concerned with being
discreet. Guinevere continues to seem none too pleasant, but she is
not simply jealous and irresponsible; tardily or not, she is concerned
with their reputations and with Lancelot's safety.[102] This combination of reasonableness of content and imperiousness of tone appears
again when the queen instructs Lancelot to make himself known to
his kinsmen and to do his best "that men may speke you worshyp"
in the "Great Tournament" section (1103.14–24), and her concern
with her lover's worship is more warmly expressed—perhaps significantly, when Lancelot is not present to hear the praise—in the
"Knight of the Cart" (1127.10–20).

That "Knight of the Cart" section is the one in which we most
clearly see the love of Lancelot and Guinevere as love. But even here
love is present in the narrative more as a modulation of chivalric
service than as a contrasting area of experience. It is almost all
summary: "they made their complayntes to othir of many dyverce
thyngis" (1131.11–12); the queen says she is as fain as Lancelot that
he might come to her. Upon entering the chamber, Lancelot goes to
bed with the queen and takes his pleasance and his liking until
daybreak; he sleeps not, but watches. This is quite different not
only from, say, Chretien's version of the episode, but from such a
tactile Malorian scene as

> And so there was ordayned grete cowchis and theron fethir
> beddis, and there he leyde hym downe to slepe. And within a

101. " 'Lancelot and Guenevere,' " *Malory's Originality*, p. 220. See Lumiansky's
discussion of these passages.

102. See also 1129.1–21, where the lovers once more argue about avoiding
"shameful noise." (There, however, the danger is somewhat different.)

whyle came dame Lyonesse wrapped in a mantell furred with ermyne, and leyde hir downe by the sydys of sir Gareth. And therewithall he began to clyppe hir and to kysse hir. [333.18–23]

The Lancelot-Guinevere love scene emphasizes what the knight does and endures for the sake of love rather than the love in itself:

And than he sette hys hondis uppon the barrys of iron and pulled at them with suche a myght that he braste hem clene oute of the stone wallys. And therewithall one of the barres of iron kutte the brawne of hys hondys thorowoute to the bone. And than he lepe into the chambir to the quene. [1131.21–25][103]

We may of course say it is Lancelot's passion which is shown when he takes "no force" of his wound and he goes to bed with the queen, but by this point in *Le Morte Darthur* Lancelot's might, suffering, and endurance are far more real to our imaginations than his erotic passion; we respond to the scene as another example of Lancelot being resourceful, strong, and enduring rather than as an extraordinary action only love could inspire.

At the beginning of the "Knight of the Cart" comes Malory's illogical and very moving "vertuous love" passage. It doesn't make sense; its unity, its poignancy, come from the earnestness of purpose which somehow shows through the murk. There, as in the other "in those days" passages, I suspect that Malory begins with the feeling of the lost greatness of Arthur's age and then looks for an idea, a specific change, around which that feeling may crystallize. Most of the serious ideas he knows about love, the ideas whose "tone" harmonizes with the grave sobriety of his hero, do not apply very well to the story of the lovers, and the result here is neither profundity nor irony but confusion. That confusion is felt not only in

103. Notice also that Malory adds to his version five lines on the practical details of getting to the queen's window (1131.6–10) and that the tending of Lancelot's wound by Lavayne—which, of course, is also original with Malory—links this adventure with Lancelot's recent nonamatory noble deeds. (See 1073 ff.; 1085–1086; 1105–1106).

his famous discussion of love, but also in the presentation of love within the narrative. Probably Malory thought at various moments that he was pointing to various morals about love, and I think he may also have been uneasily aware that those ideas did not fit together very well. But Lancelot is Malory's gyroscope; no matter what difficulties ideas may cause him, he has so strong a sense of his hero's dignity, of the kind of thing this character (that is, this quintessential knight) would do and would not do, the kind of attitude it is possible to take toward such a hero and the kind of attitude it is not possible to take, that the thing does cohere and the inconsistencies don't really matter: there is a singleness of tone created which is more important than the peculiarities of doctrine. We are told Lancelot forgets his promise and begins to act recklessly, we infer that he is lustful; none of this has any dramatic reality. Disaster will come when the lovers are put to a rebuke and a shame; but the two are reckless only as a *datum*, and they argue at some length about how to prevent such a disaster. Lancelot the lover is Lancelot the knight, and the tragedy is something that happens to him rather than something he does.[104]

104. Two points about the way Lancelot and Guinevere address one another are of some interest here. As D. S. Brewer has said, the knight and the queen normally use the second person plural to one another; the only exceptions are when Guinevere employs the more intimate singular form once in the entrapment scene (1166.25–26) and later when she tells Lancelot never to see her again (1252.17–29). [*The Morte Darthur: Parts Seven and Eight*, p. 15.] There is a quite similar pattern in the terms of address used by the lovers. Throughout the seventh tale Lancelot and Guinevere speak to one another as "madam," "sir," and "sir Lancelot." But when their love enters its tragic phase, and just at moments where the lovers seem to be parting forever, Lancelot is permitted somewhat more variety and warmth of expression. (See 1166.13; 1166.21; 1202.14; 1252.30.) Now "sir" and "madam" are of course the forms of address most frequently used by lovers throughout the *Morte Darthur*; but it is also normal for Malorian lovers to use a somewhat more affectionate vocabulary ("my fair lady and my love," "Mine owne lord," etc.) from time to time. (E.g., 341.14; 345.25; 327.18; 327.25–26; 502.13–14; 683.11; 755.32.) In the seventh tale, then, Lancelot and Guinevere are more consistently formal in addressing one another than were the lovers of earlier tales. But the way the lovers speak to one another here contrasts more noticeably with the way other characters address one another in this same tale. In the "Lancelot and Guinevere" the hero himself liberally uses "fair," "gentle," etc., in addressing Barnard, Elaine, Lavayne, Bors, Arthur, and others (e.g., 1056.15; 1067.7; 1068.14; 1074.1;

If Malory's critics have been a little too quick to understand the
adultery of Lancelot and Guinevere, they have always been troubled
by his presentation of Gawain, and especially by Gawain's behavior ✓
in the eighth tale. It is of course the sudden change after Gaherys
and Gareth are killed which is the difficulty. As B. K. Ray wrote in
1926, Gawain's love for Gareth can only partly explain his sudden
and implacable hostility to Lancelot. "The man who appears as a
moral hero in pleading for mercy on behalf of the queen and refusing
to bring her to the stake and who rises to such a height of magna-
nimity as to tolerate with equanimity the wilful slaughter of his
sons and one brother, is unable to pardon the accidental slaughter
of two other brothers in a confused mêlée . . . ."[105] I have been
suggesting that certain changes in Guinevere's behavior make
sense not in terms of the coherence of her personality, but rather in
terms of how Malory wants us to regard Lancelot. In the case of
Gawain, I think once again that it is a mistake to look for psychological meaning in his change of attitude—or better, it is a mistake
to see the significance of that change as primarily psychological. Its
meaning is essentially thematic, and to understand that change we
must look at Malory's Gareth, the news of whose death brings out
Gawain's unreasonableness.

Gareth is perhaps the most appealing of Malory's knights. He is
Gawain's *good* brother, and it is this goodness which Wilfred L.
Guerin stresses in discussing the change in Gawain: Gareth is "the
epitome of his family's best parts, an innocent victim."[106] But the
meaning of this death lies not so much in Gareth's individual goodness as in the closeness of this good knight to Lancelot the superla-

---

1082.13; 1083.32; 1084.7; 1089.26) while keeping to "madam" when he speaks
to the queen. It seems to me the way the lovers speak in the last tales is quite consistent with Malory's presentation of the adultery as we have seen it in this chapter.
In the seventh tale, where Lancelot "relapses," the love of Guinevere is experienced
as a difficult and demanding loyalty; the slightly unusual formality with which
the lovers address one another works well with this presentation of love as service.
But when love is heroic or tragic and the situation itself suggests nobility and pathos
rather than self-indulgence, Malory can let Lancelot and Guinevere speak more
warmly to one another.

105. "The Character of Gawain," *Dacca University Bulletin* 11 (1926): 10–11.
106. " 'The Tale of the Death of Arthur,' " *Malory's Originality*, p. 266.

tive knight. That closeness is a thing Malory had stressed throughout the earlier tales, and particularly in the "Lancelot and Guinevere."[107] Now, when they hear of the killing of Gareth, the major
characters think of that closeness and are bewildered. Arthur faints
when he learns what has happened, and then he says:

> "Alas! that ever I bare crowne uppon my hede! For now
> have I loste the fayryst felyshyp of noble knyghtes that ever
> hylde Crystyn kynge togydirs. Alas, my good knyghtes be
> slayne and gone away fro me, that now within thys two dayes
> I have loste nygh forty knyghtes and also the noble felyshyp of
> sir Launcelot and hys blood, for now I may nevermore holde
> hem togydirs with my worshyp. Now, alas, that ever thys
> warre began!
>
> "Now fayre felowis," seyde the kynge, "I charge you that
> no man telle sir Gawayne of the deth of hys two brethirne, for
> I am sure," seyde the kynge, "whan he hyryth telle that sir
> Gareth ys dede, he wyll go nygh oute of hys mynde. Merci
> Jesu," seyde the kynge, "why slew he sir Gaherys and sir
> Gareth? For I dare sey, as for sir Gareth, he loved sir Launcelot
> of all men erthly." [1183][108]

After the lament for the coming fall, and the attempt to prevent the
inevitable telling of what has happened, there is still the simple
incomprehensibility of the news; and what is incomprehensible is
not so much that Lancelot killed someone as good as Gareth, as
that he killed someone who loved him as much as Gareth did. When,
on the next page, Gawain does learn that his brothers are dead, he
says, "Jesu deffende! . . . For all thys worlde I wolde nat that they
were slayne, and in especiall my good brothir sir Gareth" (1184.28–
30). Then he is told it was Lancelot who killed them:

> "That may I nat beleve . . . that ever he slew my good
> brother Sir Gareth, for I dare say my brothir loved hym bettir
> than me and all hys brethirn and the kynge bothe. Also I dare
> say, an sir Launcelot had desyred my brothir sir Gareth with

107. See, e.g., Guerin, " 'The Tale of the Death of Arthur,' " p. 267.
108. Arthur's question is not in Malory's sources.

hym, he wolde have ben with hym ayenste the kynge and us all. And therefore I may never belyeve that Sir Launcelot slew my brethern." [1184–1185][109]

There are few things in Malory as poignant as the last line of Gawain's later rebuke of Lancelot:

> "Now, fy on thy proude wordis!" seyde sir Gawayne. "As for my lady the quene, wyte thou well, I woll never say of her shame. But thou, false and recrayde knyght," seyde sir Gawayne, "what cause haddist thou to sle my good brother sir Gareth that loved the more than me and all my kynne? And alas, thou madist hym knyght thyne owne hondis! Why slewest thou hym that loved the so well?" [1189]

There is no one event which makes the fall of the Round Table inevitable; but there is one central event in the tragedy, and that is this killing. In terms of plot Gareth's death is important because it means Gawain is now against Lancelot and will force Arthur to be against Lancelot; thematically, it means the basic knightly relationship, which in *Le Morte Darthur* is the basic human relationship, is destroyed.

"Why slewest thou hym that loved the so well?" In discussing the love of Lancelot and Guinevere, and in discussing the way Malory presents Elaine of Astolat (and particularly the parallel reactions of Elaine and her brother to Lancelot) I have pointed out the basic asexuality of the Malorian world or, perhaps more accurately, the shallowness of sexuality in that world. There are in *Le Morte Darthur* episodes where erotic attractiveness is imagined but we have very little sense of sexuality as a thing which colors a relationship throughout, and makes love between lover and mistress radically different from love of brother and brother or lord and knight. Now what is true of sexual relationships in *Le Morte Darthur* is true of other relationships as well. And of course this is not surprising. In this work we are interested not in what is individual in an action or speech pattern but in whether that action or pattern conforms to

---

109. Original with Malory, as are the questions in the next speech quoted. (On the latter, see Vinaver's note to *Works*, 1187.15–1190.20.)

type; human relationships are simply viewed in the same way as action or speech. For Malory there is one typical relationship, one pattern of attachment; the word *love* ties together all the loyalties in the last tale, encouraging the reader to see the likeness in various human bonds rather than look for the points of distinction.[110]

All the loyalties in "The Tale of the Death of Arthur" are similar, essentially variations on the pattern of chivalric loyalty and service. Because of this, the killing of the good knight Gareth by Lancelot, the best knight in the world and the man in the world Gareth loved best, is virtually a loss of human order. It is a sense of radical betrayal we hear in the questions of the king and Gawain, real questions underneath the rhetorical ones.

If the relationship of Gareth to Lancelot is the type of all human devotion, it is particularly the type of Lancelot's relationship to Arthur. As Guerin points out, it is only in *Le Morte Darthur* that Gareth receives the order of knighood from Lancelot, and Malory refers to this dubbing five times in the last two tales (1110.34, 1113.4–6, 1162.28–29, 1189.14, 1199.17).[111] Lancelot, of course, had himself been made a knight by the king, and Malory wants us to be aware of the parallel. Just as Gareth will never be on the side against "that man that made me knight," Lancelot tells Arthur that he ought always to be on the king's side in the king's quarrel "for ye ar the man that gaff me the hygh Order of Knyghthode" (1058.21 ff.). Characters refer to Arthur's knighting of Lancelot quite frequently in the last tale, and in its opening scene Malory juxtaposes the two loyalties: Gareth refuses to go along with the plan of Aggravain and Mordred, saying, ". . . I shall never say evyll by that man that made me knyght" (1162.28–29), and a few lines later Aggravain tells Arthur ". . . And all we wote that ye

110. See, e.g., 1169.31–32; 1186.8; 1188.24–25; 1199.21–32; 1201.9–10; 1230.10; 1233.10. The use of the phrase I've taken as the title of this section in the farewell speeches to Lancelot of both Gawain and Guinevere also underlines the place of love as the common denominator of all the loyalties in the last tale. "Love" is not an unusual word for Malory to have used in any of the passages cited, but a linking word need not be striking to be effective.

111. " 'The Tale of Gareth,' " *Malory's Originality*, p. 115. See also 1114.10, which Guerin does not mention.

sholde be above sir Launcelot, and ye ar the kynge that made hym knyght. . ." (1163.9–10).[112] As Lancelot to Gareth, so Arthur to Lancelot: both thematically and according to the cause-and-effect of the story line, to shatter one of these relationships is to shatter both of them.

There is nowhere a trust for to trust in. Once Gareth is killed by Lancelot, Gawain tries to find some order in a world where the type of order has disappeared. He turns to the loyalties of the clan.[113] When referring to Arthur, for instance, he uses the word "uncle" much more frequently now than he did before: in less than a page he speaks to Lancelot of "myne uncle, kynge Arthur" (1200.17), "myne uncle the kynge" (1200.26–27), and "myne uncle, kynge Arthur" again (1201.4). Family obligations mean that Arthur will support his warring on Lancelot; when Lancelot says he killed Gareth and Gaherys by accident, Gawain denies it, saying "thou slewyste hem in the despite of me" (1189.22–23). Kinship provides both his military strength and his explanations now: blood relations are the real ones, and he can find some kind of meaning in the killing of Gareth by thinking Lancelot was striking indirectly at the leader of Gareth's clan.

When Gawain turns to clan loyalty he is rejecting the example of Gareth himself, who again and again (e.g., in the concluding scene of the "Great Tournament") acts from devotion to knightly excellence rather than to kin, and he is turning away from his own noble behavior when he learned of the deaths of Aggravain and his sons. This new emphasis upon kinship and his almost grotesque explanation of the killings are Gawain's attempts to find a meaning to cling to. Gawain uses speech as a weapon in the last book; but he is also notably scornful of "fair language" here.[114] This scornful-

112. We find other references to the knighting of Lancelot by Arthur at 1166.16–17, 1187.26–27, 1192.17–19, 1214.10–11, 1215.30 and 1249.18.

113. See M. C. Bradbrook, *Sir Thomas Malory*, p. 34; "At the end there is a regression from the more civilized bonds of the Fellowship to the primitive ones of kinship."

114. On this, see William Henry Schofield, *Chivalry in English Literature: Chaucer, Malory, Spenser and Shakespeare* (Cambridge, Mass., 1912), p. 112. But Gawain's distrust of smooth talkers is more limited than Schofield indicates. It is not notable

ness indicates impatience, of course, and a wish to *do*; but in it there is also a fear of hearing anything which might make him doubt the new explanation of things he has found—a crude explanation, but one he needs. Gawain's behavior is desperate and pathetic rather than sinister.

Thematically, Gawain's "uncharacteristic" reaction to the killing of Gareth does make sense: if Lancelot can kill Gareth, the Arthurian values—Gareth's values and, when he is at his best, Gawain's also—may be meaningless, all order gone. But another problem involving the characterization of Gawain remains. Why is it that Malory makes Gawain so extraordinarily noble early in the tale, and why so *calmly* and *judiciously* good as he does between 1174 and 1177?[115] Malory told us in an earlier, original passage that Gawain loved fruit because he was "a passyng hote knyght of nature" (1049.1) and probably cholericness is as near to being the constant of Gawain's personality as anything else. Why is it that Malory wants a violent change in Gawain's behavior within this last tale?

A comparison may be useful here. What Malory does with Gawain in this last tale is, it seems to me, rather like what Virgil does with Turnus in Book Seven of the *Aeneid*. Juno, we recall, has sent Allecto to stir war. First Allecto goes to Queen Amata. Into her breast she casts a snake whose breath will poison her. For a few lines, before the poison entirely controls her, Amata "speaks / softly, as is the way of mothers" (1.357).[116] But soon she is altogether possessed, driven as a top is driven by boys (11.378–384); she

---

until after the killing of Gareth. (See 1189.9; 1200.13–14; 1201.1; 1216.8.) Gawain, notice, objects to Lancelot's "fair language," and Lancelot to Gawain's "fowle sayinge" (1219.5). In a world where heroic speech is normative rather than individual, the breakdown of order is emphasized by the fact that one of the two greatest heroes charges the other with (excessive) fairness of speech, and is in turn charged with foulness of speech. In language as in allegiances, Round Table unity has been replaced by what we now call polarization.

115. Here Malory is working quite freely from his sources, and the *sens* of this scene is essentially his own. See Vinaver's note to *Works*, 1174.30–1177.7.

116. *The Aeneid of Virgil: A Verse Translation* by Allen Mandelbaum (New York, 1972). (Line references are to the original and page references to the Mandelbaum version.)

"pretends / that Bacchus has her" (1.385) and leads the other women from home like so many Bacchae (11.385–405). Now Allecto goes to Turnus. She disguises herself as Calybe, Juno's priestess, and appearing to him in his sleep, urges him to arm his men and burn the Trojan ships (11.421–434). But Turnus is not to be excited this easily:

> At this, the young man mocks the prophetess:
> "I am well aware that ships are in the Tiber—
> no need to conjure up for me such terrors.
> Queen Juno has not been forgetful of me.
> But old age, mother, overcome by rust,
> fruitless of truth, has made you waste your cares;
> among the quarrels of kings, it plays on your
> prophetic spirit with false fears. Your task:
> to guard the shrines and images of gods.
> Let men run war and peace: war is their work."
> [11.435–444; p. 177]

Angered, Allecto appears in her true shape and casts a torch into his breast. Turnus wakes, insane with anger and the desire for battle. He is now possessed, as Amata is possessed.

Virgil is presenting both Amata and Turnus (as he had earlier presented Dido) as victims; Allecto changes them, maddens them. But in the case of Amata we can only contrast the "soft" but nonetheless fairly excited speech she makes while partly controlled by the poison (11.359–372) with her frenzied behavior when completely possessed. With Turnus there is a sharper contrast between a calm and sane (if haughty) speech and madness; in a moment this sensible figure—doubly so because we see him just after we see Amata—is altogether changed. He will have to be destroyed by Aeneas, but we pity rather than hate him. His fury is forced upon him, just as Aeneas himself is driven to found Rome.

Now Gawain is dramatically and suddenly changed by the death of Gareth much as Turnus is changed by Allecto. By emphasizing the completeness of the change, by making Gawain a particularly generous and fair character just before he becomes a monomaniacal revenger, Malory encourages us to perceive the vengefulness not as *no!* something that comes out because the "real" Gawain is vengeful, but as the result of an extraordinary situation. Gawain is the victim of the great anger and unhap as well as its agent; magnanimous just before his feud with Lancelot, magnanimous as he dies. Much as the Arthurian era itself becomes more idealized, the lives of the heroes more protected, in the penultimate tale than in earlier ones, so Gawain appears more generous and noble just before he too becomes part of the anger.

> "A, myn uncle," seyde sir Gawayne, "now I woll that ye wyte that my deth-dayes be com! And all I may wyte myne owne hastynes and my wylfulnesse, for thorow my wylfulnes I was causer of myne owne dethe; for I was thys day hurte and smytten uppon myne olde wounde that sir Launcelot gaff me, and I fele myselff that I muste nedis be dede by the owre of noone. And thorow me and my pryde ye have all thys shame and disease, for had that noble knyght, sir Launcelot, ben with you, as he was and wolde have ben, thys unhappy warre had never ben begunne; for he, thorow hys noble knyghthode and hys noble bloode, hylde all youre cankyrde enemyes in subjeccion and daungere. And now," seyde sir Gawayne, "ye shall mysse sir Launcelot. But alas that I wolde nat accorde with hym!" [1230.18–31]

> "Truly," sayd syr Launcelot, "I trust I do not dysplese God, for He knoweth myn entente: for my sorow was not, nor is not, for ony rejoysyng of synne, but my sorow may never have ende. For whan I remember of hir beaulté and of hir noblesse, that was bothe with hyr kyng and with hyr, so whan I sawe his corps and hir corps so lye togyders, truly myn herte wold not serve to susteyne my careful body. Also whan I remembre me how by my defaute and myn orgule and my pryde that they were bothe layde ful lowe, that were pereles that ever was lyvyng of Cristen people, wyt you wel," sayd syr Launcelot, "this remembred, of their kyndenes and myn unkyndenes, sanke so to myn herte that I myght not susteyne myself." [1256.26–38]

Guinevere, Lancelot, and Gawain take responsiblity for the ruin. They are of course right to do so; the actions of each were part of that ruin. But what Malory feels most deeply is not the blame each bears, but the nobility of the bearing. The tragedy as the reader is made to feel and share it is far more something that happens to these characters than something which they do. Each is responsible in that each could have prevented the fall, not because any one of them made it inevitable; in *Le Morte Darthur* we look at Aggravain, Mordred, Bedwere, and that adder, not past or through them. And even within the area where each is indeed responsible, the character's culpability has more a schematic than a narrative reality. An event changes Gawain before Gawain determines events; we are more aware of Lancelot and Guinevere working for and arguing about concealment than we are of their passionate recklessness.

Earlier I discussed the kind of responsibility Guinevere claims in her last speech to Lancelot; here I want to look at the words of Gawain and Lancelot. Both blame their own pride for what has happened, and this pride is worth some consideration.

Pride is one of the themes of the "Healing of Sir Urry," the last vision of Round Table nobility before the disasters begin. Pride is what works against wholeness: the wholeness of the knight, and more important, the wholeness of the fellowship. It is clear enough that whatever the pride of Gawain and the pride of Lancelot are, they too harmed the wholeness of the fellowship, and the king who held that fellowship.

The pride of Gawain is that relentless pursuit of revenge even when others think Lancelot has offered adequate recompense and more important even when his feuding puts the king in jeopardy. Gawain acts as head of his clan, he seeks to avenge a killing he interprets as a blow at himself. This is indeed pride: but is there a sort of pride for which we feel as much compassion as for this? (In a way the very difference between the grieving Gawain and our usual idea of the proud man increases the pathos: if Gawain had said, as he might have, "through me and my wrath you have all this shame and disease . . . " he would have moved us less.) Lancelot's pride is more difficult to define. His confidence in his own prowess is

associated with pride on a number of occasions.[117] Malory may be
thinking of this, or perhaps of something less specific, pride, considered as the root of every sin, almost a synecdoche for life in the
world. But the important thing is that whatever Malory is thinking
of, our sense of the culpability of Lancelot's pride hardly exists at
this point. From the moment when he leaves the queen's chamber,
all of Lancelot's actions against Arthur are urged on him by his
followers as necessary ones, yet he keeps holding back, endangering
his own reputation: when he must go out to fight Gawain, he does
indeed seem "dryvyn thereto as beste tylle a bay" (1216.5–6).
Malory is setting Lancelot against the chorus of his followers to
show how much he will tolerate. Whatever we think of Lancelot's
pride was, what is most vivid in our memories as we read his speech
of grieving is if not his humility, certainly his courtesy, kindness,
patience—a modulated form, really, of that long-sufferingness we
saw in his service of Guinevere. With Lancelot's self-accusation,
even more than Gawain's or Guinevere's it is the nobility of the act
of blame-taking the reader responds to rather than the content of
the analysis.

But there is one thing in Lancelot's speech still to look at: his
expression "my defaute." This might refer to the adultery, but it
seems too general a word to use here if this particular "fault" is
meant. Rather I would suggest "default" has several overlapping
meanings. First, it is a generalized word for responsibility: but
responsibility through omission rather than commission; a responsibility, to use Dr. Singer's terms, through failure rather than
through transgression, or as the *OED* says "failure in duty, care, etc.,
as the cause of some untoward event" (s.v., † 4). A still narrower
meaning of the word is "absence," and I suspect it is this particular
failure in care Lancelot is thinking of;[118] or at least that this meaning
enters into his use of "default." For Malory the speeches of Gawain

117. See 1081.7–8; 1083.32–1084.4; 1175.19–21; 1189.9; 1199.11–14; and in the
Grail section, 931.24–25. It is, as I have said, the possibility of appearing a coward
which Lancelot mentions in saying he will go the queen's chamber despite Bors's
warning.

118. For various usages of the word in *Le Morte Darthur*, see, e.g., the passages
cited in the *Works* glossary, and 932.10, 1084.3, 1135.31, 1136.2, 1229.13.

and Lancelot are parallel not only in that both take blame on themselves for what has happened and speak of their pride, but in that both are thinking of the same part of the disaster: the rebellion of Mordred and the last ruinous battle, which Lancelot's presence would have prevented. I think this is what Malory meant by "my default." It seems right that what Lancelot feel at this moment be a consciousness of failure, of not being there when the king and the fellowship might yet have been saved. The imaginative truth of the disaster is less the guilt of having caused than the grief of not preventing.

Many times Lancelot had rescued the king and queen, and this last time he is not there to do so; Gawain urges him to "make no taryyng, but com over the see in all the goodly haste ye may, wyth youre noble knyghtes, and rescow that noble kynge that made the knyght . . ." (1231.25–27). Lancelot and his men do prepare "in all haste that myght be" (1250.5) and cross to England; but Arthur is already lost. The last, missed opportunity is especially poignant for Malory, and there are several of these frustrations in the final pages of *Le Morte Darthur*. After the last battle Sir Lucan helps carry Arthur, who faints as he is lifted; but Lucan, an Arthurian, laconic knight, is himself mortally wounded and when the king awakes he finds that Lucan has died:

> "Alas," seyde the kynge, "thys ys to me a fulle hevy syght, to se thys noble deuke so dye for my sake, for he wold have holpyn me that had more nede of helpe than I! Alas, that he wolde nat complayne hym, for hys harte was so sette to helpe me. Now Jesu have mercy uppon hys soule!" [1238][119]

In the case of the final battle and in the case of Lucan's death, the frustration is a lost chance to do something about a situation, but the deeper pattern is of missed, last opportunities to express love. Guinevere denies Lancelot a final kiss. Later, Lancelot is told in a vision that he should go to Almysbury where he will find the queen dead. He and seven fellows go on foot from Glastonbury to Almysbury

119. This account of Lucan's death is essentially original, as is the story of Guinevere's death discussed below. The last kiss episode and the story of Ector's coming are adapted from the stanzaic poem.

"the whyche is lytel more than thirty myle, and thyder they came within two dayes, for they were wayke and feble to goo" (1255.21–24). When they arrive they learn the queen has died "but halfe an oure afore" (1255.30); she had known Lance¹ ₊ was coming "as fast as he [might]" (1255.36–37), and for that past two days—the two days that is during which the weakened Lancelot was travelling as fast as he might to reach her—she had prayed to God that she might not have power to see him with her worldly eyes. "Than syr Launcelot sawe hir vysage, but he wepte not gretely, but syghed" (1256.3–4). It is one of the greatest lines in *Le Morte Darthur*.

The last emotional focus in *Le Morte Darthur* is the threnody for Lancelot. And here too is that pattern of frustration, the last, missed opportunity. For the threnody is spoken not by one of the fellows who were with Lancelot in holy orders, but by his brother Ector, who had been searching for him all those years:

> And ryght thus as they were at theyr servyce, there came syr Ector de Maris that had seven yere sought al Englond, Scotlond and Walys, sekyng his brother, syr Launcelot. And whan syr Ector herde suche noyse and lyghte in the quyre of Joyous Garde, he alyght and put his hors from hym and came into the quyre. And there he sawe men synge and wepe, and al they knewe syr Ector, but he knewe not them.
>
> Than wente syr Bors unto syr Ector and tolde hym how there laye his brother, syr Launcelot, dede. And than syr Ector threwe hys shelde, swerde and helme from hym, and whan he behelde syr Launcelottes vysage he fyl doun in a swoun. And whan he waked it were harde ony tonge to telle the doleful complayntes that he made for his brother.
>
> "A, Launcelot!" he sayd, "thou were hede of al Crysten knyghtes! And now I dare say," sayd syr Ector, "thou sir Launcelot, there thou lyest, that thou were never matched of erthely knyghtes hande. And thou were the curtest kynght that ever bare shelde! And thou were the truest frende to thy lovar that ever bestrade hors, and thou were the trewest lover, of a synful man, that ever loved woman, and thou were the kyndest man that ever strake wyth swerde. And thou were the godelyest

persone that ever cam emonge prees of knyghtes, and thou
was the mekest man and the jentyllest that ever ete in halle
emonge ladyes, and thou were the sternest knyght to thy mortal
foo that ever put spere in the reeste." [1258.27–1259.21]

"My defaute and myn orgule and my pryde." It is not so much that
our arrogance destroys, but that our power cannot save, cannot
quite reach. The last meeting eludes the hero, and time separates
the reader from the lost great age. The limitation of mortal, sinful
man, points us to no higher goal; it defines the nobility and pity of
the world Malory knows.

Index

Italicized page references indicate comparisons of passages from *Le Morte Darthur* and French sources.